LOOK WITH YOUR EYES & TELL THE WORLD

LOOK WITH YOUR EYES & TELL THE WORLD

THE UNREPORTED NORTH KOREA

ROY CALLEY

AMBERLEY

First published 2019

Amberley Publishing
The Hill, Stroud
Gloucestershire, GL5 4EP

www.amberley-books.com

Copyright © Roy Calley, 2019

The right of Roy Calley to be identified as
the Author of this work has been asserted in
accordance with the Copyrights, Designs and
Patents Act 1988.

ISBN 978 1 4456 8794 0 (hardback)
ISBN 978 1 4456 8795 7 (ebook)

British Library Cataloguing in Publication Data.
A catalogue record for this book is available
from the British Library.

Typesetting by Aura Technology and Software
Services, India. Printed in the UK.

CONTENTS

Acknowledgements 7

Introduction 9

1. Pre-DPRK – How Did the Country Get to This Place? 13
2. The Birth of a Nation 24
3. The 1950–53 Korean War and its
   Effects on North Korea 28
4. The Cult of Personality of the Great Leader,
   the Dear Leader and the Supreme Leader 44
5. The Juche Theory 80
6. The Great Famine 97
7. Religion 106
8. Life in North Korea 113
9. Human Rights and Prisons 167
10. Terror Attacks and Unlawful Imprisonment
    Attributed to North Korea 188
11. Tourism and What to Expect as a Tourist 193
12. Defectors 207
13. Nuclear Weapons 213
14. What Will Change? 218
    Timeline 222
15. Conclusion 248

Appendix: Important Sites in North Korea 254
Further Reading 280
Index 282

ACKNOWLEDGEMENTS

I am extremely grateful to Amberley Publishing for allowing me to write this book and putting their trust in me. I have to admit though that when it was agreed, I started to have second thoughts. Not because I didn't think I could complete the book, but because I knew that the moment it was published was the moment that any hope I had of returning to North Korea had ended. It is highly unlikely I would now receive the necessary visa. That for me is incredibly sad, not just because I have fallen in love with the country down the years, but because I have met so many people there on my travels and it's now certain that I won't ever see them again; I won't even be able to contact them again either, due the ban on communication with the outside world.

North Korea is a fascinating country, something which I have tried to describe in this book, but it's also a country that evokes all kinds of different passions and viewpoints. My visits there have elicited the same sort of emotions. In my view, it is a country that should be visited if you have any curiosity about the world in which we live.

I have to say thank you to all of my guides, and I wish so much that I could mention them by name, but that would be a dangerous thing to do, so it's with sadness that I realise they will never get the chance to read this. It wasn't just the guides who accompanied me on all the tours that made the experiences what they were, but the local guides too, who are without exception some of the most pleasant and warmest people I have ever met. I will never forget the young woman who sang a propaganda hymn to me when I was touring the Revolutionary Museum. Her voice was so sweet and melodic, and her song was from the heart. She and the other guides typify the feelings of the North Korean people, who say time and again that they just want to be left alone, but also that they want to be understood.

I'm hoping that this book might lead to a better understanding of this unusual nation, and if it inspires just one person to make the journey to an unknown land, then it will be worth it. Hopefully then you can see up close the contradiction that is the society of the Democratic People's Republic of Korea and maybe embrace it as well as question it, the way I have done these past few years. If you do visit North Korea, then take the guides' advice, and *Look With Your Eyes And Tell The World*!

INTRODUCTION

The Democratic People's Republic of Korea, or North Korea as it is commonly known in the Western world, is a place that virtually everyone has an opinion on, yet few actually know. Dubbed the 'Hermit Kingdom' in the nineteenth century, it has lived up to that title ever since and has embraced its isolationism. Due to its reluctance to engage with the rest of the world, hard facts about its people, its culture, its history and its philosophy are usually absent from the media and are quite often replaced by fantastical stories about outrages that have little basis in truth. Whether it's a story suggesting that the official cheerleaders who accompanied the athletes at the 2018 South Korean Winter Olympics were the personal sex slaves of Kim Jong-un, or that the uncle of the current leader was fed to hungry wolves as part of a campaign of political purging, these reports are mostly untrue, but are accepted by people who are largely ignorant about this country that so many love to hate. When President George W. Bush described the DPRK as part of the 'axis of evil' following the 9/11 attack, its reputation was embedded in many people's consciousness, even though most would hardly have heard of it before. North Korea is a rogue state, a forbidden country, a place that is at the heart of many of the world's evils with a dictatorship that flattens any kind of opposition in a cruel and ruthless fashion. That's the image – and an image that is as much exaggerated as it is true – and that's the country that I've been fascinated by for many years.

I've been fortunate to visit the DPRK on numerous occasions, but that doesn't remotely make me an expert on the place. The former US vice-president Walter Mondale once said that anyone who professes to be an expert on North Korea is either a liar or a fool. I'll try not to be either. Indeed, on my first flight from Beijing to Pyongyang, I sat nervously next to a traveller who told me he'd been ten years in succession. He also bemoaned what the country was becoming and how he preferred it the old way, when he'd stay in hotels that had no running water or electricity – something I was to experience myself on a later visit. I could only imagine what it used to be like, but then my imagination ran riot before my first visit anyway. I was convinced I would be followed by spies, watched from every street corner, have to retire to bed early as the electricity would be turned off at 9pm and that I might struggle to find basics such as a cup of coffee. It would be a test of endurance and courage, and I would be able to boast when I returned home that I'd survived a trip to North Korea. How naïve and how utterly insulting and foolish. There were no spies; as far as I'm aware, no one was watching my every movement – although two guides have to accompany you everywhere, but as they are normally bright and attractive young women that is no hardship. The electricity kept on flowing, in the capital Pyongyang at least. In fact, I was told there hadn't been an electricity power cut in a major city since 1999 – although the same cannot be said for the countryside – and when I looked out over the capital city from my forty-second floor hotel bedroom, Pyongyang twinkled brightly like any other major city. Oh, and I did find a decent cup of coffee – in the only café in the city.

This book is not going to be a propaganda piece for North Korea. I'm not going to attempt to make it look like an attractive place to live as there are far too many problems, which have been documented, and I will certainly deal with them in here – but I am hoping to balance some of the huge untruths told about the DPRK with my own observations. I can only tell it as I see it, and I'm sure there will be people who will accuse me of having undergone some kind of brainwashing, but that's the point. I've seen it, and not many in the media have. I've been to the modern centre of Pyongyang, which is one of the most eye-catching and spectacular cities in the world, and I've travelled extensively into the countryside and seen the existence of the farmers and the peasants. I've spoken to the people, who are among the friendliest and most peace-loving that I have met, and I've travelled the deserted highways on roads that are a challenge to say the least.

Maybe the current 'fake news' obsession is relevant to this book, but I'm also hoping to explain the route that the country took to get to the place it is today, with the many, many major problems that have been encountered. The famine that killed thousands in the mid-nineties is predictably hardly mentioned or referred to anywhere in the country (it is described as The Second Arduous March for reasons that I will explain) yet still the DPRK is a place where a proportion of the people are struggling to eat. Religion is not banned, yet there have been reports of persecution for those who try to spread their faith. The one-party state is more than just that; with the Juche Theory (something which I will also attempt to explain in later chapters) being all-consuming in people's daily lives and the adoration of the Great, Dear and Supreme Leaders governing their every movement and thought, it's a place where stepping out of line is just not an option, either for the local populace or for visitors. Also, this is a place that doesn't exactly embrace any American citizens as, until very recently, the US was actively despised and any reference to the country would be prefaced by 'Imperialist' America. The story of the 1950–53 war between North Korea, supported by China and the Soviet Union, and South Korea, supported by the USA and its allies, is taught extensively in schools and a quite incredible War Museum celebrates the 'victory' of a conflict that was left unresolved until last year. In fact, the war is talked about and celebrated more than just about any other event in the last hundred years by the people and media alike.

In my opinion, North Korea is neither an evil society nor a country that's on its knees. It has technology, a fascinating culture and a cradle-to-the-grave outlook for its people. It also has food shortages, a serious world debt and an infrastructure that is far, far behind most other countries, plus a total lack of freedom of speech, so the paradox is there. I'm hoping to explain how this has come about.

Finally, the title of this book is a little obscure without an explanation. 'Look with your eyes and tell the world' could of course be a plea from both sides of the divide, but it's a saying that was drummed into me from the helpful guides when I visited. They all asked me to look with my eyes, and then return home and tell the world. All they want is to be understood. I'll try to help with that here.

PRE-DPRK – HOW DID THE COUNTRY GET TO THIS PLACE?

To understand anything about a country, you have to do a little research to see how it became what it is. North Korea (I will refer it as this from here on to make it easier) has had a long and varied history. Thankfully for the sake of this book and its readers, anything well before the late nineteenth century is not necessarily relevant to our current subject, so I will keep the history lesson reasonably brief.

The Great Korean Empire came into being on 13 October 1897 following the Donghak Peasant Revolution that had taken place during the previous two years. This was the last of many major uprisings by members of the Donghak religion and peasants against deeply unpopular and corrupt laws aimed at extracting higher taxes from an already impoverished farming community, aided by the power of the Japanese government and armed forces who had a controlling interest in the country of Korea. Japan had effectively annexed the state for economic and military reasons. In the ensuing civil war up to 10,000 civilians and soldiers were killed, Korean and Japanese, and following sweeping reforms, Emperor Gojong announced the forming of the 'Great Korean Empire'. This was only once he'd fled to Russia after the Japanese had assassinated his wife Queen Min. He was effectively attempting to cut Korea's dependence on both powerful Japan and Qing China. China under the Qing dynasty also had an interest in the country and was looking enviously at its resources.

Gojong became the first sovereign leader of Korea and so ended centuries of dynasties who had declared themselves as vassals of China. He made an attempt to modernise what was a predominantly agricultural country into the equal of Western civilisation after the industrial revolution. It was at this point that the Joseon government – Joseon is the name of the original Korean kingdom from the fourteenth century, or Gojoseon as it was known from 2000 BC – implemented a strict isolationist policy and so earned themselves the nickname that remains to this day, the 'Hermit Kingdom'.

Despite the relatively peaceful era, the spectre of the Japanese Empire was omnipresent; the rate of change in the country was slowing down to be almost stationary due to a failing economy and a military that comprised fewer than 30,000 badly trained soldiers. The strategic importance of Korea to Japan was paramount. With tensions rising and with Korea in no position to defend itself, the government were coerced into signing the Japan–Korea Protocol in 1904. This effectively gave administrative powers to Japan, forcing Korea to inform it of any decisions involving international relations. Interestingly though, the treaty was regarded as 'already null and void' as late as 1965, due to a United Nations declaration.

In 1906, two years after the Japan–Korea Protocol was implemented, the Japanese forced Emperor Gojong to abdicate after he'd attempted to send delegates to The Hague Convention, a violation of part of the treaty. He was succeeded by his son Emperor Sunjong, who became Korea's second and last sovereign in a ceremony that neither man attended. It was clear that despite the pretence of independence, the might of Japan couldn't be resisted. Although a plea was made to various nations (including the United Kingdom) to protect Korean sovereignty from Japan, the Japan–Korea Annexation Treaty of 1910 was forcibly evoked and Korea became a protectorate and annex of Japan on 29 August. There were eight articles in the treaty with the first being the most telling and dramatic: 'His Majesty the Emperor of Korea makes the complete and permanent cession to His Majesty the Emperor of Japan of all rights of sovereignty over the whole of Korea.' For the next 35 years, Korea belonged to Japan in what was a brutal and distressing time for the nation and its people, a time that even today North Koreans talk of with anger and hatred.

Japan enforced its occupation of Korea in ruthless fashion, subjugating the population without mercy. The Korean language was banned throughout the country with only Japanese to be spoken in public places. All Korean signposts and building names were replaced with Japanese ones; newspapers were printed in the language of the occupier, not in Korean. The cultural heritage of Korea was suppressed, with its history no longer taught in schools, while historical temples and buildings were either closed down or razed to the ground. Anyone who was found not to follow these draconian rules was dealt with in a ruthless fashion. The population was forced to work under military rule for the advancement of Japan's economy, with a high percentage of earnings automatically being taken by the councils of the controlling Japanese. Any resistance was mercilessly dealt with and stories of whole villages of people being rounded up, locked into a church or similar building, which was then set alight if any Korean collaborators were found in their midst, are well remembered. It's since been estimated that up to 800,000 Koreans died due to forced labour during this period, effectively meaning that every family in the country had at least one victim of the ruthless control by their oppressors. Added to that, every Korean was expected to change his or her family name to a Japanese one; failure would result in death, and usually a painful one at that. Food rations were withheld from those who didn't act quickly enough to change their surname, and in some cases rations weren't reinstated, even after the name change, leading to inevitable starvation. This era was later described as the 'Arduous March' of the repressed people who, under severe control, were losing their heritage, their language, their possessions and their ability to survive in some of the poorest areas of Korea.

It's hardly surprising that in this environment of oppression and violence, there were moments of public resistance and protest, the most famous being the formation of the March First Movement of 1919, a moment in North Korean history that is as important as the birth of the nation as we know it today. Just a walk to the Olympic May Day Stadium in Pyongyang will give you the smallest glimpse of how revered the day is in the history of the country, as well as the people who participated in it. (Although we will come to the May Day Stadium in a later chapter, the significance of every important date in the country's history is played out in what is in effect the National Stadium. All celebrations and anniversaries take place in this stadium, which is named after its opening date of 1 May 1989.) Five weeks before the March First uprising, former Emperor Gojong died amid rumours of poisoning and it was this that sparked the largest demonstration against the Japanese invaders since the annexation. Many thousands of activists gathered in the capital city of Seoul and one read out a new Korean Declaration of Independence to the crowd, stating:

> We here will proclaim the independence of Korea and the liberty of the Korean people. This we proclaim to all the nations of the world in witness of human equality. This we proclaim to our descendants so that they may enjoy in perpetuity their inherent right to nationhood. In as much as this proclamation originates from our five-thousand-year history, in as much as it springs from the loyalty of twenty million people, in as much as it affirms our yearning for the advancement of everlasting liberty, in as much as it expresses our desire to take part in the global reform rooted in human conscience, it is the solemn will of heaven, the great tide of our age, and a just act necessary for the co-existence of all humankind. Therefore, no power in this world can obstruct or suppress it!

At the same time other activists read out the same statement in various parts of the country to huge crowds who had gathered peacefully, some reports suggesting around 2 million protestors in approximately 1,500 separate locations. Radio stations had been contacted with a list of complaints, which were then broadcast to the nation, but tragically the demonstrations ended with massacres and atrocities perpetrated by the 20th Division of the Japanese military and the police. It's estimated that about 7,500 people were killed – some executed publicly after being arrested – and nearly 16,000 wounded as the authorities failed to control the crowds. More than 40,000 were arrested and kept in barbaric conditions. The Japanese suppressed the movement with brutal force. They fired into groups of Korean Christians singing hymns. Christian leaders were nailed to wooden crosses and were left to die a slow death. Mounted police beheaded young school children. The police burned down churches. If this all seems to be too barbaric to be believable, then a visit to the Korean Revolution Museum in Pyongyang might convince you, as the photographs and documents are truly chilling, even if a fellow Japanese tourist was adamant in his denial that such atrocities took place.

To give some idea of how all of this happened, it's easier to see it through an individual's eyes, as statistics and numbers can desensitise us to history. Yu Kwan-soon (or Yu Gwan-sun) was just eighteen years of age when the March First Movement took place. She was from a Christian family – her father had paid to establish a Christian school with his own money where he became a teacher – so she believed in peaceful reform and it was with that ideal that she joined the protest with five of her friends. By all accounts her involvement was not noticed at that time. Nine days later, all schools across Korea were closed down by the Japanese authorities as the independence movement grew stronger. Here Kwan-soon became the agitator who is now revered throughout the country. She visited every house in her home town of Cheonan (in what is now South Korea) and urged the population to join her in another march on 1 April. Some 3,000 did but by the afternoon the

Japanese military arrived and opened fire, killing at least ten people, including her parents. Kwan-soon was arrested and subsequently tortured in prison as she refused to name her fellow-leaders. The details of her torture are so horrific that to describe them here would be difficult. How she was able to withstand the pain and degradation is something beyond the human understanding. At her trial she was defiant, shouting 'Long live Korea' as her sentence was handed down; a policeman struck her with his sword to silence her. After twenty months of the harshest treatment, including cold water being forced into her body between her legs, her breasts being cut off and being made to stand outside in freezing conditions and constantly doused with icy water, she eventually died from her injuries. Today, she is revered as Korea's Joan of Arc by many generations of Koreans, with a special section in the Korean Revolution Museum in Pyongyang dedicated to her. All North Korean children know her story.

The reaction of the government immediately after the protests was to crack down on any more opposition, shown by events on 15 April when the 79th Regiment of the same army division arrived in the district of Suwon and assembled 300 alleged resistance fighters. They were locked into a church and burnt alive, despite one mother pleading for the life of her baby. According to a North Korean book on the history of the country in the twentieth century (*Korea in 100 Points* published by Foreign Languages Publishing House in 2002) the baby was killed by a Japanese bayonet. Whether this last part is true or propaganda, the fact is there were continued atrocities committed against the people of Korea by the ruling Japanese. The date 1 March is now designated as a public holiday in North Korea and is celebrated with mass dances and entertainment. Unfortunately the massacre wasn't recognised by the international community, with the United States, in particular, refusing to condemn Japan for its role in Korean affairs.

Despite this rule of brutality and oppression, it's fair to say that Japan did go some way to improving the the standard of life in Korea, notably in education, agriculture and transport. It's telling that by the start of the Second World War there were nearly 1 million Koreans living in Japan as immigrants with half that number of Japanese living in Korea. The northern area of Korea was regarded as a far more industrial part of the country and so workers were better educated as they were needed to run the factories and maintain the mines, and it's a fact that 90 per cent of all books published in this era came from the part of Korea that is now regarded as the North.

The hatred and anger felt by Koreans towards the occupying Japanese continued to flare, yet by the start of the Second World War, Korea was still officially an annex of the Japanese Empire. Nearly 5.5 million Koreans were conscripted to fight for Japan and out of the 670,000 who were taken to mainland Japan, about 60,000 died in appalling conditions with a lack of medical care cited as the main reasons for the large number of fatalities. It's also interesting to note how some Koreans who had risen to positions of power in the Japanese military were regarded as crueller and more barbaric than their Japanese counterparts. Judge Bert Röling, who represented the Netherlands at the International Military Tribunal for the Far East after the end of the war, noted that 'many of the commanders and guards in POW camps were Koreans – the Japanese apparently did not trust them as soldiers – and it is said that they were sometimes far more cruel than the Japanese.' Korean guards were also sent to the jungle of Burma where it was reported that they were far more severe in their treatment of Prisoners of War. Lt Col Bill Henderson wrote of his experience of them during the building of the Burma Railway:

> (They) were moronic and at times almost bestial in their treatment of prisoners. This applied particularly to Korean private soldiers, conscripted only for guard and sentry duties in many parts of the Japanese empire. Regrettably, they were appointed as guards for the prisoners throughout the camps of Burma and Siam.

During the Second World War up to 500,000 Korean 'comfort women' were snatched from their homes under the pretence of moving them to Japan to help in the war effort as secretaries or factory workers. Instead, they were forced to become prostitutes in what can only be described as appalling conditions. Only in recent years has this been admitted by the current Japanese government, but it is still astonishing that no apology has ever been offered, and certainly no recompense was made to the families of the women who were never seen again. Many Koreans were medically experimented on during the war by their 'allies' Japan, with horrifying results, in an era that is hardly referred to in modern-day peaceful Japan. It is a part of history that has effectively been erased, much to the anger of North Koreans. There is no doubt that Japan was despised by a whole generation of Koreans. Even though that hatred has been redirected to a far greater foe in the years following the Second World War, Japan is regarded with contempt by most North Koreans and the sorrow, anger and hatred that was brought about by the years of occupation still remains.

Despite the often oppressive and heavy-handed rule of the Japanese authorities, many recognisably modern aspects of Korean society emerged or grew considerably during the 35-year period of colonial rule. These included rapid urban growth, the expansion of commerce and forms of mass culture such as radio and cinema, which became widespread for the first time. Industrial development also took place, partly encouraged by the Japanese colonial state, although primarily for the purposes of enriching Japan and fighting the wars in China and the Pacific rather than to benefit the Koreans themselves. Such uneven and distorted development left a mixed legacy for the peninsula after the colonial period ended. Also, by the time of the Japanese surrender at the end of the Second World War in August 1945, Korea was the second most industrialised nation in Asia, after Japan itself.

It is interesting to note that the end of Japanese occupation is completely attributed to the efforts of the Koreans themselves and not necessarily the end of the Second World War and the victory of the Allies. There is little anywhere in the country where the combined efforts of the Allies are referred to, and even though I was assured that schools teach children that it was the USA, UK, etc., who helped to overcome the Japanese during the world conflict, I remain sceptical. Every plaque, museum, saying, book, hymn and propaganda item points towards the heroism of the Korean people as they fought imperialistic occupation. History is constantly being rewritten in North Korea in a way that duplicates the greatest fictional moments of George Orwell's novel *1984*.

Of course, once the Second World War was concluded, a shift in power around the globe took place, with borders and partitions hurriedly drawn up and implemented. Korea was one of the countries that had its future mapped out on a piece of paper. The story of the birth of North Korea is surprisingly a relatively simple one, with a Korea that was no longer enslaved by the Japanese but instead controlled by the United States and the Soviet Union. From one invader to the next, the people of Korea were again unwilling slaves of foreign empires.

2

THE BIRTH OF A NATION

North Korea as we know it now occupies around 55 per cent of the Korean Peninsula, and has a population of near 26 million, whereas South Korea has around double that number and is one of the most densely populated countries in the world. The reason for this is quite simple: after the end of the Second World War, the country of Korea was effectively cut in half. Thirty-five years of Japanese rule over Korea ended when the occupying country surrendered at the end of the Second World War, on 15 August 1945, to the combined American, British and Chinese forces. What followed was a rather haphazard way of governing the country, as it was deemed by the leaders of the three conquering nations that all Japanese provinces taken by force should be immediately released and become independent. One week before that, Joseph Stalin had declared war on Japan after promising to join the Allies following the victory in Europe. The Soviet army was strong and threatened to overrun Korea so a simple and long-lasting plan was put into place by the American President,

Franklin Roosevelt – a plan that no one at the time could have envisaged would have endured for so long. The southern part of Korea would be governed in trusteeship for five years by the United States, the United Kingdom and China, while the northern part would be under Soviet control. To implement this divide, two relatively inexperienced American army officers were given the task of defining the southern portion of the country. Dean Rusk, who would later become Secretary for State in the 1960s, and Charles Bonesteel III, literally picked up a map of Korea and drew a line across the country, dividing it along the 38th parallel. This meant there was now a North and South Korea and the country's capital, Seoul, would be under American control. One day later they passed on the plan to the Soviets, who immediately agreed, and so the countries of North Korea and South Korea were born, although the original name for the South was the short-lived People's Republic of Korea. That was disbanded after just three months by the Americans who had no intention of working with the numerous People's Committees that were common throughout the country.

The Soviets persevered for a little longer, finally ending the provisional government on 9 September 1948 when the Democratic People's Republic of Korea came into being under the Soviet-preferred leadership of Kim Il-sung. There had been local protests for complete independence, mostly from the now South Koreans, but the horror of Japanese dictatorship was now thankfully absent. The division of the two countries was now almost complete. While the South held elections (which were bloody, violent and at times unconstitutional, resulting in thousands of protestors being killed by the South Korean military) the North, under Soviet rule, implemented massive agricultural and farming reforms. These meant that previous landowners (mostly Japanese) had a large percentage of their land confiscated and passed down to their tenants in a socialist and communist purge. Many of the private industries were now nationalised and so it was estimated that due to the upheaval, some 400,000 now North Koreans fled to the South to become refugees. By the end of 1948 though, the Soviet military had withdrawn almost completely from North Korea, effectively letting the country fend for itself.

At the time, the divide was regarded as temporary and both governments believed that they were the true government of Korea. A desire for the country to be unified again swept through the populace in both the North and the South, but in such a remarkably short space of time there were two radically different points of view at government level. The North was now embracing Soviet-style socialism while the South was veering towards democracy – albeit in a bloody way – and both believed that their way was the correct way forward for a united Korea. They even had different Korean names for their country – Chosŏn for the North and Hanguk for the South – such was their now-completely disparate views.

As the tensions rose between the two, the North cut all electricity to their neighbours (they owned all the generators – a product of the Japanese industrialisation of the area) and skirmishes along the border were becoming more common. For the first time, travel between the two countries was forbidden and suddenly whole families of Koreans were separated – sadly, in some cases, never to see each other again. The constant uprisings in the South of Korea in the years between 1948 and 1950, notably the Jeju Uprising and the Yeo-Sun Incident, resulted in the loss of thousands of lives. It's difficult to believe now, but following the partition of the country, it was the North that seemed to be the more stable and economically successful, whereas the South was ruptured by protests and violent clashes, resulting in a failing economy and a disillusioned population. It is also hard to believe that a once-united nation should become so divided so quickly, but that's exactly what happened in Korea. Mistrust, envy, political interference, with families and communities separated, led to the complete breakdown of relations between the two countries. The old saying 'Divide and Rule' was never more apt than in the Korea of the post-Second World War period. As tensions rose between the two countries, more and more battles were fought at the border and eventually this escalated into a full-blown conflict. One thing the 1950–53 Korean War did for the people of the northern part of the country was to replace their hatred of Japan with a new and visceral hatred of the United States of America.

Hindsight is of course perfect vision but the cutting of Korea into two brought about the divide, not just geographically, but spiritually and emotionally, of the Korean people. If in those tumultuous moments after the end of the Second World War the United States and its allies, and the Soviet Union and China, had come to a more long-lasting agreement, then maybe the dream of all the people of Korea would no longer still be being yearned for; they talk of reunification – without the partition, the dream wouldn't exist. The day the two soldiers, Rusk and Bonesteel, drew a pencil line across a map, was the day they unwittingly caused misery to thousands of families in a very proud nation. Such are the moments of history and fate.

3

THE 1950–53 KOREAN WAR AND ITS EFFECTS ON NORTH KOREA

There is a war museum in Pyongyang called the Victorious Fatherland Liberation War Museum. No, let me rephrase that. There is an absolutely amazing museum in the centre of Pyongyang called the Victorious Fatherland Liberation War Museum. It was built in 1963, after being relocated from a previous site, and in 2013 it was completely renovated. It is frankly one of the most awe-inspiring tourist attractions I've seen and a complete tour of this huge complex could take up two days at least, if you were allowed to have the time. The building is so large that it spans the Botong River, which runs through the capital city. The building has numerous floors, seemingly hundreds of rooms and displays laid out in the most eye-catching fashion, and is topped off by an incredible 360-degree panoramic revolving room in the tower at the top of the building showing the war in all its 'glory' with animation and the most up-to-date CGI (computer-generated imagery). Berthed next to the museum, alongside the many fallen American and British tanks, jeeps and helicopters, is the USS *Pueblo*, a US Navy ship captured in 1968. This is kept in exactly the same state as when it was taken and is an essential part of the tourist trail. The whole experience is quite surreal as the mock-up battlefields and the accompanying films almost make you feel as if you've just experienced a day in the life of a North Korean soldier during the war. Unfortunately, photographs are not allowed inside the museum, for reasons that were never explained, so you'll just have to take my word for its excellence, unless you decide to visit. Alongside the captured enemy equipment there are Soviet T-34/85 tanks, naval craft and warplanes.

The museum seems to be a major part of children's education in the capital, as there were numerous groups of youngsters being led around the rooms and displays listening earnestly to their guides or teachers, and the reason I've mentioned all this is because the 1950–53 Korean War effectively defines the country today. Unlike in the United Kingdom, and most other nations of the West, war is celebrated there for its glory, and victory in the Fatherland Liberation War is spoken about time and again to children and it's the victory that is the main focus of the museum. Whatever we believe in the West about the 1950–53 Korean War, the North Koreans are told and believe that their country defeated 'Imperialist America' and her allies and they will do so again if they have to. I remember as I left the museum the first time I went and was met by my official guides, one of them asked what I thought. I told her how much I enjoyed it, but then said that the truth was probably midway between the American and North Korean versions. She smiled indulgently. A guide on a subsequent visit told me that she believed absolutely everything in the museum without question. As she said at the time, 'North Korea has never invaded another country. Even when we went over the border to the South, it was still part of Korea.' Such is the complete and total reliance on the official view of North Korean history that absolutely nothing is questioned or challenged.

Later, as I was perusing the local bookshop in the capital (actually, the *only* bookshop in the capital) I bought a book that told the history of the war. The opening page contained this:

> Kim Il-sung, the ever-victorious and iron-willed brilliant commander and outstanding military strategist, inspired the entire army and all the people to turn out in the sacred war to ward off the invaders and led the three-year Fatherland Liberation War to victory. Under the leadership of President Kim Il-sung and Chairman Kim Jong-il, the DPRK beat off all the challenges of aggressors from the 1960s to the 1980s, when the dark clouds of war hovered over the country due to the incessant arms build-up and military provocation by the US... The geopolitical position of the country is the same as ever, but it is no longer a weak country of yesterday, which was trodden underfoot as a theatre of wrangling among big powers to expand the sphere of their influence. It has turned into a proud political and military power and its people are demonstrating their dignity as an independent people whom no one dares to provoke ... as it is led by Kim Jong-un, the DPRK will emerge victorious in the showdown with the US, a confrontation between resources, which has continued century after century.

The war began on 25 June 1950 but it's unclear who exactly started it. Traditionally it's been agreed that the Korean People's Army crossed the 38th parallel, but obviously that is not the way the North Koreans see it, as they insist it was the South Korean army that intruded 2 kilometres north. There's even a doubt as to which side fired the first shot, but what was not in doubt was the superiority of the North Korean military with nearly 200,000 soldiers, effectively double that of South Korea and far superior air and land forces of fighter jets and tanks. Within two days the South Korean capital Seoul was captured by North Korean forces and the DKRP flag was hoisted on the top of the Capitol Building. At the time there were about 200 American troops stationed there, and through sheer force of numbers they had to flee (described in the book *DKRP–US Showdown,* published by the Foreign Languages Publishing House in Pyongyang, as being 'like startled cattle and horses ... who took the clothes of civilians at the point of guns and joined the crowds of refugees') as indeed did President Syngman Rhee, but not before ordering the Hangang Bridge to be destroyed to stop advancing North Korean forces.

The book says when the bridge was blown up, approximately 4,000 refugees were killed as they were crossing it. The next day he ordered the massacre of political opponents in the country. Even in this his darkest hour, the North Koreans have found a way to ridicule him, describing his retreat from Seoul in a third-class train compartment that had blacked-out windows so that he couldn't be seen.

The scale of the invasion was such that within two weeks, the South Korean army had been reduceed to fewer than 22,000 from the original 97,000. It was at this point that the United States and its allies, backed by a UN resolution, entered the war on the side of the South, with China and the Soviet Union supporting the North. America's involvement was apparently a reactive response as President Truman admitted that he didn't expect an invasion and the concern was that a victory for North Korea could fuel the rise of communism, especially in the fragile peace of Europe. With many South Korean soldiers defecting to the North, the US intervention effectively saved the South from being governed by Pyongyang.

America's first skirmish since the end of the Second World War was in the Battle of Osan, but it couldn't have been more disastrous. The US Forces, weakened since the Second World War, and heavily outnumbered, put up little resistance to the well-trained North Korean army. Lt Col Charles Bradford Smith took the 21st Infantry's First Battalion to Osan in an attempt to halt the invading army, but his men were inexperienced in battle, some straight from the training ground, ill-disciplined but extremely brave. They stood little chance. The 440 soldiers, each equipped with only 120 rounds of ammunition, managed to hold Osan for seven hours but found themselves completely overwhelmed. Smith ordered a retreat and despite the North Koreans stating that only 85 American soldiers survived, the actual figure was closer to 280.

Many of the retreating soldiers were captured and executed, some shot in the back of the head with their wrists tied behind their backs with wire. It had become a complete rout of the bloodiest kind. Smith was quoted in the North Korean newspapers as saying afterwards: 'Victory was impossible from the beginning. The reality proved that the KPA was really far stronger than we had expected, whereas we were not so strong an army as we had pretended to be. I believe that the Korean War will remain forever as the first record of the shameful US defeat in its history of war (sic).' These words seem unlikely to have been spoken by a serving American military leader.

The relentless march of the Korean People's Army (KPA) continued as American forces fell further back, suffering significant losses in the Battles of Pyongtaek, Chonan and Chochiwon with approximately 3,600 soldiers killed. Kim Il-sung then ordered all South Korean civil servants and intellectuals to be killed, something that was condemned by the United Nations. By August of 1950, South Korea looked as if it was to be governed by the North as the Americans, backed by their allies, mostly British, suffered defeat after defeat and were being pushed further back on a daily basis. The Korean War wasn't being received well in American homes, and so a huge deployment of troops was sent, while China boosted North Korea's numbers along the Korean border, but in the decisive battle in the early months of the war, the American forces outnumbered North Korean by two to one.

In the book *DPRK–US Showdown*, there is absolutely no mention of the Battle of Inchon, the battle that saw the pendulum swing away from the KPA. The only brief reference to it is on page 38 with the words 'The KPA was compelled to start a strategic temporary retreat while holding in check the enemy through an adroit mobile defence and a continuous war of attrition...' In fact, my guide in the Victorious Fatherland Liberation War Museum also pointed at a huge map on the wall and made it clear to me that the events of 16–19 September 1950 were part of a master plan by the Great Leader, and that he had personally sanctioned a retreat. The facts are that the Americans and Canadians launched a surprise amphibious landing at Inchon near the capital Seoul and with 75,000 soldiers at his disposal General McArthur managed to drive out the KPA and recaptured Seoul. Only 30,000 North

Korean soldiers managed to escape the attacking forces and Soviet Premier Joseph Stalin called an emergency session of the Politburo to completely denounce the leadership of the KPA forces, effectively Kim Il-sung.

No matter how many times the history books in North Korea write it and no matter how many times the guides tell you that North Korea was victorious in the 1950–53 War (bearing in mind it has never actually ended) the fact is that China's intervention played a huge part in preventing the northern part of Korea from being overrun by the southern. With the advance of the UN forces led by the Americans, China's leaders started to become concerned, stating that 'Korea is our neighbour ... the Chinese people cannot but be concerned about the solution to the Korean problem.' With that, on 25 October 1950, some 200,000 Chinese troops of the People's Volunteer Army (PVA) entered North Korea and managed to march to the combat zone south of Pyongyang within nineteen days. They were joined shortly afterwards by the Soviet air force, which provided cover for the land-based soldiers. At the same time America started the 'Home-by-Christmas' offensive, but this turned out to be overly optimistic.

The defining moment in the early months of the war was at the Battle of the Ch'ŏngch'ŏn River in the week from 25 November to 2 December 1950. This tributary ran alongside the UN front line some 80 kilometres south of the Sino–Korea border and was heavily fortified by the allies, but unfortunately for them it was a battle that was fought during the coldest winter in over a century, with temperatures falling to below −30°C. The American troops appeared to be completely unaware of the massive Chinese opposition awaiting them. Add the freezing temperatures to the lack of artillery for such an offensive and the 'Home-by-Christmas' push was over by the beginning of December. Some 11,000 or 23,000 UN casualties (depending on which side you believe) meant that a retreat described by *Time* magazine as 'the most disastrous one the US has ever suffered' was inevitable.

One of the most remarkable events that took place during the retreat was the evacuation of approximately 14,000 refugees from the advancing Chinese army by a ship, the SS *Meredith Victory*. This was quite amazing mainly because the vessel was originally built to hold twelve passengers and its crew of forty-seven. As the UN forces retreated, they razed the city of Hungnam and the adjoining port to stop any more landings of Chinese troops and, on 18 December 1950, President Truman declared a State of Emergency in the area. At the same time, despite since being lauded as single-handedly directing the victory over the Americans and being described as an 'outstanding military strategist', Kim Il-sung was removed as the commander of the KPA by the Chinese.

The victories for the PVA and the KPA continued into 1951 as the UN allies retreated further following another devastating attack during what was originally called the 'Chinese New Year Offensive' by General Ridgway. The PVA took Seoul, meaning the capital city was under the control of the North once more. Unfortunately for them, it became logistically difficult to push further forward owing to the immense difficulty of managing food and ammunition supplies from Pyongyang and Beijing, and following failed ceasefire negotiations, the UN condemned China as an aggressor and demanded its troops be withdrawn from Korea.

General MacArthur, ever a controversial figure who at one stage suggested the use of nuclear weapons against North Korea, had been replaced by Matthew Ridgway, which gave the beleaguered American troops a boost, and in February the combined US, South Korean and French troops recorded an astonishing victory by overcoming 25,000 Chinese troops who had surrounded them. The fact that the allied forces numbered hardly more than 6,000 shows how impressive the victory was and it became a turning point in a war that was now claiming so many lives on both sides. Add this to the fact that the population of the battered and ruined Seoul was suffering from massive food shortages (estimates at the time suggested there were only around 200,000 people left from a pre-war count of 1.5 million) and efforts were of course made to bring the suffering to an end. Sadly, it continued.

The Korean War carried on for two more years with both sides suffering huge losses, especially the Chinese who were now struggling with the logistics of a war that they had thought would end quickly. The lack of support from the Soviet Union had hindered their progress and the North Korean army was virtually now that in name only.

On the opposite side the Americans could call on all of their UN allies for support with the British, French, Turks and of course South Koreans to the fore. Their weaponry was superior even if their manpower was lower than the Chinese, and they had the financial muscle to sustain a war thousands of miles from home, something the Chinese certainly didn't have. Neither side could claim to be making any real headway and the desire for a victory waned appreciably as both sides looked for a way to end the conflict. The new American President, Dwight D. Eisenhower, visited Korea in 1952 in an attempt to find a solution to end the war – the main problem being the repatriation of thousands of Prisoners of War on both sides –

and finally in 1953 an armistice was signed, with a ceasefire agreed at the 38th parallel. This of course was another huge propaganda moment for North Korea; the events were described thus by the DPRK:

> ... the Fatherland Liberation War ended in a brilliant victory on the part of the Korean People's Army and the Korean people. Kim Il-sung, chairman of the Central Committee of the Workers' Party of Korea, premier of the Cabinet, chairman of the Military Commission and supreme commander of the KPA, devised outstanding strategic and tactical policies and unique fighting methods, based on Juche-oriented military ideology at every stage of the war and led the KPA to victory by translating them into practice.

The war was one of the most devastating in history. The statistics bear testament to this, as America in the three-year conflict dropped 635,000 tons of bombs on the country and 32,500 tons of napalm, compared to about 500,000 tons of bombs in the Pacific during the entire Second World War. Eighteen of the twenty-four cities in North Korea were virtually obliterated with Curtis LeMay, who succeeded General MacArthur, writing: 'We burned down just about every city in North Korea ... and we killed around one million Koreans and drove many more from their homes.'

This kind of destruction was not easily forgotten by the North Korean people; it was estimated that approximately 2.5 million civilians had been either killed or injured. These figures are a testament to what was suffered in the region, and that suffering has been constantly referred to ever since.

Armistice

The armistice was signed on 27 July 1953 in what is now known as the Demilitarised Zone (DMZ) by the United Nations Command with delegates from the United States, North Korea and the Chinese People's Volunteers present. An immediate ceasefire was called for and the governments of North and South Korea, China and the United States were tasked with continuing peace talks. The armistice brought an end to one of the bloodiest wars with an estimated 1.2 million soldiers and civilians being killed over a three-year period. For North Korea and its fledgling government, the armistice was perceived – and still is today – as a victory for their country. All literature, the teaching in schools, propaganda films and of course the aforementioned Victorious Fatherland Liberation War Museum point to a famous and defining victory for the armed forces of Kim Il-sung. He was described as '… defeating (them) single-handedly … the most ingenious military strategist and greatest military commander ever known in the world.' This view is constantly referred to in propaganda broadcasts on State television, plus 27 July is now an annual celebration when the population of Pyongyang enjoy a public holiday and take part in mass dancing before the spectacular fireworks displays are set off.

The DMZ is an astonishing place to visit. The actual length is around 250 kilometres and although it crosses the 38th parallel, it doesn't run along it, while the width is in the region of 4 kilometres. Any tourist visit is a moment to savour as the security is as intense as just about anywhere in the world, certainly confirming its title as the most heavily militarised border on the planet. Soldiers from both sides stand guard and patrol the Joint Security Area and inevitably there have been many excursions over the zone resulting in deaths on both sides. One famous occasion, as far as the North Koreans are concerned, was the axe incident in 1976 when two American soldiers were despatched to cut down a tree that was obscuring the view for the UN observers. This tree was, according the North Korea propaganda, the very tree that Kim Il-sung had planted and, in a brief skirmish, the soldiers were killed by the North Korean guards and the axe was confiscated. This axe is now proudly displayed in the tourist section of the DMZ where the story is retold with enthusiasm.

Far more dramatically though, a 'second Korean War' took place along the DMZ over a three-year period, and despite being referred to as a list of 'skirmishes' by both sides, about 700 soldiers from both sides of the divide lost their lives. The DMZ does appear to be a source of pride to North Korea, and as I travelled along the main highway towards the first of numerous checkpoints, my guide pointed out the flag that was flying in the countryside to my right. I was told that the North Korean flag was higher than the South Korean flag I could see in the distance, as a proof of the country's superiority over its neighbour. However, a guide on a subsequent visit confirmed that South Korea's flag was bigger! To continue this theme of one-upmanship on both sides, broadcasts from loudspeakers were played at high volume, either exhorting their opposite number to stand down or proclaiming the advantages of living in either the North or the South. Both sides also regularly flew balloons over the border filled with propaganda leaflets. These acts have now all but ended since the movement towards reconciliation in recent times, but they go to show that there was mistrust and misunderstanding on both sides.

As the 250-kilometre zone is now a no-go area for humans, it has become one of the most natural and well-preserved habitats in the world, with various plant species, animals and birds returning to an area that was once a battlefield and is now still filled with unexploded mines. A few brave – or foolhardy – soldiers have crossed the border at this point, but it was pointed out to me that mines line the DMZ at regular intervals, so it's a gamble to say the least. The returning fauna and vegetation has made it a haven for wildlife that would struggle to exist elsewhere. The black bear, musk deer and rare Amur goral (a species of wild goat) can now be seen roaming the wilderness if you stand and stare for long enough, and there are now nearly 2,000 types of vascular plants and numerous fungi and lichen growing in an area that rarely sees a human footprint.

Despite the heavily armed border, no weapons are allowed within the DMZ itself except for handguns. This is one of the reasons why soldiers fleeing the north have been fired upon without too much success, as machine guns are strictly forbidden by both sides. Rather bizarrely there are actually two villages *within* the DMZ where citizens can live under the scrutiny of guards on both sides. There has always been a suggestion that the North Korean Peace Village called Kijŏng-dong and located next to the flagpole, was in fact a Potemkin village, a place that was an empty shell but gave the impression of having inhabitants who were living there and enjoying a full social life. This was a view put forward by the South, but I was taken to the outskirts of this place and it looked pretty real to me.

Before we continue to explore the North and how it has become the country it is today, there is another telling example of the anti-Americanism that is rife within it, and that involves the ship USS *Pueblo*. In late January of 1968 this American Navy ship, described as an environmental research vessel or, according to the North Koreans, a spy ship, was captured after straying into North Korean waters – although this was vigorously denied by the Americans. The stand-off between the two sides was brutal and one American sailor was killed when a submarine, backed by Soviet-run MIG 21 fighters, opened fire, with the end result being the capture of the ship and the surrender of its remaining 82-man crew.

The accusations and denials that followed were as contradictory as they could possibly be, with the Americans refusing to admit to any spying activities, and the North Koreans refusing to back down until an admission of guilt was received. This had come just three days after North Korean soldiers had breached the DMZ and exchanged fire with South Koreans. Their target had been the president's mansion – the Blue House – in Seoul, so the tension on both sides was high.

The ship is now proudly berthed alongside the Victorious Fatherland Liberation War Museum on the Taedong River and is a huge tourist attraction. It has been renovated and the interior is the same as when it was captured but with the added explanations of the incident and video footage posted everywhere. I watched the video in what is described as the 'code room' with the eyes of the North Korean sailors firmly fixed on my facial expression as the story of the incident was replayed for me from their point of view, and of course this is the paradox. The two points of view do not tally.

From the North's perspective, this was an act of American aggression and the capture of the ship was essential for national security. It is claimed that at the time that all sporting events and planned artistic performances were cancelled, although in the same propaganda explanations it was confirmed that Kim Jong-il (the son of the Great Leader who was to become the Supreme Leader in 1994) had insisted that the more loudly the people sang and the better they played at games, then the bigger shock it would be to the American government. According to the book *DPRK–US Showdown*: 'America ... finally gave in to Kim Jong-il, who had composedly dealt with the situation, never being daunted by the formidable enemy. On 23 December 1968 Washington finally admitted the illegal intrusion and espionage activities of the *Pueblo* and formally apologised to the DPRK government.'

Of course, nowhere and at no time during my tour did I see or hear anything about the dreadful, inhumane conditions the poor sailors had to endure. They were held for eleven months in what is now described as a 'concentration camp' and regularly tortured and starved. Their captain, Commander Lloyd Bucher, was psychologically tortured by facing a mock firing squad and only after his crew were lined up and made ready to be executed, did he give in and 'confess'. Once the release was formalised by the two governments and the crew returned across the DMZ (the 'Bridge of No Return') America immediately retracted every statement it had made about admission of guilt and apology. After the men returned to America there were suggestions of Bucher having to face a court martial but the Secretary of the Navy, John H. Chafee, intervened on Bucher's behalf and no action was taken against him. He was never found guilty of any indiscretion and continued to serve in the US Navy until he retired.

This is just one of the many incidents that have taken place between North Korea and 'Imperialistic America'. If I was to write a list of every event, then this book would be significantly longer than it is, but this one serves to show how much hatred the North Korean government had for the US following the 1950–53 war, right up to the present day. I found it interesting that when I was first taken to the museum, I was introduced to my guide, a female soldier, who at first thought I was

American (all Europeans appear to be regarded as American at first contact) but when she was told I was English, a huge smile appeared on her face and she linked arms with me as she personally conducted me around the museum. I somehow think I wouldn't have received the same attention if I was from New York or Chicago.

4

THE CULT OF PERSONALITY OF THE GREAT LEADER, THE DEAR LEADER AND THE SUPREME LEADER

If you walk through the streets of Pyongyang or any other town or city in North Korea, (yes, you can, as long as you are accompanied by two guides) there are many things that stand out that are different to places elsewhere. The streets are immaculately clean, there is little traffic compared to, say, London or New York, there is music played from loudspeakers on virtually every street corner consisting of propaganda hymns, there are billboards that have slogans that praise everything about the country and its leaders, and of course one of the most striking things is just how many statues and portraits of the country's first two leaders, Kim Il-sung and his son Kim Jong-il, there are. These images are everywhere – so these two people dominate just about every waking thought and action of the North Korean population. In front of every public building in every major city or town, huge larger-than-life bronze and gold statues of the two men stand side-by-side guarding the entrance and dominating the immediate area. On every public building, especially entrances to train stations or metros, their portraits are clearly visible. Even in the carriages of the trains and in the underground system, you will sit quietly with the music in the background with the two leaders staring down at you. As you walk past apartment blocks you can see their portraits hung on the walls in exactly the same position in each room, with the Great Leader on the left and the Dear Leader on the right. These portraits have to be hung at a certain level so that they are higher than the sightline of people looking at them. They have to be hung at exactly the same position with the correct space separating them. If the images of the two leaders are in any newspaper or magazine, the page they are printed on cannot be defaced or folded or thrown away, otherwise a severe prison sentence will follow. When walking past the statues, it is customary to bow, and this includes tourists, and you must never cross your arms when standing facing the monuments. If anyone wants to take a photograph, then it has to be a full image – it cannot focus on the face alone – and every statue, portrait and picture has to be scrupulously clean without a hint of dust or dirt. These two people are not just glorified in North Korea, they are worshipped in an almost frenzied fashion.

To Western eyes there is nothing remarkable about either figure. The original Great Leader is a portly man with a rather drab wardrobe, while his son standing alongside him has a similar appearance, but their posture, smiling and pointing towards some wonderful future, is the one image that every North Korean has grown up with, from preschool days right through to old age. These are the men who have guided and will continue to guide North Korea to a wonderful and prosperous future in which the country will be completely self-sufficient and one of the major nuclear powers in the world. Despite the fact that both these men are dead, every member of the population is taught that they are still being protected and guided by both the leaders and will never be abandoned by them. The expression 'cradle-to-the-grave' care is more apt here than any other place on earth, as everything is apparently provided; no man or woman should be wanting for anything. So how has this happened? How has one family effectively captured the hearts and the minds of a whole nation, where any kind of transgression against them would be unthinkable, no matter what deprivations parts of the population may endure? How did this cult of personality come about? How is it that both of these ungainly and unremarkable-looking men have transfixed a nation, so much so that the third generation of the Kim dynasty – Kim Jong-un – is just as revered? To answer these questions, we need to return to the end of the Second World War to truly understand.

Kim Il-sung

'It's like a religion. From birth, you learn about the Kim family, learn that they are gods, that you must be absolutely obedient to the Kim family. The elites are treated nicely and because of that, they make sure the system stays stable.' This is how the dynasty was described by a refugee who had fled North Korea in the early part of this century.

Kim Il-sung was born on 15 April 1912, the same day that the *Titanic* sank, in a small village called Namni (now called Mangyungbong) near Pyongyang into a Presbyterian family. Which one of these two world-changing events has become the more relevant today is certainly open to question. He was the oldest of three sons and at his birth, there was nothing remarkable to be seen in the infant. His birthplace has now been lovingly recreated as a tourist destination in the capital city where the relative poverty of his surroundings are apparent. His father, Kim Hyŏng-jik, who is described in official history as being a farmer, was actually a Protestant minister who dealt in Korean herbal medicine and had founded a missionary school, while his mother, Kang Pan-sŏk, played a major part in the anti-Japanese protests that were sweeping the country during the brutal regime's occupation. It's also mentioned in the official history of the Great Leader that the young Kim would warm his mother's fingers with his breath during the winter months and refused to play outdoors for fear of tearing his clothes and adding to the economic burden on his parents. This may be an apocryphal story, but it is the start of fashioning the image.

By 1920, when Kim Il-sung was only eight, they fled to Manchuria to escape persecution, and it's clear that these early days of the young boy's life were to shape him for the future, especially in his loyalty to his nation. According to North Korean history, at the age of fourteen he founded the Down-with-Imperialism Union or DIU, the forerunner of the Workers' Party of Korea. This is extensively referred to in his autobiography, written in 1994, and it seems that he and a handful of other students in the school he was attending, Hwasong Uisuk School of the Chinese schooling system, did in fact found the fledgling party. He was later trained at the Whasung Military Academy before leaving due to their 'outdated' methods and lack of communist understanding. By the time he was seventeen, he'd been arrested for subversive activities and then joined the Communist Party of China. Although his personality cult has certainly exaggerated many of his earlier achievements, it's clear that by his twenties, Kim Il-sung was a rising star in the country and was soon a prominent member of the Northeast Anti-Japanese United Army.

In 1935 he changed his name. His birth name was Kim Sŏng-ju, Kim being the family surname, but he became Kim Il-sung, meaning 'Kim becomes the sun', a far more evocative title for a man who was now becoming a respected leader in the military. Of course, as with everything surrounding the life of the Great Leader there is truth and there is myth. This is how he describes it in his autobiography, *Reminiscences: With the Century,* published by the North Korean Publishing House:

Around the time the song 'Star of Korea' was being spread, my comrades changed my name and began to call me Han Byol ... meaning 'One Star'. It was Pyon Tae U and other public-minded people in Wujiazi and such young communists as Choe Il Chon who proposed to change my name into Kim Il Sung. Thus I was called by three names, Song Ju, Han Byol and Il Sung... I did not like to be called by another name. Still less did I tolerate the people extolling me by comparing me to a star or the sun; it did not befit me, [as a] young man. But my comrades would not listen to me, no matter how sternly I rebuked them for it or argued against it... It was in the spring of 1931 when I spent some three weeks in prison, having been arrested by the warlords in Guyushu, that the name Kim Il Sung appeared in the press for the first time. Until that time most of my acquaintances had called me by my real name, Song Ju. It was in later years when I started the armed struggle in east Manchuria that I was called by one name, Kim Il Sung, by my comrades. These comrades upheld me as their leader, even giving me a new name and singing a song about me. Thus, they expressed their innermost feelings.

There are suggestions that in fact Kim Il-sung took his complete identity from a dead North Korean activist called Kim Kyung-cheon, while others point to another Kim Il-sung in the North Korean army, but whatever the truth, from 1935 until his death in 1994, this is how he was referred to, as the 'Kim who becomes the sun.' I questioned this twice with two of my guides, and they forcefully insisted that his story was the correct story, and everything else was a lie. There were no further conversations on the subject.

At about the same time as his name change, he was appointed as political commissar with responsibility for around 160 soldiers, all at the age of just twenty-three. A year later he had his first military success, when 'Kim Il-sung's division' captured the Japanese-held town of Poch'onbo, a feat that is now widely regarded in the country as one of the greatest military victories of all time. Unfortunately, his success brought about tragedy as it was reported that one year later his wife, Kim Hye-sun (a familiar name in the country and also the same name as a famous Japanese actress of recent years) was captured by the Japanese, held hostage and finally killed. Again, this is a type of story that is shrouded in mystery as the 'official' history of the Great Leader doesn't refer to her at all. Instead he is credited with only having had two wives in his life. The first, Kim Jong-suk, gave him two sons then died in childbirth while delivering a stillborn girl, and the second, Kim-Sung-ae, gave him three children. There is a story of how in 1935 he and his fighters came across a locked log cabin in the mountains in central Manchuria. Upon opening it, they discovered numerous orphaned children who were survivors of the Chinese and Japanese attacks. The woman who cared for these orphans ultimately became his first 'official' wife, and together they worked to create the country of North Korea as we know it today. They also created numerous orphanages throughout the north of the country as a tribute to the ones discovered on that day, and that in turn led to the creation of the Revolutionary School that his grandson went to attend. Eventually, being pursued by Japanese troops, Kim Il-sung fled to the Soviet Union and was soon made a major in the Red Army, serving throughout the Second World War.

The cult of Kim Il-sung didn't really begin until after the 1950–53 war, but the seeds were sown immediately following the end of The Second World War. After Japan surrendered, and the country of Korea was split in two, Kim was recommended to Stalin as a future communist leader of the North. It was from this moment that the man the North Koreans now idolise became the Great Leader, even if not in name at that time. Rather surprisingly though, and something which is not acknowledged in Pyongyang today, he was created 'from nothing'. He couldn't speak Korean as his formal education was in Chinese. He could neither write, prepare nor read a speech in his country's language and his grasp of political affairs was completely driven by his admiration of Stalin and his policies. When he was presented to the crowds in Pyongyang wearing his Soviet army captain uniform, the people were seemingly unimpressed as all they saw was a rather short, chubby young man who didn't appear to have the look of a leader. Yet from this rather lowly starting point, Kim Il-sung became the creator of the nation. The pro-communist *Pyongyang Times* described him as '... the incomparable patriot, national hero, the ever victorious, brilliant field commander with a will of iron ... the greatest leader that our people have known for the last several thousand years ... a man equipped with exceptional powers.' This was hardly the general feeling among the public at the end of the 1940s, yet now the place where he made that first speech – the site of the modern Kim Il-sung Stadium – is honoured and revered with such gravitas that it begs the question why on earth they built a football ground on it? There is no doubt though, that his personality was being 'constructed' for the people in the immediate aftermath of the Second World War.

One of his first acts was to create the Korean People's Army, helped enormously by the backing of the Soviet military, as well as soldiers who had battled against both the Japanese and Chinese – with land, sea and air equipment all being supplied by the Soviet Union. This army soon became one of the largest in the world and is today regarded as the biggest per capita in any country. His enthusiasm for creating a huge land army means that today just about every family in North Korea has a relative who is in the army.

On 9 September 1948, following independent Soviet-led elections (not immediately recognised by the United Nations, which wanted to conduct its own Korean elections), the Democrat People's Republic of Korea was proclaimed, with Kim Il-sung as its leader. At the age of thirty-six this young man was now in a position of such power that he could dictate the future of his country, albeit not the full Korea as the South had recently achieved its own statehood and was called the Republic of Korea. This didn't stop either him or his Soviet backers from claiming sovereignty over the whole country, something which is still adhered to today. It was at this time that Kim self-styled himself as 'Great Leader' and the cult of personality was born. Within two years of his election, Kim started the sweeping reforms that were to completely change the country. Every industry was nationalised, land distribution started with more than half being shared among the peasants of the countryside, working days were strictly administered and a country-wide health system was introduced. The land sharing took the form of wealthy landlords, mainly Japanese, being forced to hand over large swathes of their holdings in return for a much smaller area and little in the way of financial recompense. Unsurprisingly, many chose to flee North Korea and rebuild their lives elsewhere. As previously mentioned, at the time of the start of the Korean War, it was the DPRK that was more prosperous and certainly more successful than its southern neighbour.

Despite the fact that the Chinese had replaced Kim Il-sung as leader of the KPA, the end of the Korean War is now seen in the country as a victory that was almost single-handedly achieved by him, and his military exploits are not only constantly referred to on state media but are also a staple part of children's education. This extract from *DPRK–US Showdown* is a perfect example:

> Kim Il-sung ... devised outstanding strategic and tactical policies and unique fighting methods based on Juche-oriented military ideology at every stage of the war and led the KPA to victory by translating them into practice... Portuguese President Gomes said at the time when he was chief-of-staff of the Portuguese forces in Macao during the war... 'General Kim Il-sung defeated them single-handedly and I saw it with my own eyes and came to know that he was the most ingenious military strategist and greatest military commander ever known in the world.'

This obviously seems ridiculous to Western minds, but I had a glimpse of the level of adoration that everyone in the country has for the Great Leader when my guide at the Victorious Fatherland Liberation War museum told me the very same story with tears welling up in her eyes. To change the people's perception of him is an almost impossible task, and that is surely the main reason why no other country could be remotely successful in implementing regime change.

Kim Il-sung's hold on power became absolute when in 1956 he aligned with China's Chairman Mao. Any obstacle in his way was removed in a ruthless fashion, with the leader of the Korean Communist Party, Pak Hong-yong, being one of the most high-profile executions. He was killed at a time when the purging of political opponents was widespread. This included a show trial of twelve activists who were then publicly killed as a lesson for anyone who might feel they could challenge the leadership.

By 1955 the Great Leader had introduced the Juche Theory to the country (something which will be explained later in the book) although it wasn't completely put into effect for another eight years, but to understand the level of his control we have to look at the August Faction Incident in 1956. Every opponent of Kim Il-sung was put to death following a brief attempt at the removal of the Great Leader. The Soviet Union was becoming increasingly concerned at the level of personality cult that was surrounding Kim. At that stage they were going through an anti-Stalin propaganda campaign coinciding with the arrival of the new President, Nikita Khrushchev. Kim was summoned to Moscow for the whole of the summer period of 1956 where he was threatened with forced removal if his policies didn't change. Of course he was unmoved and when he returned to Pyongyang he was informed of several plans to overthrow him, especially by the likes of the Soviet-sponsored Pak Chang-ok and Choe Chang-ik. They were due to denounce him at the next communist plenum but when they stood to make their speeches criticising his power over the State, and his policies which were leading the peasants into starvation, they were roundly heckled by Kim's supporters who had been forewarned of what was to come. The scenes at the plenum became ugly and threatening, and eventually his opposition fled the building. What began immediately, and followed in the later months and years, was an absolute purge of every political opponent of Kim Il-sung. Every member of a different faction was rounded up and killed, or thrown into prison, even those who played absolutely no part in the attempted removal of the Great Leader. Such was the complete cleansing during the purges that only those who were completely loyal to Kim were left, including those who had joined the Workers' Party of Korea under him. It's been reported though that even among those loyal and trusted members there were some who were also almost certainly executed in the following years, such was the complete power that Kim Il-sung had in the country.

As the years passed, Kim Il-sung became a micromanager in virtually every aspect of North Korean life. He would make 'on the spot' visits to farms and factories throughout the country. When he offered advice, it would immediately be acted upon – whether it was right or wrong – although any suggestion that he could be giving wrong advice was complete anathema to the people of the country. Any failure to follow his wishes would result in punishment, although this was not necessarily death, as in the common theme of Western journalists. I recall being shown around a school outside of Pyongyang and my helpful guide told me of its construction and how quickly it was being built in the 1960s. She then said that the Great Leader had visited unannounced one day and informed the workforce that they had the capacity to work much harder and finish it within a month. This 'advice' was heeded by the workers and of course the school was finished within the week. This story was told to me without even a hint of irony or sarcasm, but with genuine pride.

During the 1960s Kim Il-sung was turning North Korea into an independent and non-aligned country, despite its obvious connections and links with the Soviet Union and China, and despite him rarely ever travelling outside of the country (he only travelled twice to non-communist countries during his leadership) he received leaders and statesmen from around the world who were keen on forging an alliance with the country. The state of North Korea, especially economically, was at that time stronger than the South and it was this standing that made Kim a leader who was respected, if not understood, abroad. At home he was the complete controlling force of the country, yet those who met him described him in normal terms, in that he seemed to be approachable. There didn't appear to be the effect of power about him, despite the cult of personality that had now transformed him into a deity. The fact that he had ruthlessly held onto power was seemingly lost on the commentators.

Some four hours' drive north of Pyongyang, on a highway that can only be travelled at a maximum speed of approximately 30 miles an hour due to the condition of the surface, there is the International Friendship Exhibition in Myohyangsan in the North Pyongan Province. It is not an easy place to get to; after traversing the highway, we veered off into a dark and rather eerie forest, crossed a bridge that seemed fragile at best, before finally winding up a track that led to our tourist destination. Ours was the only vehicle in the car park, which wasn't necessarily a surprise. The International Friendship Exhibition is housed in an extraordinary building – as are all the buildings associated with the Great Leaders. Heavily protected and fortified, this traditional North Korean palace is an amazing collection of rooms and halls (over 150, yet I was only able to see around twenty in the three hours I was there) holding thousands of presents and gifts given to Kim Il-sung and Kim Jong-il by other world leaders and dignitaries down the years. It is only accessed by invitation, it is spotlessly clean inside and out, and is predictably flanked by the huge statues of the Great Leaders. After entering through an enormous thick steel double door, you walk across a marble floor while above chandeliers are burning brightly, then you are greeted by a line of female guides dressed in their traditional North Korean costumes. Despite what is claimed in some reports on the internet, you are not asked to remove your shoes or change any part of your clothing, but you are gently asked to observe silence when entering each room and of course bow in front of any statue of the Great Leaders.

Each room has a theme, either by nation or state, and each room is guarded by stern-faced soldiers. Gifts are displayed in huge glass cases and set out in such a way that they tell their own story, without words, of the meetings between either the Great Leader or the Supreme Leader and their guests. In the 70,000-square-metre complex, a 'breathless' guide will talk you through as many of the 200,000 gifts as she can, explaining when they were given, by whom and why. I describe the guide and her colleagues as 'breathless' because when talking of their Great Leaders, their natural speech is replaced by an awestruck worshipping tone; the subject of their descriptions could clearly do no wrong. The gifts vary from the well-known and often ridiculed outside of North Korea, such as the stuffed bear head from Nicolae Ceausescu of Romania, a bulletproof car from Joseph Stalin, a private plane from Chairman Mao, to the more intimate items such as a tea set from Germany, paintings from France, a ceremonial sword from South Africa and, bizarrely, a rugby football from the Wigan Warriors Rugby League team in England. It is an incredible collection and is there primarily to show the people of North Korea, and tourists, that the Great Leaders are as popular around the world as the propaganda dictates. There is another similar building in the capital city, which has all of the gifts from within the country, and this too is an impressive sight.

Unfortunately, photographs aren't allowed inside either of the buildings, but the impression a visitor gets is so memorable that it's the kind of place you want to return to time and again, if of course circumstances allowed. To top off the half-day tour, visitors are then taken to a terrace at the top of the building overlooking the most beautiful scenery of forests and mountains, where you can listen to the birds and watch the mist roll down the hills while sipping an almost undrinkable cup of coffee. The whole complex was opened in 1979 and when you search for its details on the internet, you find it was built in only three weeks; when I asked my guide, she proudly proclaimed that it had taken 'just a year'.

The reason I mention this tourist attraction is to give another example of how Kim Il-sung was, and now more than ever is, worshipped in North Korea. This shrine-like building shows the populace, should they ever dare to doubt it, that the Great Leader is the most revered anywhere in the world, as evidenced by the staggeringly large number of gifts that he and his successor have received. It also shows any tourist willing to make the journey that whatever we may think, the Great Leader and the Dear Leader were and are loved all over the world, so it serves two purposes at once.

To give some idea of how Kim Il-sung is revered, it's interesting to hear how he is described now. No, he isn't dead, he continues to look down on the people and guide them. Buildings are adorned with slogans saying those words. As you travel through the countryside, distant towns first come into view mainly because of the huge signs that proclaim love for the Great Leader and declare his protection of the people. One of my guides, a very intelligent and fluent English speaker, told me that she'd cried for three days non-stop when Kim Il-sung died and she too believes that he is still there, guiding the country down any path it takes.

In official literature there is no one else at all who has contributed to the birth of the North Korean nation. There are no assistant leaders, there is no political party, and there are no army generals who have guided the country since 1948. They just don't exist. All records have been changed in a style reminiscent of George Orwell's novel *1984* (published in 1949) as the only person who gets the credit for anything that has happened in the country that has benefitted the population is Kim Il-sung.

The image was of course enhanced by the Great Leader himself. One of his favourite parts of his biography was a tale about a teacher who asked one of his pupils to buy wine for him each day. One day the pupil returned with the wine and saw his teacher lying drunk in a ditch, and he immediately lost all respect for him. With that, the student (Kim Il-sung – for it is he) destroyed the wine and the teacher was forever afterwards humble in his behaviour, saying that no teacher should be seen in such a position by his pupil. Rather interestingly, when I recounted this story to a guide on my last visit, she didn't actually know what I was talking about!

By 1972 Kim was in complete control of the DPRK, able to issue edicts independently, grant pardons and sign treaties. He was in a position to oversee virtually every aspect of life in the country, including the military and the economy. During this time, he kept up relations with both the Soviet Union and China yet he had little compunction about criticising both as and when it suited him.

Chairman Mao's *Little Red Book* – a best-seller around the world, not least because it was more or less mandatory to have a copy in China during the Cultural Revolution – was banned from

North Korea following a particularly critical Chinese newspaper article about Kim Il-sun and his country.

After being re-elected as President of the Seventh Supreme People's Assembly (an election that involved just one candidate) Kim Il-sung effectively retired from public life and handed duties to one of his sons, Kim Jong-il. Kim Il-sung had failing health, his eyesight was poor and a huge benign tumour had grown on his neck (all photographs of him subsequently were taken from a sideways angle with the Leader staring to his right so that the bump the size of a tennis ball couldn't be seen), meaning that he retired as a recluse to his favourite retreat of Kumsusan Palace in Pyongyang. The Great Leader died on 8 July 1994 after suffering a heart attack. He was eighty-two. It wasn't until three days later that his death was announced to the North Korean people, who then went into a deep and intense period of mourning. This was due to last officially for just ten days, but it's no exaggeration to say that it continues to this day. Whereas many leaders of totalitarian states have had their legacy destroyed by subsequent inheritors, in North Korea there is no anti-Stalin, anti-Mao or anti-Ceausescu style feelings. He was, and to this day continues to be, adored despite the fact that his death occurred on the eve of the greatest national catastrophe the country was to face. Thousands attended his funeral in the capital city and his body was placed in a mausoleum at the Kumsusan Palace of the Sun – his favourite residence in later years.

The Kumsusan Palace is another extraordinary place to visit. Open only on Thursdays and Saturdays to tourists, it is over 115,000 square feet in size and was renovated in 1994 (following Kim Il-sung's death) at a cost of nearly $900 million. I have been fortunate to visit there twice, in February 2017 at the time of the 75th anniversary of the Great Leader's birth, and in November 2018, and they were experiences never to be forgotten. To be allowed access, you have to go on an official government tour with your existing guides. There are extremely strict guidelines as to what you can and cannot wear, with jeans and trainers forbidden. All personal items are taken from you (including handkerchiefs) and placed in storage for the duration of your visit. You are searched again and again as you arrive at each new room and the soldiers on duty don't take kindly to any flippant comments, facial expressions or gestures. Looking stern and passionless is certainly a skill worth acquiring at moments such as these. During the three-hour visit you are led through numerous dust-filtering machines and are told quite strongly that at no time must you walk quickly or indeed move at all when being transported by travelators.

Each room has yet more mementoes and souvenirs of the lives of both leaders (Kim Jong-il is also laid to rest here) including the train carriage where the Dear Leader suffered his heart attack. This is perfectly preserved and left in exactly the same state as when he died. The guides tell you in awed tones of the work he was doing when he collapsed.

Eventually you arrive at the mausoleum where the Great Leader, Kim Il-sung, lies in state. His head rests on a Korean pillow, with the flag of the Workers' Party of Korea by his side. All visitors are expected to bow at his feet, and once either side of him, but it is strictly prohibited to stop or bow at his head. The sense of tension is great and you are made very aware of being watched at all times by the soldiers and the equally humourless female guides who stand at the doorways. It is quite amazing to hear that one year ago an American student had actually done a handstand as a 'dare' in that room and was, of course, immediately arrested. Even the thought of doing such a thing is incomprehensible in such a forbidding atmosphere.

Unfortunately, despite it being the anniversary of his birth, the room where Kim Jong-il lay was closed on my first visit, with no explanation given, and on that day we were rather hurriedly shown the exit. On my second visit to the Palace, the room was open again and I was able to see Kim Jong-il lying in state. Once outside again, we were finally able to take photographs (they are completely banned inside the Palace) and the tension and stress disappeared from our guides and there were smiles all around again.

There is definitely the feeling that a visit to this building is a serious test for the government-trained guides as any infringement would be taken very seriously and their privileged positions might then be at risk. The gardens that adjoin the Palace have been extensively renovated and they make for a pleasant attraction for locals and tourists alike with, of course, the two huge statues of both the Great and the Dear Leader dominating the area. It was certainly the highlight of my first visit to Pyongyang, despite the overwhelming solemnity of the occasion.

The cult of personality was effectively started not necessarily by Kim Il-sung, but by one of his sons, Kim Jong-il, who was to eventually become his successor, and in a way that explains the transformation of a human being into a god during the 1960s. It was Kim Jong-il who looked to the future when his father would be too old to govern while he eyed the position for himself against his much better-educated brothers.

Kim Jong-il

The Dear Leader was apparently born on the sacred Mount Paektu (the birthplace of Korea over 5,000 years ago) on 16 February 1942. When this event took place, a double rainbow appeared followed by a new star glistening in the sky. A nearby lake burst its banks and lights filled the surrounding area.

Swallows passed overhead and immediately passed on the news to the population of the country. That is the official story of his birth, which is taught in schools and broadcast on television. In reality he was born in Siberia after his father had fled to the Soviet border while being pursued by the Japanese in the Second World War. He was Kim Il-sung's firstborn son, with a second arriving two years later, but who died in a swimming accident when he was only three. The official version of the Dear Leader's birth is still taught in schools as mentioned, and it's reasonable to believe that it's a story that is not questioned by the populace. To our minds it feels almost ridiculous, but to a country that depends almost entirely on the benevolence of the family in power, it makes perfect sense. As one might expect, Kim Jong-il had all the trappings of advantage as he was being schooled, firstly at the Number 4 Pyongyang Primary School, followed by the Mangyongdae School for the Children of the Revolutionaries and then the Namsan Senior High School in Pyongyang. In May 1964 he graduated from the Kim Il-sung University with a degree in political economy and was now being referred to as 'The Premier's Son'.

At this point in his life, it wasn't certain that he would succeed Kim Il-sung, especially as his uncle, Kim Yong-ju, was the more experienced and worthy candidate, but Kim Jong-il had a way of ingratiating himself with his father. He'd kneel as he helped to put on his father's boots, regularly showered him with gifts, and once he had joined the Propaganda and Agitation Department, he used all his skills in promoting his father's cult of personality. His interest in the cinema was huge and his ability in production was seemingly high. It was a perfect scenario for the son to promote the father in such a way that the masses started to believe in the Great Leader as someone more than a mere human being.

Kim Il-sung's 60th birthday celebrations were entirely conducted by his eldest son, with Kim Jong-il writing songs, producing plays, printing literature and also making sure that everyone knew that he was at the helm. The schoolboy who had 'corrected' his teacher's errors and helped to design a new school for himself and the pupils was now using these talents to glorify his father and put himself in the strongest possible position to succeed him.

Eventually he was given command of the 'Three Revolutions Movement' – cultural, technical and ideological – and he used his power like a machete cutting through a forest. Young soldiers would visit factories and farms, government agencies and even schools, sweeping through them looking for any resistance to the Great Leader and any suspected failings. They forced workers to self-criticise themselves publicly, and those who refused, or who failed to impress the guards, would be arrested and imprisoned. A network of spies within the factories would immediately report anything untoward to their government official, meaning that workers turned against workers and family members had no loyalty to each other. Only one person mattered, and that was the Great Leader. In 1976 the Vice Prime Minister, Kim Dong-gyu, criticised these actions and was immediately arrested. His mansion was taken from him and he was transferred to a notorious prison camp where he died of injuries following torture.

As his father's health waned, so the son blossomed. Kim Jong-il had all of his father's telephone calls intercepted and listened to, plus he diverted a great deal of money into what was called 'Office 39' or 'Division 39', the organisation that became infamous for its 'gangster economy' where funds were used for purposes that would benefit the government. This was an organised network of companies entrusted with procuring hard currency through all kinds of secret transactions. In Kim Jong-il's case, this meant he could afford such luxuries as new models of cars and boats, fine clothing and jewellery, all of which weren't available at that time in North Korea. A lot of the trafficking of money and goods was done via the diplomatic bag – a bag that cannot be searched by any customs officer – and even now it's suggested that this is still a way for top government officials in North Korea to access the goods they cannot get by normal means. 'Office 39' has been accused of being involved in money laundering, drug running and forgeries, yet it also has a legitimate business front. It appears that it was set up in the 1970s by Kim Il-sung, yet it seems it was his son who benefitted the most.

When Kim Il-sung died, his son disappeared from public view, apparently in deep mourning for his father. When he returned he announced that the title of President, or Great Leader, would be retired so that his father would be called that for all eternity. He would be described as the 'Dear Leader' instead. The legacy of North Korea that was left to him though was disastrous, with a catastrophic famine that claimed the lives of thousands following his elevation to power. We will deal with this in another chapter, but it was owing to Kim Il-sung's failed economic policies that the country reached the point of starvation. Although we will look at the famine – or 'The Second Arduous March' as it is described in North Korean history – in the next chapter, it is interesting to look at the lavish lifestyle that the second leader of the country enjoyed while his people were starving. It's believed that he owned more than 20,000 videos, which he would watch in his own purpose-built cinema, with James Bond and Hong Kong police films being his favourites. He owned numerous Harley-Davidson motorcycles as well as over 100 luxury cars that he stored in a five-storey building. He paid in the region of $700,000 per year for imports of his favourite Hennessey Paradis Cognac and had a 'Joy Division' in which his favourite Scandinavian and Japanese women would be flown in to pamper him in any way he wanted. It was also reported that he had about US$4 billion deposited in European banks. He was reportedly a food and wine expert and had the best chefs from Japan to prepare his sushi, although the official history states that his favourite meal was the Korean national dish of cold noodles. He loved tennis, swimming and horse-riding and played the piano expertly. He had a mistress, Koh Young-hee, but she was involved in a car crash in 2003 and died a year later in Paris. There were also tales of his ruthlessness. A member of his security guard was banished to the horrendous conditions of the coal mines after being found with one of Kim Jong-il's cigarettes, and was stoned to death by his fellow workers when they found out about it.

The Dear Leader wore platform shoes at all times as he was self-conscious about his height. His love of the cinema was his greatest passion. He directed a number of Korean plays, which of course are now regarded as classics in the country, *The Daughter of the Party* being one that is mentioned constantly by any tour guide. As well as all of this he had his own satellites that could pick up any news broadcast from anywhere in the world, including the BBC, CNN and China's CCTV. This at a time when people were lying in the fields and ditches of the country overcome with starvation.

There is also the rather disturbing story that he had the famous South Korean actress, Choi Eun-hee, kidnapped and held under house arrest for eight years so that she would make films for the Leader. She'd recently been divorced from her husband Shin Sang-ok, who was a well-known film director, and she had gone to meet a mystery businessman in Hong Kong who was keen on setting up a new film company using her name. She was then held against her will and taken to Pyongyang. Once her ex-husband learnt of her disappearance he spent some time and lots of money looking for her, but he too was then kidnapped and held under house arrest for four years. While there they remarried, at Kim Jong-il's suggestion, and they then went on to make films together; one of them, *Salt*, giving Choi the best actress award at the Moscow International Film Festival. They eventually escaped during a visit to Vienna and later wrote a book, *Kidnapped to the North Korean Paradise,* which unfortunately was never translated into English. In 2016 a documentary called *The Lovers and the Despot* was released, chronicling their time in North Korea. Choi died in April 2018 at the age of ninety-one.

This last episode shows the inner workings of a man who was protected from an early age by his father and had no idea of how to treat other people. There were reports that he was awkward around others and preferred smaller gatherings while making 'on the spot' visits. He rarely travelled abroad, apart from diplomatic visits to both Russia and China, and preferred the North Korean way of dressing with high-buttoned suit jackets and wide trousers – something his son Kim Jong-un has also adopted. As well as being the successor to Kim Il-sung, he was also the sole interpreter of the Juche Theory, and in 1982 had an eighty-five-page book called *Kim Jong-il on the Juche idea* published by the Foreign Language Publishing House in Pyongyang. This is not an easy read, should you ever get a copy, but it perfectly describes the reasoning behind Juche and the way it controls every aspect of North Korean society. We will explain Juche in a later chapter. As an aside, Kim Jong-il seemed to be a prolific writer as, according to official records, he published 890 works and his *The Selected Works of Kim Jong-il* has now reached twenty-four volumes and continues to be expanded, despite the fact he's been dead since 2011.

It was while Kim Il-sung was in power that the cult of personality reached epidemic proportions. His childhood and teenage years were rewritten with the accent on military successes, despite absolutely no evidence whatsoever that he was involved in guerrilla warfare. His mother, Kim Jong-suk, was now described as a revolutionary, with the ancestors of the family portrayed as resistance fighters against the Americans and Japanese in the nineteenth century. She now has the title of 'Mother of Korea' with her own museum in her birth town of Hoeryŏng. In fact in the International Friendship Exhibition, she has her own room and a statue of her against a backdrop of towering mountains and a cloudless sky dominates the scene. Again, tourists are expected to bow before her image. Virtually every member of the Kim family has positions of power in the government, although of course the famous assassination of Kim Jong-un's half-brother Kim Jong-nam in February 2017 at Kuala Lumpur airport shows that not all family members have protection, especially ones who openly criticise their leader.

It was during Kim Jong-il's tenure as Great Leader that laws were announced prohibiting any questions about the personality cult. There are severe punishments for anyone who doesn't follow the party with the utmost obedience. The ratings of the punishments are from 'No. 1 case', involving defamation of the Kim family, to 'No. 9 case', which involves the defaming of the family tree. It was when the laws were enacted that it was established that no one was allowed to deface the image of the two leaders, every household had to have the photos of the two leaders on their walls, and even the names of each Leader could only be written completely and not separated if the text was finishing at the end of a line on the page. During this period, the statues appeared all over the country and it's calculated that there are now approximately 35,000 of the same image, with the Great Leader and the Dear Leader standing side-by-side. Add to that the numerous buildings, schools and factories named after them, and you can understand the sense of their total domination over the country. If that doesn't convince you, then the relentless playing of *No Motherland Without You*, a song aimed at the Great Leader, over loudspeakers on every street corner of Pyongyang will surely enter and stay in your consciousness for some time. There is even a flower, the *Kimilsungia begonia*, which was presented to the Dear Leader as a mark of friendship by a Japanese botanist. This flower now adorns virtually every public building and is made to bloom in February, the anniversary of Kim Jong-il's birth. There is a very large exhibition hall that displays the flower in its thousands called the 'Kimilsungia and Kimjongilia Flower Exhibition'. I visited it in February 2017 and it's an overwhelming sight to say the least. While there I was photographed and interviewed by the North Korean press (I never did get to see the printed story) and also given my own begonia seed to take home to grow. I can only assume that it was my lack of green fingers that resulted in it being buried in the soil never to be seen again.

Everyone who lives in North Korea is also expected to wear a lapel badge showing one or both of the leaders (there are no restrictions as to which one you wear) and it's worn on the left breast and must be visible at all times. It cannot, however, for reasons unexplained, be worn on an overcoat.

The level of flattery and obsequiousness towards the Dear Leader was far more evident than it had been even to his father. All went out of their way to show a higher level of loyalty and the pictures you see today of hundreds of military generals sitting at a conference enthusiastically applauding the Supreme Leader, Kim Jong-un, have their roots in the cult of personality that took over the country through State media during this time. In 1997 there was a full-page advert in the *New York Times*, paid for by the North Korean government, extolling the virtues of the Dear Leader and describing him as 'The Lodestar of the Twenty-First Century', but unsurpisingly that didn't help his cult to be accepted outside of the DPRK. Whereas some of the rather unsavoury leaders of the past, such as Mao, Stalin and maybe even Hitler, had their supporters outside of their countries, there doesn't appear to be anyone outside of North Korea who actively supported or supports Kim Il-sung, Kim Jong-il or Kim Jong-un unless they are of North Korean origin.

The human rights record that Kim Jong-il presided over is appalling. Human Rights Watch estimated that there were more than 200,000 political prisoners during his tenure as Dear Leader, with freedom of the press completely restricted and an atmosphere of fear pervading every part of North Korean society. Families would be the worst affected as the 'Three Generations' rule existed then and exists even today. Basically, it means that any crime committed by a family member would trickle down to other generations and they would all be punished. The only exception would be daughters or sisters who have married, as it is deemed that once a woman is married she has effectively left her blood family.

The concentration camps, of which there were at least ten under Kim Jong-il's rule, but are now down to four, were the harshest anywhere. Conditions were horrific with many prisoners starving to death. Punishments were basic but cruel with inmates being forced to stand in one position for hours on end. Any movement would result in beatings. The stories of torture and cruelty are mainly from fortunate defectors who somehow escaped, but it certainly seems to be a system in which once you enter the gates of a camp, there is effectively no hope left.

By the start of the twenty-first century, North Korea was economically on its knees, with the Juche Theory completely entrenched into the nation's consciousness and yet destroying any hope of a better future. It was due to this that in 2001, Kim Jong-il announced that the run-down town of Sinuiju on the Chinese border was to be the forerunner of an extraordinary experiment. It was to be regarded as a Special Administrative Region (SAR), effectively a self-governing area that would embrace capitalism. They would use US dollars as currency, have their own police force, town hall, civil servants and even their own flag. The government of North Korea would not interfere with the acts of Sinuiju but would obviously benefit from any trade surplus and profit made in the future.

The town was chosen as it was close to China and the benefits of trade between the two countries was the deciding factor, but one thing the North Korean government failed to do in this rather unusual plan was to inform any of the existing residents of the town about the idea. There were reports of as many as 30,000 people being forcibly 'relocated' as they didn't fit the profile of the population that would bring prosperity to the area. Where they were taken to was never made public. It was also decided that around 200,000 people would be chosen to relocate there (most of them from the armed forces with computer, construction and economic abilities) and that the existing town would be completely flattened and replaced by a city of the future.

The running of the town, which was heavily based on a similar project that had been successful in China called Shenzhen, was given to a Dutch citizen, Yang Bin. He had a controversial reputation as a businessman in China, with failed ventures alongside some startling successes, but it seems Kim Jong-il applied no 'due diligence' process before Yang was given a blank sheet of paper to create a new and prosperous town. It failed spectacularly.

Yang Bin had made a fortune in China, but there was a serious case of tax evasion hanging over him. He'd also created, in an act of breathtaking self-aggrandisement, an amusement park in the north of the country dedicated to Holland. This included windmills, tulips, a re-creation of Amsterdam train station, and basically anything that connects to the Netherlands. Its effect was completely lost on the average Chinese citizen, who even if they were interested would have had to drive for three hours from the nearest town to see it. It was eventually demolished after losing too much money to be sustainable. This though was the man to whom Kim Jong-il had ceded sovereignty of a part of North Korea, such was the insanity of the scheme. There was no investment, no real infrastructure and hardly any idea how it was going to work, just a forlorn hope that a major hotel chain, a huge conglomerate or major business corporation would be charmed and enticed, and pave the way for riches and wealth. It didn't happen. Sinuiju is still the small trading town that it was before, relying on the Yalu River to import and export all kinds of goods, not all of them legal, and Yang is still in a Chinese prison after being sentenced in Beijing following his tax evasion prosecution.

The Sinuiju story perfectly encapsulates the problems that Kim Jong-il had when dealing with the economy. He'd once been described as being 'comically inept in all matters of economic reform' and during his tenure, his country had fallen far behind the South after it had embraced investment from the United States and Europe, whereas North Korea had isolated itself even more. Add that to the now-ongoing nuclear threat that the country had become to the Western world, and it explains why any economic reform was put on hold as the DPRK turned its back on the world again.

Kim Jong-il's death was announced on 19 December 2011. He had died on his personal train while working. It was reported that as he was dying, a fierce snowstorm stopped and a red glow appeared in the sky above Mount Paektu. A nearby lake, which was covered in ice, suddenly cracked with such a noise that heaven and earth shuddered, and a heron stood before the statue of the Dear Leader and stared.

Kim Jong-il was only sixty-nine and of course the mourning by the people was immediately frenzied and dramatic. Over the next few weeks, millions of citizens paid their respects to his body as he lay in state in a separate room to that of his father. His rather self-indulgent lifestyle could have been the reason for his early death, but that is something that would never be even considered by the average man or woman in Pyongyang. There had been numerous rumours outside of the country about his ill-health for at least five years leading up to his death, with some suggesting that body doubles had been used at public meetings. Different reports said that he had epilepsy, or diabetes, he was paralysed in his left leg, or he was confined to a wheelchair.

The place of his death, unanimously agreed in the country as being on his personal train just outside of Pyongyang, has also been suggested as having really been in the main hospital in the capital. My guide told me that he died while quietly reading documents in the personal carriage of the train (as referred to earlier, it is kept in pristine condition in Kumsusan Palace) meaning his last act was to the benefit of the nation, yet other sources say that he was in a fit of anger over a delayed power plant project and he was stressed over the stalling negotiations with the US over nuclear capabilities. Whatever the truth, North Korea had lost its second Leader and now faced an uncertain future. Meanwhile, South Korea put its troops on emergency standby for fear of an attack from a leaderless North.

Kim Jong-un

In 2013 it was announced that according to Clause 2 of Article 10 of the Ten Fundamental Principles of the Korean Workers' Party the 'Baekdu Bloodline', basically the Kim family, would carry the country for eternity. That in effect secures the future of the country for the next few decades. Kim Jong-un was elected Supreme Leader on 17 December 2011, being described by North Korean media as an 'outstanding leader of the party, army and the people ... great person born of heaven ... We vow with bleeding tears to call Kim Jong-un our supreme commander, our leader.' It wasn't a straightforward decision though to allow him to succeed his father, as his elder brother, Kim Jong-nam, had been the favourite. He fell out of favour with his father though when, among other indiscretions, he was found to have faked a passport in 2001 to visit Disneyland in Tokyo. This enraged his father. Kim Jong-nam left North Korea and following numerous criticisms of the current leadership, both privately and publicly, he was assassinated in 2017 at Kuala Lumpur's airport, seemingly on the orders of Kim Jong-un.

The Supreme Leader was born on either 8 January 1982 according to North Korea, or the same date but a year later according to the South, or maybe even 8 January 1984 if the US is to be believed. His upbringing is also clouded in a certain sense of mystery and uncertainty. He was, according to many witnesses and any official North Korean biography, schooled in Bern in Switzerland, where he was an outstanding pupil. Recent records though have suggested that in fact it may have been his eldest brother, Kim Jong-chul, who went there, as they have similar facial features.

Teachers at the numerous schools he was reported to have attended have described him as shy, awkward, a poor pupil, who had an obsession with basketball, especially the player Michael Jordan. What is definitely known is that between 2002 and 2007 he attended the Kim Il-sung University, an officer training school in Pyongyang. He was later given the military title of 'Grand Marshal', which belies the fact that he has never served in the army and has no guerrilla experience. For most of this time he was completely unknown to the North Korean people, yet it's now clear that he was being groomed for the succession, often travelling with his father to public events without being noticed. It's now also believed that there was a certain amount of purging taking place to rid him of any political opponents and the supporters of his half-brother.

On 15 January 2009 he was officially named as successor, being described in glowing terms by Kim Jong-il as 'exactly like his father' in that he had physical gifts, drank heavily (seen as macho and therefore a good thing) and never gave up. At the same time, a newly composed song was played through all the loudspeakers in Pyongyang praising him, with the population expected to learn the words and the tune so they could sing it at any time. After Kim Jong-il's death, Kim Jong-un was publicly declared Supreme Commander of the Korean People's Army on 24 December 2011 and two weeks later a public demonstration of support took place outside the Kumsusan Palace as he waved from the balcony. Shortly afterwards a half-a-kilometre banner was erected on a hillside in Ryanggang Province that reads 'Long Live General Kim Jong-un, the Shining Sun'. North Korean legend says that the sign can be seen from space, but when I saw it from a distance, it actually didn't look that impressive, even if it was unusual. Again, I wasn't allowed to take a photo. The then UK Foreign Secretary William Hague announced: 'This could be a turning point for North Korea. We hope that their new leadership will recognise that engagement with the international community offers the best prospect of improving the lives of ordinary North Korean people.'

Oddly the cult of personality doesn't appear to have touched the Supreme Leader, as his biography hasn't been rewritten with tales of extraordinary events at his birth, or exaggerated claims of his physical exploits. He seems to be a reasonably normal human being (albeit with health issues due to his weight and lack of exercise) who is happily married and wants a wealthy and prosperous future for his beloved country. His jovial image, with his unusual haircut and fashion sense, however, masks a ruthlessness that shouldn't be overlooked. He has continued to build nuclear weapons at an alarming rate, has tested nuclear warheads that have landed dangerously close to South Korea and China (despite repeatedly stating that the DPRK would never start a nuclear war but would look to defend itself) and he has re-introduced martial law to the country.

He was also responsible for the mass purging of the family of his uncle-in-law and one-time mentor, Jang Song-thaek. Jang, who had held the 'number two' position under Kim Jong-il, was arrested for 'anti-state, counter-revolutionary actions' and also accused of gambling and womanising. He was executed by firing squad (although many Western newspapers decided to make his death more dramatic by reporting that he'd been fed to starving wolves) and all of his family, including young children, were killed too. The reasons were simple according to the government: 'The discovery and purge of the Jang group ... made our party and revolutionary ranks purer.' It also meant there was little opposition within Kim's closest circle. In May 2015 it was widely reported that the execution of North Korea's senior defence minister had taken place. Hyon Yong-chol was apparently killed by an anti-aircraft gun while being watched by senior cadres. Whether this is true or not is open to conjecture. As someone who has travelled extensively throughout the country, I find it hard to believe that anti-aircraft gunfire would be wasted on one individual, bearing in mind the economic difficulties that currently exist. When I asked one of my guides about the story, he just laughed and started talking about Brexit!

The defence minister was apparently one of at least fifteen members of the senior military to be executed within the month, and it was noticeable that not a single member of the pallbearers at Kim Jong-il's funeral was still alive. All had been executed on Kim Jong-un's orders.

There was also the rather comical hacking of a Hollywood film studio after it released a movie called *The Interview* that lampooned the Supreme Leader Kim Jong-un. This caused untold damage to the studio's finances, yet absolutely no evidence was found linking the sabotage to North Korea. The publicity certainly helped the film though.

It may also be noted that the United Nations continue to name North Korea and Kim Jong-un as the perpetrators of the worst human rights abuses anywhere in the world. He himself has been ordered to appear in front of an International Criminal Court, yet the likelihood of that happening is remote to say the least, and as recently as June 2017, North Korea's abuses were under the spotlight again when the American student Otto Warmbier was returned to the United States after apparently suffering terrible torture. He was to die shortly afterwards, although there is mystery surrounding the story.

So what are we to make of the current leader of North Korea? A man who commands the undying loyalty of his people, who worship him the way they did his father and grandfather. A man who seems to be attempting to open up the borders of the country to economic change, looking to bring 'products to the masses', yet still has an iron grip on everything. A man who willingly met the South Korean leadership and then American President Trump in an attempt to find a peaceful solution to the years of tension. He seems to be a simple man in his pleasures. There are no reports of womanising or gambling or financial obsession. He loves basketball and has invited a former great of the sport, Dennis Rodman, to the country on numerous occasions. Kim Jong-un has a wife, Ri Sol-ju, who is much younger than him, and they have at least one child, a daughter, but none of this is confirmed by North Korean officials. According to the same people though, he is a leader who has far more empathy with his people than either his father of grandfather.

In my visits to North Korea, the subject of Kim Jong-un isn't an easy one to bring up. Official guides seem reluctant to talk about him, except to say that each day he works for the good of the country, constantly travelling and visiting farms and factories to help aid progress. Talking to anyone in the street is in itself almost impossible, so the chances of discussing their Supreme Leader are virtually nil. Due to the fact that he is still alive, there are no statues or photographs of him anywhere in the country and as he is still relatively young, that's unlikely to change in the near future. Asking why there aren't any monuments to a current living leader is one of the taboos of conversation; the response is more of embarrassment than fear because trying to explain that there won't be any until he's dead forces an admission of human fallibility – mortality – and one that won't endear you to the person you're talking to.

The Supreme Leader is revered though and this article from *The New Yorker* gives a revealing glimpse as to how he is following in the footsteps of the Great Leader and the Dear Leader in the affections of his people. The account is by reporter Evan Osnos about a visit to an orphanage in Pyongyang:

> I stood in front of a large photo of Kim Jong-un touching a fuzzy red blanket. The principal stepped aside and, with a flourish, revealed, in a Plexiglas box, the blanket. 'He personally touched it,' he said. So it was with the other specimens – the white painted chair that he blessed with his presence in the lunchroom; the simple wooden chair from the language lab, on which he rested from his labours – all preserved under glass, like the relics of a saint. I asked Pak Yong Chul how it felt to be visited by the leader, and his eyes widened. 'That moment is unforgettable. I would never have dreamed of it,' he said.

I too have experienced an astonishing example of the adoration of the leaders. While visiting the Korean Revolution Museum, I was shown, among thousands of others, a particular glass case which contained a schoolbag, a calculator and a milk cup. These, I was told, came from the Pyongyang Taedongmun Primary School and had been seen by Kim Il-sung on a visit. Yes, *seen*. They hadn't been donated or used by him while he was a schoolboy himself and they hadn't been touched by him. They had been *seen* by him, and that event inculcated them with such significance that they could sit proudly among the other materials that represented the great revolution, such as tanks and flags. This is the level of devotion that the country has for its leaders.

If North Korea is to change, then you get the sense it will under Kim Jong-un's leadership, yet for it to happen a whole culture would have to be abandoned. The Juche Theory dominates every facet of the society of the DPRK.

5

THE JUCHE THEORY

The driving force behind everything within North Korea is the Juche Theory. This is a mode of living that dictates absolutely everything to do with society, the economy and the culture of the country. It is so totally and completely entrenched within the consciousness of every single member of the society that its abandonment would destroy the very essence of North Korea, but what is the Juche Theory?

The explanation involves varied cultural and historical references, and can be confusing. Paul French, in his best-selling book *State of Paranoia*, describes it as a 'progression of Marxism', even though there is no mention whatsoever of either Marxism or Leninism in the constitution of the country, owing to the fact that all connections to the two have been erased down the years. It is an ideology that aims to move the country toward complete self-reliance, no matter how far away that may seem at any one time.

There are so many differing explanations as to what it is and how it came in to being and how it was based on not just the

Lenin and Marx ideology but China's Confucius, that the simplest way of finding out for me was to ask one of my guides. She gave me the most concise explanation that I have found anywhere:

1. Total self-reliance. The country will never be at the behest of any other nation as everything that is needed to sustain it will come from within its borders.
2. Military first (officially called Songun). This means that the military will benefit from the greatest expenditure of national economic resources to ensure a strong armed force. They will not take second place to anything else in society.
3. This was the most enlightening. Man is completely master of the planet and everything on Mother Earth is there to be controlled and utilised by man. There is no God or any benevolent force to watch over you, man is the only one who can dictate what happens and when. Everything on the planet is for the benefit of man.

If you want a rather more convoluted and less comprehensible explanation, then this is the way it is described in Kim Jong-il's book, *On the Juche Idea*:

The Juche idea is a new philosophical thought which centres on man ... the Juche idea is based on the principle that man is master of everything and decides everything. The Juche idea raised the fundamental questions of philosophy, by regarding man as the main factor, and elucidated the philosophical principle that man is master of everything and decides everything...

Man, through material existence, is not a simple material being. He is the most developed material being, a special product of the evolution of the material world... He exists and develops by recognising and changing the world to make it serve him, whereas all other material lives maintain their existence through their submission and adaptation to the objective world...

As history advances, man's position and role as master of the world is strengthened, and the extent of people's domination over the world increases daily through their independent, creative and conscious struggle. In our time the masses of the people have emerged as true masters of the world, and through their struggle the world is being changed more and more to serve the masses. Today the position and role of the masses of the people as masters of the world are becoming stronger than ever before. This reality proves more patently the validity and vitality of the principle of Juche philosophy that man is the master of everything and decides everything.

Of course, all three of the above explanations are worth further investigation as it's clear that this paradise that the North Korean government aspires to isn't anywhere close to appearing, so I'll try to unravel the mystery as best I can, bearing in mind most of the North Korean population would have difficulty in summarising it.

Total self-reliance

Of the three, this is the one that is failing almost completely. North Korea cannot sustain itself, as was proved by the famine in the 1990s, or the 'Second Arduous March' as it is described in the country. This is something we assess in the next chapter. The country's economy is on its knees. Compared to their neighbours in the South, the people have a far tougher life, with few of the material adornments that typify a progressive society. It relies heavily on imports with little in the way of exports to balance the books, and with constant sanctions implemented (especially from the United States) this is having a deeply unsettling effect. This was exemplified on one of my visits when walking through the main street in Pyongyang from the train station. This is a street that by North Korean standards is bustling with activity. My guides and I passed what looked like a shop that was closed, with empty shelves clearly visible through the window. Without asking, one of them said it was 'a fruit shop, but this month there was no fruit'. Of course, if North Korea was the self-reliant nation that it aspires to be, there would be no empty shelves.

On a much larger scale, the idea of self-reliance looks fairly ridiculous when you think that the nation was effectively created by the Soviet Union and has benefited down the years from Russian aid, whether in military economic, but this is the fundamental drive behind the Juche Theory. As it is described in Article 34 of the constitution: 'The State shall formulate unified and detailed plans and guarantee a high rate of production growth and a balanced development of the national economy.'

The problem was, and still is, that only around 11 per cent of the land in North Korea is arable and from the very early days of the nation's existence, its trade with the Soviet Union was one-way: exports were virtually non-existent and imports were costly. However, despite that, by the mid-1970s it was estimated that the DPRK was in the top twenty of the world's wealthiest nations, owing to the propping-up of the economy by the Soviet Union.

It all started to go badly wrong when technology was imported into factories and farms, but the workers weren't well trained enough to use it. It became clear that by the 1980s (at a time when the Soviet Union was dismantling itself and China was turning a blind eye to North Korea) that it was easier and cheaper to import goods as opposed to attempting to make the same components at home without any hope of selling them abroad due to their inferior quality. The workforce was willing but their skill levels were lacking. The isolationist policy that was implemented meant that there were now fewer exports than ever; the country was forced into self-reliance, but with little to rely on.

Kim Jong-il in a speech, which was later printed in his book *On the Juche Idea*, explained the vision of the future:

Building an independent national economy means building an economy which is free from dependence on others and which stands on its own feet, an economy which serves its own people and develops on the strength of the resources of its own country and by the efforts of its own people. Such an economy makes it possible to develop the productive forces quickly by utilising the nation's natural resources in a rational and integrated way, improving the people's living standards continuously ... and increase the nation's political, economic and military power. It also ensures the exercise of complete sovereignty and equality in political and economic affairs in international relations and contributes to strengthening the world's anti-imperialist, independent forces and socialist forces. It is vital to build an independent national economy particularly in those countries which were backward economically and technically because of imperialist domination and plunder in the past. Only when they build an independent national economy in these countries, will they be able to repel the new colonial policy of the imperialists, free themselves completely from their domination and exploitation, wipe out national inequality, and vigorously advance on the road to socialism.

Brave words but the problem of course is that it hasn't worked. The North Korean Won (pronounced 'Wan') is a closed currency and cannot be used anywhere else, and in fact is rarely used within the country now as either Euros or US dollars are preferred. Chinese currency is also now accepted and there are occasionally farcical sights of women queuing at a desk outside a department store where they can change their North Korean currency for Chinese before they can enter and buy goods. Such is the paradox of self-reliance.

The shelves in the shops are reasonably full, but they are full of goods that are inferior versions of bigger brands, and not sold for a profit, so that there is no incentive to improve. The chances of anyone outside of the country buying these items in large numbers is slim to say the least. Self-reliance was a political ideal when it was first mentioned by Kim Il-sung in 1955 as he introduced his Juche thinking (which actually wasn't taken seriously until around 1962, when his ideas became a matter of law) but there was little in the economic way of life to back up his arguments. Even less so now.

Of course, for self-reliance to work, products have to be either made or grown, and there again is the problem. Travelling through the countryside of North Korea is like travelling back to the Middle Ages. There is absolutely no technology whatsoever available to the farmers working in their fields, and it is still a common sight to see ox-drawn carts carrying bags of cabbages, radishes and bundles of wheat. Their pace is laboriously slow and so any attempt to reach modern production levels is fanciful at most.

It is also not uncommon to see whole families ploughing the fields as winter approaches, including children as young as seven or eight. This is a necessity as without the manpower, the crops would not be planted and then people would have nothing to eat in the cold winter months. This is self-sufficiency of a desperate kind. At the side of the road, usually collected by members of the military, are huge urns that contain the cabbages and radishes soaked in vinegar, which after a month of fermenting, give a family enough food to eat until spring.

There are no corner shops to visit for essentials, there are no home deliveries and there is no internet to order any product that becomes desirable. This is living in what we would describe as a miserable existence, but it is living in a North Korean self-sufficiency environment. The Juche Theory describes self-reliance in a hectoring tone as the people are constantly surrounded by signs and slogans as they go about their everyday lives. One that stands at the entrances to the many metro stations states:

> The economy is the material basis of social life. Economic self-sufficiency enables one to consolidate the independence of one's country and live independently, provides a sure guarantee for Juche in ideology, independence in politics, and self-reliance in defence and ensures rich material and cultural lives for the people.

The fact that every North Korean has to memorise these words perfectly and repeat them over and over again is probably not lost on those who are below what the West would call the poverty line. That line is higher up the scale than most countries, but it's still a guiding influence in the minds of the population who totally believe in the Juche Theory, or believe in the effects of the Supreme Leader's ability to implement it for the good of the nation.

Military first

Unlike number one in our three-part list, this is the aim that has been totally successful. North Korea is the world's most militarised country with up to 1.2 million soldiers (and that figure not only masks the unemployment figures but also takes away men and women at an early age from gaining the skills needed to aid the economy) and is regarded as the fifth largest fighting force in the world. It's also estimated that around 4 million citizens are under arms too, with the Militia of Worker-Peasant Red Guards, Red Guard Youth and many College Training Units. One of the more noticeable things you'll see when visiting North Korea is the huge number of soldiers in the streets, either marching to some unknown destination, or being transported in large and cumbersome trucks. Many of the soldiers appear to be involved in unskilled and mundane tasks, such as repairing fences at the sides of roads, or digging ditches for hedgerows to be planted. This is not an elite and combat-ready fighting machine.

It seems that any menial task is given to the army as a way of keeping the vast numbers occupied. Sometimes the threat posed by this huge military is perhaps exaggerated by the West. The overwhelming impression one has of the fighting force is of men carrying shovels or peering into the engine compartment of another broken-down jeep or lorry. Though one thing that stood out for me when I visited was that the soldiers were correctly attired in smart and clean uniforms, contrary to the many reports of shabbiness. It has been suggested by people outside the country that the military suffered the most from the famine and soldiers were close to starvation, leading now to physical requirements to serve being laughable (i.e. the minimum height was allegedly reduced to 4 foot 11 inches), but I saw no evidence of this. The military are omnipresent, yet their presence isn't intimidating to the locals. They aren't seen as arbiters of justice or keepers of the peace; they are seen as another pair of sturdy hands who help to keep the wheels of the country's industry turning, albeit at a snail's pace.

'Military first' didn't really come into effect until around 1994, despite its origins coming from a much earlier time, and it was Kim Jong-il who confirmed it in 1999. Basically, its creed calls for 'giving priority to military issues over everything ... a line, strategy and tactics of putting the army before the working class'. It also states that, 'The army is held to be decisive in achieving and protecting sovereignty, in economic construction. Implementing the principle of self-reliant defence means defending one's own country by one's own efforts ... only when one is strong, will foreign aid prove effective. In national defence, therefore, one should rely on the efforts of one's own people and one's own defence capability before anything else...'

To help achieve this the KPA gets priority when it comes to provisions, resources and rations, above anyone else in the country. The percentage of spending on the military is higher in North Korea than any other country on the planet, and that gives it almost complete power at its highest level among the generals and officers. There are even suggestions that many higher members of the army have the ability to dictate policy, despite the presence of Kim Jong-un. One of the least-reported facts concerning the Supreme Leader's rise to power is that he had many opponents in the military, and even now there are suggestions of criticisms of his policies, despite the number of political adversaries who have recently disappeared.

Nearly every family in the country has at least one member in the Korean People's Army. Conscription is for three years, or for four if one joins either the Korean People's Navy or the Korean People's Air Force. Military service is then around thirteen years for men and ten for women and every reserve soldier serves up until he or she reaches the age of forty. Armed Forces Day (traditionally the day that huge processions are shown around the world of soldiers, tanks, aircraft and missiles parading through the main square in Pyongyang) is an official public holiday and one that everyone throughout the country is obliged to take part in.

The people of North Korea are extremely proud of the military as they are regarded as the one thing that will always defend them from 'Imperialist America', and that is the declared philosophy of the armed forces. They are there to 'defend', not to 'attack'. I have had numerous conversations with guides who have said the same thing. The country doesn't want war, but they will defend themselves should it come. The Juche Theory states that 'we do not want war, nor are we afraid of it, nor do we beg peace from the imperialists.' North Korea (or Korea) has never invaded any other country in its existence, yet it has had to defend itself against numerous invaders down the centuries. The presence of the military in everyday life in the country is a comfort to the population, yet this vast militarised nation is in effect a peaceful one that just wants to be left alone. As an aside, no soldier (with the exception of official guides) is allowed to speak with any foreign tourist, and when you encounter their stern and near-aggressive stance, there isn't really the desire to engage in any conversation. For their part, they are regularly monitored and live an extremely disciplined life.

To give some idea as to how important the army is to North Korean culture, here are the words of Kim Jong-il in 1982: 'Such armed forces must embrace the sons and daughters of the working people. An army whose men and commanding officers come from among the workers, peasants and other working people, and between superiors and subordinates, and become a truly self-reliant people's army which safeguards national independence and revolutionary achievements and serves the people ... it is necessary to arm all the people and fortify the whole country. When all the people are under arms and the whole country becomes a fortress, all the people can be mobilised to crush the enemy as soon as it comes in to attack from any quarter...'

Of course, the spending on the military far outweighs anything else in the country, and as a result there is not only a huge army, navy and air force, but also a workforce that can be moved from province to province in order to do the work of the government – whether that be helping to complete the construction of a new power plant or waterway, or the planting of seeds alongside the peasants in the country, the army is there driving the country forward. There is, of course, the counter argument that (according to the South Korean government) if the North were to reduce its spending on the military by as little as 5 per cent, then the constant food shortages could be avoided.

'Military first' is unlike anything anywhere else in the world. The military comes first in everything. They are given more provisions than anyone else, they are paid at a higher rate than anyone else, they have the right to call up any citizen at any time for any task. Having said all of that, there is absolutely no sense of the country being a military dictatorship, no 'jackboot' domination and no fear of the armed forces. This is mainly because the military is essential to the economy of the country and everyone at some stage feels as if they are part of this vast force that is there to defend it. To the citizen, one thing is for certain: the military and 'military first' will always be there.

Man is dominant

The third part of the Juche Theory is certainly the one that arouses the most interest in the West. According to Juche, man is in total control of the planet. Everything that is in this world is there for the betterment of man. The resources from the earth, the animals that roam the planet, the air and the water that we rely on, are all for the exclusive use of man. There is no God to protect us, no higher energy to dictate our thoughts and no benevolent being to guide us – unless you count the constant presence of the Great Leader and the Dear Leader. The earth is not a living organism and the crops we plant and the animals we raise are for one purpose only, and that is for the survival of man.

In addition, Kim Jong-il included this in one of his many speeches to the population; 'Man is the most powerful being in the world, and man alone is capable of transforming the world. It is man and none other that requires its transformation and performs this work. Man acts upon and transforms the world as he desires, drawing on the objective laws. The world is changed for the benefit of man only by his energetic activity. For this reason, it is an absolutely correct viewpoint and attitude to the world to approach its change and development from the standpoint of man's positive activity to transform nature and society purposefully and consciously to meet his own desire.'

There can be no doubt that this philosophy is what drives the Juche Theory. To give a small indication of how this plays out on a day-to-day basis for all North Koreans, I have never once in my visits seen anyone with a pet. Although it's not official policy, it seems that all animals are there for either work or sustenance. You will never see dogs being walked on a lead, cats roaming the streets, or for that matter horses kept simply for riding pleasure. There is an argument that most people are so busy in their working lives that they just don't have time to keep a pet, but it's a strange experience to see a country that effectively doesn't have any. The concept of having an animal companion as a pet is completely alien to the average North Korean. Man is everything and there is not a single thing that man cannot do to change the world and the future. On my second visit to the country, I was invited to see a circus that had 'dancing bears' and 'smoking monkeys' as part of the entertainment. I didn't actually attend, and it would have been incomprehensible to those who invited me that I might see anything worng in such a show.

The Juche Theory has also rewritten history in North Korea. Anything before the birth of the Great Leader is unimportant; very little of the story of Korea is taught in schools. Basically, North Korea started in 1948 and nothing before that date is relevant, except for the struggle against Japanese occupation. Even the calendar is now dictated by a Juche-date system. When Kim Il-sung was born in 1912, that became the Juche Year 1 and so every year is now calculated from then. In 2019, the year in North Korea is 108. Any reference to a time before Year 1 is written as in the traditional Christian calendar (such as 1911), and any set of years that might range across Year 1 are written in the Christian way also.

This is only a relatively recent change as the Juche calendar wasn't officially implemented until 9 September 1997 after being decreed on 8 July of the same year, the third anniversary of the death of the Great Leader and the official ending of the three-year mourning period. The date 9 September is of course the anniversary of the Foundation of the Democratic People's Republic of Korea. By the way, any date mentioned before the birth of Christ, is still referred to as BC, which for a nation that has turned away from God and religion, is rather strange.

As an act of celebration of Juche (or as a reminder to the population) the Juche Tower stands tall in the capital of Pyongyang. It was built in 1982 and is a huge monument, 170 metres in height. Its design has been attributed to the Great Leader and the Dear Leader, but this seems unlikely, surely yet another example of the cult of personality at work.

The tower stands alongside the River Taedong and directly faces the Kim Il-sung Square, dominating the skyline during the day and especially at night when it is lit up. It comprises 25,550 bricks (or blocks), which account for every one of the days of Kim Il-sung's life (365 × 70: one for each day of Kim Il-sung's life, excluding supplementary days for leap years) and is topped by a 20-metre high red torch that can be seen for miles around. The view from the balcony at the top of the monument is spectacular and a 'must' for a 5 Euro fee. At its base and at the entrance there is a gallery of plaques and signs given by supporters of the country from all over the world, and I have to admit to being quite surprised to find one from my home city of Nice in France. These plaques are a source of enormous pride to the people and my guides were more than keen for me to stand and read all of them, although with there being eighty-two pinned to the wall, I deployed some speed-reading skills.

Once inside the tower you are asked politely to sit and watch a video of the history of its construction before getting the lift to the viewing platform at the top. I did ask what was on the numerous floors that we passed as we ascended but was told they were not open to the general public, without any further information being given.

The views from the top are breathtaking as you can see over the whole of Pyongyang and further, but on my initial visit the temperatures were below freezing, so it was certainly an act of will to stand there. Looking down, you can see another monument that is associated with the tower, and that is the statue of the Workers' Army. This consists of three figures cast in bronze, each holding a tool that symbolises the struggle of the people. One holds a hammer to signify the worker, the second a sickle, to signify the peasant, and the last a writing brush, which symbolises the working intellectual. Immediately behind are two apartment blocks that I was informed were built in the shape of the North Korean flag, both symmetrical on either side. I have to say that was completely lost on me and no amount of staring at the two buildings could conjure up an image of a flag.

It's all incredibly impressive, yet it seems to be a place that is completely ignored by the local population. I have visited it on numerous occasions and never once seen a North Korean anywhere near it, never mind paying the admission price to reach the viewing platform. It is possible that it's one of those exhibits that are invisible to locals, such as the Blackpool Tower or Edinburgh Castle in those cities, but there could also be another and rather bizarre, even sinister explanation.

From the platform, the Kumsusan Palace can be looked down on quite clearly, the place of rest for both the Great Leader and the Dear Leader, and therein lies the problem. From the top of the Juche Tower you can *look down* on the Palace and that is something totally alien to the North Korean people when regarding their leaders. Any thought of looking down on them, even in the presidential palace, is an anathema, and so this is maybe the reason why only the occasional tourist takes the rickety lift to the top of the tower.

The Juche Theory is an ideology that completely dominates every aspect of North Korean society, and if you were to ask anyone in the country about it (something which is forbidden by the way) they would probably say it was successful, yet there isn't another single country in the world that has followed the DPRK's example. Unlike Stalinism, Leninism, Communism or the ideas of Confucius, Juche has not expanded beyond the borders of North Korea. Unlike just about every other radical political and ideological force, the Juche Theory doesn't appear to have any supporters anywhere in the world. Even the once-isolated state of Albania described North Korea as an 'unbelievably closed society'. The Soviet Union and now Russia have long given up their attempts at trying to change the system, especially as the Kim dynasty has progressively distanced itself from the 'mother country', while China, which has of course itself gone through the painful transition from a barren and backward state with thousands of its people suffering starvation to one of the world's major powers, now looks upon North Korea as a neighbour that sometimes has to be indulged.

There is one uncomfortable link that could be made between Juche and the outside world; not a link perhaps, but more of a parallel. As geologists debate whether mankind has fundamentally altered the earth and therefore whether we have entered a new age, the Anthropocene, the human epoch, does not the ruthless exploitation and potential destruction of the planet echo the third concept of Juche?

Isolation and Juche are virtually the same thing as neither can exist without the other. It will certainly be interesting to see if

Juche can survive if the new openness that is being promised by Kim Jong-un actually takes hold. These final words from the Dear Leader (admittedly spoken in 1982) show that change is a long way off:

> Our Party and people who have traversed the glorious path of struggle and victory following the banner of the Juche idea under the guidance of the Leader, should hold high the banner in the future too, and fight on energetically. Our revolution has not as yet ended. We are still confronted with complicated and difficult revolutionary tasks. Only when we continue with our struggle upholding the banner of the Juche idea, will we be able to overcome all difficulties and trials, speed up national reunification and achieve final victory in the cause of socialism and communism.

6

THE GREAT FAMINE

If there is one subject that is hardly ever likely to be mentioned in North Korea, it is the great famine of the 1990s. This was a catastrophic time for the country when it's been estimated that between 250,000 and 3.5 million died in a four-year period from its effects; such a wide spread of course means these figures are open to interpretation. Every single person who lives in North Korea has almost certainly had a member of their extended family who would have experienced the famine, yet it is a time that is almost completely erased from the nation's consciousness and very rarely mentioned at any tourist destination or in any literature.

When there are any references to that time, then it is as 'The Second Long Arduous March', a propaganda title chosen by the government at the time as a way of mobilising the masses to rise up and beat hunger, similar to the mythical way in which the Great Leader rose up against Japanese oppression in sub-zero temperatures before the birth of the nation. With the population dying of starvation, the completely inflexible and inept leadership at the time could only exhort its people to 'eat two meals a day' as a way of prolonging limited food stores, when most in the outlying areas of the country were unable to feed themselves at all.

The reasons for the famine appear to be threefold. In the 1980s the country was reasonably self-sufficient and wealthy, but the rigidly enforced central planning of the agricultural system was one of the main reasons for the complete collapse of the food chain in the country. Agriculture has always taken second place in the country behind industry, following the example of the Soviet Union and the well-known, but now discredited, Soviet agronomist Trofim Lysenko. He was a huge influence in his native country and had advised the Kremlin that the way to better production was to plant seeds closely and heavily fertilise them. This turned out to be a complete disaster in the Soviet Union. Despite this, Kim Il-sung was a great admirer and followed Lysenko's ideas, ignoring the lack of success they'd had. Add to that the fact that many of the collectivised small landholdings that had been redistributed in the Land Reform Act of 1946 had failed to produce the minimum required output, and there was a disaster waiting to happen.

Only about 20 per cent of North Korea is arable land and it produces on average about 25 per cent of the country's GNP, not helped by a complete lack of modern agricultural methods and machinery throughout the country. To watch the farming practices in North Korea is like inventing your own time machine and transporting yourself back a number of centuries. It's highly likely that the scene I witnessed in twenty-first century rural North Korea is probably the same as it was in thirteenth-century Korea. There has been absolutely no technological advancement of any kind. Also, the Juche Theory demanded that to achieve self-sufficiency, changes had to be made in traditional agricultural production, meaning that crops such as millet and potatoes were replaced by maize, so that a total lack of diversity put the country at risk should there be a crop failure. This is of course what happened. With the reliance on heavy fertilisation, once the Soviet Union withdrew its provision of fertiliser following its collapse (the second reason for the famine) then the lands that had been heavily reliant on such farming methods withered away, with crops being replaced by weeds. Soil erosion, silting and contamination contributed to the huge flooding that took place (reason number three) meaning that there was no hope of the country being able to feed its people. Basically, the land died at the start of the 1990s.

While this was happening, the leadership seemed unable to react. There is the tale of Kim Il-sung actually advising farmers on the spot to plant corn on hillsides that had become barren, only to see those same crops washed away during heavy rains. He had no experience in agriculture, yet his suggestions had to be obeyed. The government was aware of the problems, but looked away, extolling the people to plant small crops in any piece of land they could find, also closing its eyes to the black market that was beginning to develop in rural areas. This, in a way, was a small solution to the lack of food distribution.

With the collapse of the Eastern bloc at the end of the 1980s and start of the '90s, the USSR demanded repayment of debts from the past that North Korea just couldn't honour. Before then, the Soviet Union had been the main supplier of aid to North Korea, including oil and machinery for the agricultural sector, but as change and political reform started to take place, it called in its marker. On 26 December 1991, the Soviet Union fell and so North Korea suddenly found itself without the benevolence of the former superpower and the cheap oil that it had so depended on in the past now stopped flowing. It's estimated that from that date, energy imports fell by as much as 75 per cent and the economy went into free-fall. Mines and factories relied on oil to run and with the lack of electricity, these all but came to a halt. There was no other source of supply.

Once the fuel became unavailable, families resorted to cutting down trees to burn the wood for heating, leaving huge areas barren and so open to flooding. It's estimated that 16 per cent of the forests were destroyed in the two-decade period of the famine, and so when the storms arrived, there were no trees to stop the land becoming flooded.

Reason number three was the biblical-scale floods that affected the northern part of the country in the early to mid-1990s. These were of such cataclysmic proportions that it's estimated that nearly 900mm of rain fell in one area in a 7-hour period, and the Amnok River on the Korea/China border had about 4.8 billion tons cascading between its banks in a 72-hour period. Most countries would struggle to cope with an environmental disaster such as this, but North Korea was completely helpless as lands had been cleared of trees for crop-planting and most of the stored reserves of grain had been hidden underground, resulting in nearly all of it being destroyed in the floods. The United Nations suggests that up to 1.5 million tonnes of grain were lost in the floods of 1994 and 1995. Another serious flood took place in 1996 and one year later there was a lengthy drought, adding to the ravaged countryside's problems.

At first the famine wasn't noticed by the government or the outside world, but in 1993 there were a few reports from Non-Government Organisations (NGOs) of people starving in the mountainous north-east regions. Stories emerged of people eating grass, acorns, berries, tree bark and rice roots, while illegal fishing of crab and shrimp was becoming commonplace. A black market selling household goods for food was burgeoning and any livestock was being eaten prematurely without reaping the benefits of traditional animal farming. A goat or a cow that could provide dairy products for a family was prematurely slaughtered for its meat in what was a desperate short-term solution. Eventually, the famine spread throughout the country and by the time it hit Pyongyang, the government could no longer attempt to keep it a secret, as it had done up until then.

In Sinuiju there were food riots. Mass graves near Hamhung were revealed by aerial photography, and orphaned children wandered the streets of the capital city. According to Paul French's book *State of Paranoia*, these children, some as young as eight, were put to work on the construction of the Youth Hero Highway running from Nampo to Pyongyang. As someone who has travelled that road on numerous occasions, it disturbs me greatly that the very tarmac we drove on was probably laid by a malnourished and starving young orphan who had been roaming the countryside in search of food. Melodramatic words, but here is the problem with North Korea; sadly, it's a nation that can elicit vivid emotions.

During all of this, public executions became commonplace – according to reports. This capital punishment was apparently for crimes of desperation, such as stealing food, although there seems to be no evidence of these incidents actually happening. They certainly aren't referred to anywhere in the country, but then that is not surprising. Also, the stories that circulated in the Western media of cannibalism in the northern regions again don't appear to have firm evidence to back them up, although that isn't to say they are untrue. At the time the North Korean government stated that cannibalism was punishable by death, so there must have been some kind of problem to prompt that reaction.

What was confirmed though was that there were many people in the mountainous regions who were now close to starvation. Malnutrition was everywhere and the Minister of Foreign Affairs admitted that the country was now suffering famine. It could no longer feed itself and so the government did something that completely belied its self-sufficiency ideology. It asked the international community for help.

That help came primarily from South Korea, Japan, China and the United States. After a while China became the country's leading aid supplier, replacing the old Soviet Union, but constant criticism from the Kim dynasty of China's changing political climate caused more than a few hiccups in the process. Eventually the famine was beaten after four years of intense hardship for the people, yet at no stage did the government admit to any failings. The famine (or Glorious March to Paradise as it was later renamed, alongside the phrase The Second Arduous March) was down to environmental disasters due to the inefficiency of the antiquated farming practices and poor leadership.

The failing agricultural practices are still in operation today and food aid is still a part of everyday life. To walk through the streets of Pyongyang today, you wouldn't know that there was, and to a fair extent still are, food shortages. Each time I stay in a hotel in the country, food is plentiful for obvious reasons, but there is always that underlying feeling that the food you are eating has been taken off the plate of someone who needs it more than you do.

Of course, statistics tell one story, but it's the personal tales that make it real and alive. I spent a very enjoyable few hours in the company of a Buddhist monk in his home at the Woljong

Temple in a UNESCO Biosphere Reserve during my last visit. He had been the senior monk at this stunningly beautiful and peaceful retreat for over thirty years, and through my guide he told me of the hardships of the famine. This was a man who had virtually nothing to eat for days on end, who was forced to eat the leaves from a tree or weeds from the ground, who had a distended stomach due to near-starvation and had virtually lost the ability to walk due to his weakness. Only when you hear testimony in the personal words of a survivor of such a horror, can it really become a reality to you. His humbleness and gratitude for life, made me ashamed at times to be a Westerner who lives in a society where the desire for the trappings of wealth can be paramount.

The actual number of deaths during the famine is hard to confirm. Many people believe that the higher number of nearly 3.5 million from the North Korean government is, in a way, used to extend and increase the aid to the country. Many experts have said that about 800,000 is a fairer number. Interestingly, certain international aid agencies have stated that despite the number of deaths, the population didn't appear to fluctuate and the figures stayed stable, suggesting that babies were still being born into a starving world.

The aid has continued since the 1990s, even though North Korea made an official request in 2002 for the food supplies to stop. Food shortages are clearly still an everyday part of North Korean life, and the former US President Jimmy Carter, on a visit to the country in 2011, said that he believed that one-third of all the children were malnourished. North Korean defectors have regularly reported that people are starving again in the rural areas and a Japanese newspaper went as far as to report in 2012 that more than 20,000 had starved to death in the South Hwanghae

Province. On the other hand, the World Food Programme has stated there is now no famine in the country, but there are still cases of malnutrition.

My heavily guided trips throughout the country certainly can't disprove or prove any of the reports referred to above, so all I can say is that in all of the schools, farms, factories and countryside areas that I visited, I saw no evidence of people or children being malnourished or on the edge of starvation. Of course, I was taken to specific locations where singing and dancing was put on for my benefit, and it is entirely possible that behind closed doors the food shortage is still a problem, but one thing is for certain – ask a guide about either the famine or the Second Great Arduous March, and the subject changes rather quickly.

In a world where we have seen famines in Africa on a regular basis, where the international community has acted with compassion and concern, the famine of North Korea in the 1990s is one that relatively unknown around the world, and certainly not recognised by the government of North Korea. I quote from Paul French's *State of Paranoia* as he describes the current situation perfectly.

Despite the obvious failure of the system, the collectivised nature of the agricultural economy remains officially in place even though it is increasingly fraying at the edges as people are forced to adopt survival mechanisms that conflict with official policy. Agricultural production remains extremely problematic, and hence feeding people without aid is impossible. Drought and flooding have persisted, further adversely affecting the rural economy. The longer Pyongyang refuses to make significant changes in the organisation of agriculture the more risk increases of famine returning... The continued adherence to Soviet-style agriculture combined with another major crop failure, compounded by donor fatigue reported by NGOs, would be truly catastrophic for North Korea, its people and its neighbours.

North Korea failed to feed its people once, and only recently. It could fail to feed its people for a second time, and the question is who would help? Despite the image given to tourists as they travel from one site to the next and stay in impressive hotels in the cities with luxurious accommodation and a seeming abundance of food in the restaurants, the fact is that the country is still on the edge of another human disaster unless the government acts and changes its agricultural practices. That will take a lot of money and education. The latter would be difficult to put in place but not impossible, the former is scarce.

7

RELIGION

One of the great myths about life in North Korea which is constantly reported around the world is that religion is banned in the country and that no religious worship takes place. This is just not the case at all. Religion is allowed in the DPRK and is tolerated, but – and it's a large but – promoting religious belief in the country is strictly prohibited.

Before the creation of North Korea, and while the peninsula was under Japanese occupation, Korea was essentially a Christian country but it also observed Shamanism, its indigenous religion. Japan attempted to impose its state religion, Shinto, on the population, but Christians refused to take part in the Shinto rituals as part of their defiance of the Japanese oppressors. State Shinto was effectively an ideological use of folk traditions promoted by the Japanese in an attempt to make the Emperor into a 'divine being', which is ironic bearing in mind the way the two North Korea leaders are now recognised as such in the

DPRK. Whatever their beliefs, the people of Korea refused flatly to embrace state Shinto as a way of life.

Christians were found in the greatest numbers in the north of the country, in the mountainous regions, and among the peasant community, although Seoul did have numerous churches and places of Christian and Buddhist worship. Following the division of Korea after the Second World War, many of the Christians who lived in the North fled from the communist regime of the Soviet Union to the non-communist South.

Meanwhile the approximate 1.5 million Chondoists, a religion that is based on Confucianised indigenous shamanism from the nineteenth century (which is about as far as I can take this explanation) remained in or moved to the newly formed North Korea. This status quo continued until the end of the 1950–53 Korean War, when a complete change of mindset affected the population of the North with the arrival of the 'cult of personality' surrounding the first Great Leader, Kim Il-sung.

It's a very simple explanation to say that the people of North Korea became so completely conditioned by their love and awe of the Great Leader that they just turned their back on organised religion, but in a way that's exactly what happened. Christianity was associated with the US and following the horrors that befell their nation during those three years of war, it is not difficult to understand why people rejected a religion that was essentially part of 'Imperialistic America' in their eyes. The same fate befell the other religions that had been followed up to that point: Korean Shamanism, Chondoism and Buddhism. All four of these religions are still practised today in North Korea, but the numbers of followers have dwindled drastically and in some cases they have virtually disappeared.

If you look on the internet and search for 'religion in North Korea', you can find all kinds of facts and figures about the number of people who still follow God or gods in the country, but simple research doesn't back this up. According to sources quoted in Wikipedia, a total of 35.7 per cent of the population believe in the four religions I've mentioned, but frankly this is absurd and not remotely close to the truth. In my travels in the country and speaking to my guides, I can honestly say I didn't come across a single person who had any religious faith (with the exception of the aforementioned Buddhist monk) or indeed had heard of any of their family members who followed a religion either. That isn't to say that there is no religious following though.

On my second visit I went to a different Buddhist Temple, near Pyongyang, and spoke to the lovely official guide who explained that the government continue to fund the upkeep of the area as it is now a successful tourist destination. The place and the surrounding areas were some of the most beautiful and peaceful I have ever seen and the Buddhist monk was happy for me to take pictures and ask questions via the guide. Although I'm not sure how accurately my questions were being translated, I was given the distinct impression that life in the Buddhist temple was as serene and unhindered as you would be likely to see anywhere in the world. According to figures (again impossible to verify as they are placed on the internet without any official sources mentioned) there are 5 Christian churches, 60 Buddhist Temples and about 800 Chondoist churches in the country. One of the subjects that I raised when I was at the Woljong Temple with the monk was why he still wore the badge of the Great Leader on his lapel, despite his obvious faith. He replied that it had been Kim Il-sung who had personally visited the temple when it was being rebuilt and proclaimed that it would be protected for evermore. The fact that it is also a UNESCO Heritage Site helps too.

Although it's well-known that during his reign as Great Leader, Kim Il-sung persecuted Christians particularly, despite his mother being a Presbyterian deaconess, that persecution started to fade by the time Kim Jong-il started to take the reins of power. The majority of North Koreans are atheists and believe in their own deities, the Kim dynasty, but here is a brief resume of the four religions that are practised in the country, from the most to the least popular.

Chondoism

Chondoism was founded in 1860 by Choe Je-u, a member of an aristocratic family, as a way of combating foreign religions that were having such an effect on Korea. He started the religion after apparently being healed of a serious illness by the god of the universal Heaven in shamanism. This religion became so popular with the common people that Choe Je-u was actually sentenced to death four years later by the Joseon government as divisions grew in society. The movement flourished though and gave rise to the Donghak Peasant Revolution against the royal family and government. The Chondoist community stayed in the north of Korea following the partition, and it's fair to say that this is the one religion that is favoured by the North Korean government today. There is political representation as the Party of the Young Friends of the Heavenly Way and today it is recognised as a revolutionist and anti-imperialist religion.

Korean shamanism

This was once the main religion of the Koreans. The shaman priest was an intermediary between the spirits and humans, enacting rituals to solve the problems of human life. Central to the faith is the belief in 'the source of being' and the gods of nature. The priest (or mu as they are described) are descendants of the 'Heavenly King' and the 'Holy Mother'. This religion was certainly widespread right through the nineteenth century, but Protestant missionaries demonised it with physical oppression and by the time of the Second World War it was very rarely seen. Having said that, the numbers of people in North Korea who still follow this religion are supposedly relatively high, but again as no official figures are available from the country, it's a matter of conjecture. I know that I never once heard Korean shamanism being mentioned in any of my visits.

Buddhism

Buddhism has been in Korea since the fourth century, yet it has suffered more persecution than any other religion in the country. During the Joseon kingdom, which lasted for over 500 years until the occupation by the Japanese in 1910, Buddhism was suppressed as Korean Confucianism was installed as the State religion and ideology. It was only once the country was divided that Buddhism re-established itself, albeit in a small way. North Korean Buddhists have different traditions from their southern counterparts and are entirely reliant on the benevolence of the government to continue their faith and work. They are paid a salary and have to reapply regularly for state authorisation. There are still many temples in the country, and as previously mentioned, these are in pristine condition, but that is more to do with the benefits of tourism than the promotion of religion. Only a very small proportion of North Koreans now follow the Buddhist faith and that was shown clearly to me when I visited the temples. I did see a coachload of North Korean women enjoying a 'Mother's Day' trip, but they completely bypassed the temple and climbed the nearest hill to have a picnic there. There were, however, numerous tourists.

Christianity

Christianity was introduced to Korea, especially the northern areas, in the late eighteenth century and within about a hundred years a huge proportion of the population had been converted by Protestant missionaries and Catholic priests, so it is surprising to see how few people in the country now follow Christianity. During the early part of the twentieth century Christians established schools, hospitals, orphanages and churches and were at the forefront of the struggle against Japanese colonisation leading up to the Second World War. Following the division of the country they still played a large part but as the North became communist many Christians fled to the sanctuary of the South and so Christianity started to fade in North Korea.

Despite writing in his autobiography *With the Century* that he 'did not think the spirit of Christianity that preaches universal peace and harmony contradicts my idea advocating an independent life for man', Kim Il-sung was instrumental in the state following a policy of persecution against Christians after the Korean War. This was mainly due to the perceived association Christians had with America, as it was 'their' religion.

There has been a subtle change over the past thirty years though, especially following the succession of Kim Jong-il. A North Korean translated Bible was made available to the population, although it was strictly regulated in terms of availability (I certainly didn't see one for sale in Pyongyang's sole bookshop), and a new Roman Catholic Association was formed in the 1980s. The American evangelist Billy Graham visited the country and met the Dear Leader, something which would have been inconceivable fifty years ago, and new churches have been built in the capital city. This is all very welcoming, but Christianity in North Korea is strictly state-controlled and according to a Human Rights organisation, 'Open Doors', Christians are still persecuted in the country.

My experience of religion in the country is vague, as repeated questions to my guides about the state of faith in North Korea were normally met with bland and uninformative answers. I did establish that Christmas is definitely not celebrated anywhere in the country, despite what has been reported, and I was also taken to an outdoor Buddhist museum where I was shown artefacts from centuries ago. I found all of this fascinating, but my guide didn't. Out of all the destinations and tourist spots that we visited where she showed undying enthusiasm for educating me in the delights of North Korean culture, this was the one where she showed the least interest. While the Kim dynasty continues, religion is always going to have a difficult time in North Korea.

8

LIFE IN NORTH KOREA

So, what is life like in North Korea? How does the average North Korean man, woman and family spend their days? What are their working habits? What are the schools like? How do they amuse themselves? All of these questions have been asked by the Western media, with varying answers, many of which have little basis in fact. Hopefully I'll try to explain in this chapter that in fact North Koreans are just like you and me. They live their lives and want the same things, but in a rather unique environment. Having said that, life in the cities and towns and life in the countryside for North Koreans could not be any more different.

A *normal day in the city*

I've always been an early riser, so it's not unusual for me to be awake at about 5am. Add to that the effects of a little jet lag, and it's not surprising that on my visits to North Korea I can be found standing at my bedroom window on the forty-second floor of the rather grand hotel looking over the city of Pyongyang before the dawn has risen. The city is lit up just like any other. There don't appear to be the regular power cuts that are constantly referred to in newspapers back in the UK as the street lights are still blazing and slowly you can see the place coming to life. The first thing you notice though are the strains of the patriotic hymn 'Onwards Toward the Final Victory' wafting through the air from the numerous loudspeakers positioned on every street corner. This song will be heard by every single citizen of Pyongyang (and indeed every single citizen is expected to know the lyrics by heart) and is almost like an early morning alarm call. At the same time, workers will be cleaning the empty streets of any dust or leaves that may have fallen during the night. This is done with traditional twig brushes and they are perfect for the job, although they would be pretty useless in cities like London or New York where the night's detritus would probably consist of pizza boxes, empty beer bottles and cigarette stubs; these things just don't appear in North Korea's capital.

There will also be many workers, mostly women it has to be said, who will be attending to the neatness and tidiness of the pavements, trimming grass verges or replacing loose stones from slabs of concrete that pave the walking areas. All of this is done in a clean-air environment as the relative lack of vehicles in Pyongyang means that there is less pollution in the city than virtually any other capital in the world. As the sun rises and the daylight arrives, it is amazing to look to the sky and see how clear it is. As no planes fly over North Korea, unless they are domestic flights, the familiar vapour trails or air streams of jet engines are completely absent. It is like looking up into the sky of the seventeenth century. The clear and fresh air is something that is instantly noticeable because it is without a hint of any toxic aromas or smells.

Gradually the streets start to fill up with people making their way to their offices or factories. This is not like a rush hour on the A3 in London though. There are far fewer cars, albeit nearly all of them the expensive top-of-the-range vehicles such as Mercedes and BMWs, imported from China, but there are also many lorries crammed with soldiers, plus the rattling tram system which emits sparks of electricity from the wires above and always seems to be on the edge of completely collapsing. These non-air-conditioned relics of 1970s Czechoslovakia are crammed with people as the public transport system is ridiculously cheap. You can only imagine the discomfort of travelling to and from work each day like that, unless of course you travel by London's Underground.

Watching over all of this activity are traffic controllers who have absolute authority on the streets and are the kind of people you simply cannot afford to get on the wrong side of. Eighty per cent of them are young women wearing the familiar blue-and-white uniform who actually march to their spot in the streets, salute the person they are relieving and then stand to attention making sure the traffic moves smoothly. It's been said that Kim Jong-un chooses these young women personally, but as there are so many it's probably unlikely as it would take him so long, and again is just another myth surrounding the Supreme Leader. One thing is for certain though, this is a highly prized position for any young female, especially if she is good-looking (I was told that this was a pre-requisite for the job), and all of them seemed to be more than happy to have their photograph taken by any interested tourist.

Joining the traffic is a constant stream of men riding bicycles to work. This is about the most popular way of getting around the city and bikes are highly prized in North Korea. There are actually at least three types of bicycles that denote status among men, so they are cherished at all times, with bicycle theft about the most common crime in Pyongyang. Even the walkways under the road intersections have a special flat surface alongside the steps where men can push their bikes instead of carrying them up and down. It is a predominantly male activity as women on bikes have been frowned upon for many years. This is mainly due to the fact that any woman in North Korea riding a bicycle would almost certainly wear trousers for modesty reasons, and that is not something that is totally accepted in the country, apart from in the military. Having said that, in the countryside women can be seen riding bicycles, but the equality of the sexes is far greater in the harshness of rural life.

Underground there is the same type of bustling activity. Pyongyang boasts sixteen metro stations and they are truly a wonder to behold. As I was taking the escalator down to one of them, I was told very proudly by my guide that the underground system in the capital city was the deepest in the world. This I can believe, especially as I'm not exactly the biggest fan of travelling through underground tunnels, but the stations are incredible.

After descending an escalator that seems to be nearing the centre of the earth, you finally get to the metro stations. Each one has two platforms separated by a marble concourse with chandeliers hanging above. The trains are controlled by two female conductors who decide when the train can leave and who can actually board it too. There doesn't appear to be a timetable, but they do seem to run efficiently and regularly.

While waiting, the Pyongyang worker can idly stand and read the copy of the national newspaper that is pasted to the hoardings (no advertising here of course and the newspaper is not on sale anywhere) and then once inside he or she is whisked through the dark tunnels at all of around 10 miles an hour in a wooden creaking train that was also bought from what is now the Czech Republic, with the portraits of the two leaders staring down at them while listening to the same hymn again. That part is not a pleasant experience, yet it is accepted by the population of the city with resignation it seems, judging by the unsmiling faces I encountered.

Of course, the streets of Pyongyang have absolutely no advertising hoardings, so no one is delayed while deciding whether to buy the latest iPhone or book tickets to see a new film at the cinema. All hoardings have the same images, and that's of the two leaders, plus the latest propaganda message such as 'Long Live General Kim Jong-un, The Shining Sun of the DPRK', and of course the constant background noise of the propaganda hymns that are absolutely everywhere. There are also numerous big television screens dotted around the city playing news feeds from North Korean stations extolling the success of the latest wheat yield or images of another satellite being blasted into space. Most of the time, all of this is ignored as everyone makes their way to work.

Unlike the reports that have created an image of a sullen and scared population walking zombie-like under the watchful eyes of spies and the police, most people appear to smile a lot – unless they are travelling underground, and that is something I definitely do understand! In fact, my overwhelming impression of the North Korean populace, whether in the capital or the surrounding countryside, is that they all have a ready smile. They no longer seemed to be fazed by tourists and I found that I could walk down any main street (accompanied by my guides of course) and hardly be noticed.

As for their clothes? Well they don't all walk around with the latest Kim Jong-un haircut or indeed wear his favourite full-buttoned bell-bottomed trouser suit. The men are smart in black suits, white shirts and black ties, and the women are in a similar black-and-white business suit outfit that nearly always incorporates a rather shorter skirt than is expected with black tights and high-heel shoes. This was either the latest fashion when I was there on my visits, or people genuinely do take a great pride in their appearance.

The one thing that does stand out though is the fact that everyone wears black-and-white and virtually no other colour. The only time that is changed is when there is a national anniversary and the women put on their traditional Korean costume, which is a riot of colour and rustling fabric. These outfits are called *hoejang jogori*, and are basically a woman's jacket whose collar, strings and sleeve ends vary in garish colours. The wide flaring skirt is of bright colours too, making the whole ensemble a riot of contrasting pinks and reds and greens and blues. It's certainly an eye-catching outfit.

There is a myth that jeans and training shoes had been banned in the country as they were too 'Westernised' but I was reliably told that this just wasn't the case. These 'must-have' items in the West, are just not available in North Korea due to the constant economic sanctions against the country. Also, the men can wear their hair long if they so wish, but this again doesn't appear to be part of the fashion in the country.

I was told by another of my guides that the reason for every young boy and girl having similar hairstyles was that this meant they 'fitted in' and they had no distractions when studying for the betterment of the country. Individualism is something completely alien to the North Korean people.

Meanwhile, the women must have their hair tied up at all times when in public, unless in an official role – both my guides were able to flout this rule as they were official tour guides and so they wore their hair down in a way that other women weren't allowed to do.

While the men and women are making their way to work, the children are being collected by official government buses and coaches and taken to school. Their uniform is predominantly white with a red scarf and, like their parents, they are expected to wear the lapel pin showing either or both of the two leaders. What awaits them is a completely different school day from anything offered in Europe. While their parents are starting their working day at 8am with exercises and then a half-hour session of Juche reading and what is called 'self-criticising' (essentially a tool by the management to pick up any failure the previous day in reaching the day's goals) the children are taken to their schools where they have a half-day of the basic educational needs (maths, reading, writing, etc.) before then transferring to another larger building – the Mangyondae Schoolchildren's Palace – where they meet other pupils and study the history of the country, the Great Leaders and Juche.

I've been taken to a few schools in Pyongyang where the teachers and pupils have put on shows for me to illustrate the advancement of education in the country. One of the schools was in the centre of the city and was so architecturally impressive and huge that I actually wanted to start my schooling all over again there. It had the most amazing reception area with blue-and-green marbled floors and huge spiral staircases. I'm not naïve enough to believe that they're all like that, especially as I've been to quite a few, but what is being taught does look impressive to untrained eyes and ears.

During the course of several visits, I saw classrooms of children reciting English phrases, typing on the intranet (the internal North Korean network, not the internet) and playing musical instruments. I'll never forget one young boy of around twelve or thirteen who played the drums like Keith Moon! Unfortunately, I can't imagine seeing him in the future playing on stage in a rock group, but he certainly had rhythm. It's fair to say that children are highly treasured in North Korean society as they are obviously regarded as the future, so their education is as good as most places in the world, if you ignore the indoctrination.

During the day Pyongyang is a virtually deserted city; everyone is at work. There are few shops and restaurants, so the streets don't have the hustle and bustle of other cities, even at lunchtime. Most workers tend to eat their lunch in the office or factory canteens, with only a few venturing outside to eat a packed lunch. The pavement café culture certainly doesn't exist in the country. There are no Starbucks, McDonald's or indeed any other food chain. As far as I'm aware there is only one coffee shop in the city (I've visited it twice, the room was the size of a small studio flat, the coffee was ok) and there are no bookshops to browse apart from an official government one that appears to be open to tourists only and sells North Korean propaganda and nothing else. Apart from the very attractive gardens and play areas, there are no inducements for the workers to leave their factories or offices and have lunch outdoors.

The working day for the average North Korean is around eight hours, and that is actually fewer than in South Korea, where workers have notoriously long shift patterns. At the end of each day though, all workers go through a 30-minute exercise drill, and a quick recap on the day's activities, before leaving for home at about seven pm. There are many reports that have almost become accepted as fact in the Western media, such as that families have to go to bed at nine in the evening as that's when the electricity is turned off, and their apartments are so under-heated that it wouldn't be possible to enjoy any type of social activity. I have no idea as to what the domestic conditions for North Koreans are like, as it is totally against the law in the country to allow any foreigner into one's home, but my experiences of looking into the windows of the apartments and talking to my guides suggest to me that in fact the living conditions are nowhere near as horrendous as reported. In fact, they seemed to be quite pleasant without being overly luxurious.

When I've asked about what utilities they have in their homes, I've been told that the usual goods are part of every household, such as washing machines, television sets, microwaves, etc. I also know that the night-time entertainment in the capital is quite vibrant, if you know where to look. There are numerous restaurants where locals have family dinners (with the national dish of cold noodles in abundance), and there are many bars where it is a regular thing to see men suffering the effects of one too many bottles of Taedonggang beer (which, by the way, is excellent).

There are of course many karaoke bars, although they don't appear to be that popular and the word *Eumjugamu* (meaning drinking, music and dancing) can be seen at the entrance to many of these establishments. Drinking alcohol seems to be essentially a male-dominated activity and a solitary one too, as wives don't appear to join their husbands on a social night out.

The family dynamic is one that sees the husband and wife initially living with his parents until they can afford an apartment of their own. Once the woman is joined in marriage she is effectively saying goodbye to her natural family and moving to another one. There she is expected to work a full day shift at whatever employment she has, and then in the evening cook, clean and wash while her husband is usually out drinking. In many ways, North Korea is still some way behind other cultures around the world, and gender equality is all but absent. I travelled on a busy bus and gave up my seat to a lady who was weighed down with bags of shopping. It certainly caused a few amused comments as it seems that that act is completely alien to the man or woman in the street.

Divorce by the way is possible, but just about the most shameful thing a couple can bring to their extended family, with the female especially carrying the stigma of separation far more than the male. There must be many loveless marriages in North Korea, as indeed many arranged marriages too. Most weddings are politically motivated and the supplying of a dowry always rests with the bride's family.

As explained, once married, the woman then becomes part of her husband's family, so the thought of a young bride marrying someone from outside of Pyongyang is unheard of, as there would be little reason for her to leave the capital city. Once a couple decide to get married, they are then put on a lengthy waiting list for a small apartment. This could take up to three years until quite recently, but there is now a huge building and renovation project in the capital city where new high-rise buildings are going up quicker than anywhere I've seen previously.

Once the couple have their new home, it is effectively theirs for life if they continue to be employed by the unit which has supplied it. That is not quite as risky as it sounds, as a job in North Korea is nearly always a job for life and you would have to do something profoundly bad and stupid to lose that 'career', if a job for life can be described as a career.

I had a quite interesting conversation with one of my female guides when talking about marriage. She was a young woman and her mother was going through the whole process of trying to arrange a match for her, but with little luck. When I asked her about falling in love, she gave the impression that it really wasn't important, and then she was stunned when I told her that, unlike in her country, we didn't normally have blood tests ahead of a marriage to see if we were a suitable match. Her shock was because having a blood test before marrying someone could ensure healthy children. That indirectly brings me to another observation. I have never once seen anyone who may be partially or completely disabled in North Korea, and there are certainly no provisions anywhere, either in buildings or on the roads, for wheelchair access. Obviously, there could be some kind of a terrible explanation for this, perhaps not.

Home entertainment appears to be limited. The television channels will only show the state propaganda programmes that run in the evening from around 6pm, these being documentaries and dramas telling the familiar story of struggle to victory for the North Korean people. Some of the titles of the most popular give you a clue to their subject matter: *The Story of my House, Oh Youth, Forever Striving Together*, and *Nation and Destiny*. The latter was recommended to me by one of my guides, so I actually bought a DVD of the programme at Pyongyang airport before leaving for Beijing. I was rather astonished to find that it was part of a series of thirteen 3-hour episodes. I watched it and found it hard going (not helped by a lack of sub-titles), although *The Story of my House* was a far better film and actually starred my guide, who clearly had had a change of career in her earlier years.

North Korean households can access South Korean TV, but it's a time-consuming and rather dangerous thing to do, so most just accept what they have. Even my guides on my second trip, staying in the same hotel as me and on the same floor, couldn't access the television stations from China, South Korea and Japan the way I could and had to rely on my recounting the previous night's news bulletins to get a better and more balanced view on world affairs. There was also certainly no way at all they would risk being in my room watching the stations, as that would incur serious punishment. Having said that, there is a big black market trade in 'Western' films via DVD and more recently memory sticks, and South Korean films in particular are very popular. There is absolutely no access to the internet, but the country's intranet is widely available as a substitute. I have no real knowledge as to how open this is as it is written in Korean, but I was told, naturally, that everything anyone in the country needs to know can be found on those pages. What is on those pages though remains a mystery to me.

There are certain areas of the country, although I'm pretty sure are not in Pyongyang, where some streets have electricity on one side and none on the other, depending on the power shortage at the time. I have heard stories (although completely denied by my ever-smiling guides) that neighbours would discuss at the start of each week which home would cook and serve the evening meal as they were the ones with electricity that day or evening. The other unfortunate families have to make do with candles or kerosene bottles to light the gloomy evening. This is something that was definitely prevalent in the 1990s when the country was on its knees, but as I said earlier, I have seen Pyongyang at night, and it is as sparkling as any other major capital city in the world.

As I have previously written, there certainly doesn't appear to be any provision for pets in North Korean culture, and this is almost entirely down to Juche; I have never seen a single domestic animal in any of the streets of the country.

Instead of going to see the travelling circus in the capital city mentioned earlier, the selling points of that afternoon's entertainment being the dancing bears and smoking monkeys, I was taken by my guides – bemused at my missing out on the bears – to what was called a 'circus act', which turned out to be a magic show in a small theatre, with North Koreans of all ages including young children delighting in the performers. I felt embarrassed to be shown to the front row where a burly security man effectively pushed a young family out of the way so that I could sit down with my two guides, but the show was entertaining if rather old-fashioned by Western standards.

One thing that struck me though was how much everyone enjoyed themselves. From two-year-old children to grandparents in their later years, they all laughed loudly and constantly and applauded every trick and every telling of every gag. It was a true family day out and the kind of thing that at times seems to be lost in the West.

What about mobile phones? They are available in North Korea and are used regularly. They can receive the intranet, just like we can receive the internet, and texting is a big activity among younger people, but all of the satellite apps and social media sites that we take for granted are not available, or even heard of, in the country. South Korean phone providers can be reached near the border, but the punishment for using one is harsh enough to deter most people.

All of this describes what is essentially a normal day in Pyongyang, and all of the major cities, Sundays excepted. On that day the whole workforce takes the day off and nearly everyone heads to the municipal parks if the weather is warm, with family picnics and a rather large amount of alcohol. Either that or they go to the local amusement park, the Kaeson Youth Park, which is very popular, and which, annoyingly for me, has always been closed every time I've visited.

The capital city in particular is surrounded by gorgeous parks and hillside treks and trails that are extremely popular, especially in the spring and summer. Sunday is a day for the family, so mothers, fathers, brothers, sisters, grandparents all get together on that one day of the week. Family is extremely important and the expression 'He/she's like family to me' which we use regularly, is completely lost on the North Korean people as family is just about the most important thing in their lives – behind their adoration of the Great Leaders. There are special anniversary days too, which I will describe later in the chapter; but outside of the capital city it is a completely different story.

A normal day in the country

I have been driven through the countryside of North Korea numerous times, and each time it's a similar experience. Apart from the highways being almost impossible to navigate due to the thousands of untended potholes, plus the many, many checkpoints with unsmiling, stern soldiers checking every bit of paperwork possessed by the guides, the overwhelming sense is of desolation and a life that is miserable at best to our Western eyes. There is no one around near the main highways and great distances can be travelled with barely a sighting of another vehicle, but once you get to the heart of the farming countryside, it is a hive of activity.

In the distance, as you are travelling, a small town or a clutch of houses that make up a village will be pointed out to you, but these are all some way from the highway and so seeing anything closer is difficult. I have visited other cities/towns in the country and in some cases, they are spartan at best and almost uninhabitable at worst, with a road system that is virtually unusable in parts.

I've been fortunate to stay in a sensational hotel deep in the heart of the forests and mountains and well away from any town, one which would be regarded as five star in Europe, and I've stayed in hotels that are that in name only. The hard beds, cold showers and electricity cuts are certainly prevalent there. In fact, one of my hotels didn't have running water at all and my bath was filled before my arrival with cold water for washing and flushing the toilet.

All of this gives a glimpse at the degree of difference in the lifestyles of the people in Pyongyang and the major cities, and the people of the countryside.

Although there is no possible way that a tourist can see inside the small, squat buildings that the peasants inhabit in the country, it must be fairly certain that they live a difficult existence. Electricity is powered by a generator as the grid is unreliable at best, and running water is not taken for granted, never mind the possibility of hot water. So life in the North Korean countryside looks to be a miserable existence, yet everyone I saw – and in some cases there were hundreds of people working in the fields – seemed to be genuinely content. It's possible that a lack of knowledge of what life is like in the outside world contributes to this sense of happiness. I simply didn't see anyone who looked genuinely unhappy.

I have witnessed men pulling an ox-driven cart along a dusty path, and I have seen many farmers and workers squatting at the side of the highway waiting for lifts from the once-an-hour vehicle that may arrive, as there is no other way of travelling around the country unless on a bicycle. The train network is slow and cumbersome, it doesn't really connect the towns and it is rather expensive for the average farmer. It is also one of the most exhausting of activities attempting to buy a ticket for any journey. An ID is required for the local populace as well as proof of the reason for the journey, while for tourists it is strictly governed.

There are few cars or lorries or buses on the roads, the main highways are completely deserted and the one 'service station' on the main road southwards out of Pyongyang towards the DMZ and the border with South Korea had a man waiting with a kettle and instant coffee for us, as the restaurant had clearly never been opened since the building was built owing to lack of visitors. It's an eerie and uncomfortable if fascinating experience.

One thing is for certain though: If you live outside of the main city of Pyongyang, or any of the other large towns and cities, then you are almost inevitably living in poverty. A lot of the older generation of farmers and country workers will never have even visited Pyongyang and have probably never left their small enclave.

Government projects

Every North Korean family, whether living in the cities and towns or the countryside, have to send one member for at least two hours a day and six days a week to help to support government projects. This can be in the form of building structures to cleaning the roadsides.

In a society where there are no taxes, this is the equivalent of keeping the nation moving. Everyone feels it is their duty to help the country grow, and it's represented very strongly in one of their mottos: 'The one who eats rice must plant rice.' I might also add that North Korea has some of the most beautiful countryside anywhere in the world, and as it is effectively 'unscathed', it retains its natural wonder. It has been left essentially unchanged down the centuries with no farm lands carved into its face. It's wild and rugged and undisciplined, and that is what gives it its alluring beauty.

There are inevitably areas of heavy industry and these are the places that are the least attractive and welcoming. Passing coal stations belching out fumes with huge engineering machines straddling a river was like a glimpse into 1900s Britain. I visited the West Sea Barrage, a huge dam near the town of Nampo, some 8 kilometres long and one of the most impressive engineering successes in the country that was built in the 1980s, but it was also one of the most forbidding and overwhelmingly depressing structures. Watching the video of the building of the barrage – compulsory when you visit as a tourist – it's striking to reflect on the hardship the workers had to endure to reclaim land from the sea before building the monstrous concrete dam. I could only speculate as to the number of people who must have been injured or likely killed during its construction, yet this film was accompanied by the usual propaganda hymns of success and victory.

In general, I can only say that life on a day-to-day basis in Pyongyang and the major towns and cities seems to be acceptably comfortable, yet once in the beautiful countryside, the conditions are harsh and existence a struggle. North Korea is effectively two countries in one, and the two societies live almost side-by-side yet with barely a flicker of recognition from one another. This for me is the essential problem with the challenges the country is facing and has always faced. There is not enough productivity within the cities to create goods that can be exported, as workers' output merely serves to keep the domestic market supplied, while the peasants and farmers in the country have even less chance to create a surplus, they simply survive.

Cuisine

It's always an interesting insight into a country's culture to look at their national cuisine, and of course with the Great Famine of the 1990s as part of their history, even more so for North Korea.

The main dish, which is eaten virtually every day and served in every restaurant, is cold noodles served in a large brass bowl. Firstly broth containing seasoned meat shreds is warmed up over a naked flame, before the noodles, made of buckwheat, are then coiled and dropped into the liquid. They are accompanied by boiled egg, cucumber, radish and red pepper, mixed together to enhance the flavour. There then follows some of the noisiest eating outside of China as trying to eat noodles with chopsticks is neither quiet nor dignified, but it is enjoyable. I personally managed to develop a liking for them in vegetarian form but struggled with the same diet each day. The mung bean pancake, which is served with them, is quite delicious.

Another favourite is onban. This is a dish of rice in hot chicken broth, which is regularly served, often at breakfast. There is also fish porridge, which seems to be an acquired taste from what I could see, and mullet soup with roasted ribs of beef, served with a cake called nochi. This is a popular treat made from steamed powder of glutinous rice that is fermented with malt before being fried. It's not for the diet-conscious.

As a vegetarian I worried about my diet when I first visited, so I was surprised to learn that quite a decent number of North Koreans are indeed vegetarians, although their reasons are far different from mine. A lot of the population who survived the Great Famine had to exist on roots and vegetables grown locally and so meat left their regular diet. It seems that quite a few of the older generation just never reverted to eating meat and they continue to have their vegetarian meal of choice, maybe due to the inability of the stomach to digest meat any longer. My first guide, in her early thirties, was certainly a vegetarian and would never consider eating any type of meat.

As has been mentioned though, the countryside offers a rather different experience to the city, with rice, cabbage and radish being the staple diet of peasants and country workers. These foods are grown extensively throughout the countryside, and it's not uncommon to come across a road or street that has virtually no traffic covered in rice that is drying out ready to be stored for the winter.

The staple vegetables, cabbage and radish, are collected and stored in huge vats of vinegar from which they will then be eaten in the cold winter months. The local rice wine, seemingly very popular and actually 70 per cent proof, is drunk sparingly for obvious reasons, but is certainly a way of enhancing a bland meal on a cold winter's evening. I tried it once, and 'strong' is too weak a word to describe it!

Public holidays

The only real time that life changes in Pyongyang is during one of the many public holidays; there are officially seventy-one public holidays in North Korea, but these include Sundays which are regarded as such and not just a workers' day off. The two most important holidays of the year celebrate the birthdays of the first two leaders, Kim Il-sung on 15 April, and Kim Jong-il on 16 February, plus the Day of the Foundation of the Republic on 9 September and the Party Foundation Day on 10 October. On these days the populace comes out and spends the day singing and dancing, enjoying huge feasts with lots of alcohol involved; but there are also sombre events too.

I was present on the Day of the Shining Star (Kim Jong-il's birthday celebrations) in 2017 and I witnessed the whole city effectively come to a standstill. In the main square in Pyongyang, there are mass dances involving thousands of men and women in a choreographed tribute to the Dear Leader. Women dress in their traditional North Korean costumes, bright and voluptuous dresses with a riot of colour, while the men are in a more sombre grey and black. The women dance in circles singing and holding hands, with the men as back-up marching and chanting propaganda songs in unison.

These dances and marches can actually go on for most of the day, yet they never seem to lose their intensity. To an outsider like me it looks incredible and, in fact, the rehearsals start days beforehand. On my second visit to the country, I came across such a rehearsal and the people were standing listening to instructions bellowed out from a loudspeaker for hours on end (I've no idea how they were allowed to do this on what was a working day, but I'm guessing it is felt to be far more important than attendance at a factory or office). This was done in intense heat as the temperatures had rocketed, but no one seemed unhappy or uncomfortable, and the one thing that stayed with me was the amount of laughter I heard. This was a genuinely enjoyable experience for the people. For those who read the Western reports that the people are physically forced to participate in these events, I can testify that it just isn't true. Everyone enjoys it and everyone looks forward to the days when the mass dances take place.

Of course, there is a more sombre side to these celebrations. On 16 February I joined thousands of silent people as they climbed the hill to the Korean Revolution Museum, where the statues of the two leaders dominate the surroundings and city. The people then stood in groups of approximately 100 as they bowed deferentially to the monuments. I was also expected to do this. The overwhelming feeling was of complete servitude to these two leaders shared by all, and the total silence was extraordinary. This is certainly not something that 'regime change' can undermine, as has been suggested. These people are so completely in awe of the Great Leader and the Dear Leader that virtually nothing is likely to change it.

Compare all of that with the images you see regularly on television, when North Korea displays its military hardware in the same central square with the Supreme Leader, Kim Jong-un, and his military advisors watching from the balcony. This is normally on Army Day on 25 April and provides not just an impressive sight as tanks, military hardware and missiles are paraded along the main street, but also gives the North Korean people a sense of safety through the sheer scale of the demonstration. Thousands of soldiers take part too, and it's not just an exhibition of strength for the population of the country, it's also regarded as a timely reminder to the outside world that North Korea has an extremely powerful army.

As mentioned, Sundays are also seen as public holidays, and are also meant as walking days. As well as family entertainment in the parks, children are encouraged to walk everywhere, so most forms of public transport are cut back on these days. Also, with a nod towards the environment, occasionally these days coincide with tree-planting days, which are exactly what they say. Families are encouraged (ordered to be more correct) to plant a tree seedling in an attempt to make the city a greener place. I have to say that as I strolled around the parks of the city with my guides, I was struck by how environmentally clean it all looked. There is a huge park and woodland in the centre of the city in which I spent a pleasant few hours, just strolling along the pathways that criss-crossed the woods leading up to a hill that overlooked the city and the Botong River. It was so peaceful and serene and the views at the top were so spectacular, and all of it completely at odds with the image the country has outside its own borders.

It's also on these days that you'll quite regularly see the Art Propaganda Troupes – the same group who performed at the 2018 Seoul Winter Olympics and which later one British newspaper described as Kim Jong-un's 'sex slaves'. These troupes consist of about ten to twelve student girls dressed in smart clothing who sing in the streets, mostly propaganda songs and hymns, but it's very melodic and enjoyable and certainly extremely popular with the crowds.

It's on these days that I think you see the real side of the North Korean people. They are not the oppressed zombies being herded into factories by machine-gun toting soldiers and spied on by shady characters in raincoats and trilby hats. They are men and women, young and old, couples and families, just enjoying the freedom that a day off from the routine of work can give. I've seen couples on park benches canoodling and kissing, just as you would in the parks of London, children giggling as their fathers push them on swings and roundabouts, and grandfathers and grandmothers sitting peacefully as they survey their family, probably telling the same stories to their grandchildren time and again. The point is, they are normal people, just like you and me. They don't appear to be scared of authority, although granted the punishment for wrong-doings against the state can bring about a retribution far greater than most other places, they have a genuine affection and gratitude for their leaders, and they *seem* to be happy in their lives. There is an old saying in North Korea which translates quite easily into 'Nothing to Envy', and this is aimed at the rest of the world. Despite their deprivations, and the majority of North Koreans aren't exactly sure what it is they're missing out on, they don't appear to envy anyone else. It's a simple life, without any of the pressures of commercialism and capitalism, and certainly a cradle-to-the-grave society.

Their hierarchy is straightforward. They go to school, they are given a job based on their abilities and merits and they expect to stay in that job for the rest of their lives, they are given housing, they marry and they have children. It's all pretty well mapped out for them, but the opposite side is there seems no hope of betterment as careers are decided, marriages are mostly arranged (as previously mentioned) and the day-to-day routine is not likely to change. Money is never abundant, food can be in short supply and hopes and expectations are minimal, but there is a genuine contentment among the people.

To illustrate this, I spoke to one of my guides and asked her what she wished for in life. She didn't really understand the question as she had everything that had been planned for her. She had a good job, and being a government guide is certainly ranked among the highest, she was recently married and was in the process of receiving her first living accommodation away from the ties of family, yet there was one thing she admitted that she really wanted. She confided in me that she wanted to travel to see Switzerland. I didn't really understand why, but she'd seen it on a television programme and had fallen in love with the idea. I told her that I hoped one day she would be allowed to, but the look on her face suggested otherwise. So that is the problem. On these relaxing and restful days, the people are content and happy, yet that is as far as they are likely to travel away from the confines of their working and personal environment. That is North Korea.

Below are two of the important and enjoyable public holidays that are celebrated by families and that have no political connection, should you wish to visit the country on these dates; and days out in Pyongyang recommended by the state.

Lunar New Year's Day (*Jongwoldaeborum*)

15 January. This is celebrated from early morning and the major events of the day are the memorial services for ancestors, paying respects to elders of families and villages, relatives and teachers, the serving of food to young people and children, exchange of greetings between friends and playing games in the public parks. These games are normally for the children such as kite flying or sledding. In the evening families climb the highest hill by torchlight to view the first full moon, and then would predict their future by its light and wish for a happy harvest in the year ahead. They then end the night by dancing in the fields, holding torches, until the midnight hour has struck.

Harvest Moon Day (*Chuseok*)

On this day people visit their ancestors' graves with various foods prepared with the new crops of the year, trim the grass on the graves and make any repairs. This is a very respectful day for all North Koreans and it is observed without fail. Drinks are prepared, and special cakes are made and exchanged. These are half-moon shaped rice cakes stuffed with beans and flavoured with pine needles, plus chestnut dumplings, which are a delicacy in the cities and towns.

By tradition, there are also 'Eight Famous Scenes of Pyongyang', which locals are urged to experience during the year. They are, and in no particular order:

- The view seen from Ulmil Pavilion, where in the spring there is a spectacular view of the first full moon. This is a place where young couples enjoy the first moments of romance.
- Visiting the monks at Yongmyong Temple, a historic relic that is awe-inspiring in its beauty and serenity. I have been there and I can confirm that it's as marvellous as it is described.
- Seeing off guests at the Pothong Gate. This is a gateway to the northwest of the old Walled City of Pyongyang that can still be seen today. By waving off their visitors, they are mirroring the good manners of Koreans of the past who used to stand at the old entrance until their guests were no longer in sight.
- The boating at Komun Ferry is particularly popular during the summer months as individual boats are hired for lazy trips on the Taedong and Pothong rivers. As the tourist literature given to me described it: 'You can hear the sounds of ripples beating against the side of the boats and see the water birds fly in the blue sky.' It sounded idyllic, but each time I've visited it has been closed. Frustrating.
- Listen to the patter of raindrops at the Aeryon Hall. This is recommended as the noise the rain makes as drops fall onto the lotus leaves in the pond sounds like a pipa, a lute-like musical instrument from centuries past. It is seemingly very enchanting, but sadly I didn't hear it.
- Observe the lush greenness of Mount Ryong as the pine woods there and the neighbouring Mount Taesong stay green even in late autumn.

- Watch the thawing of the Ma Rapids in early spring as the Taedong River rises with the onset of the warmer months.
- Watch the full moon rise from Pubyok Pavilion.

All of the above are regarded as wonders by the locals of Pyongyang, and there are indeed some spectacular sights and sounds, but don't be surprised if you are looked at strangely if you wave to an invisible visitor from the Pothong Gate, especially as it is now surrounded by old tenement blocks and building sites.

Shopping

If you ever catch a flight from Beijing to Pyongyang, you can be guaranteed that sharing the check-in queue with you at the Air Koryo desk will be numerous North Korean and Chinese men accompanied by huge trolleys that contain boxes and boxes and boxes. All of them are sealed and all have to be checked in individually, much to the frustration of other passengers. These boxes, I have been told, contain just about every variety of goods that can be sold on through the black market in North Korea, or directly to the highest bidder once the goods have cleared customs in Pyongyang. They are all being imported from China by groups of traders who make the journey between the countries on a regular basis. Such is the way the market operates in the country.

It's a well-known fact that North Korea has severe shortages of goods, including the basics such as food and medical supplies. This is mainly down to the sanctions imposed by the US and other allied countries, but of course it is also down to the almost complete failure of the Juche self-sufficiency concept. Having said that, I was taken on numerous occasions to an extremely busy supermarket in the centre of Pyongyang, where virtually every item you could think of was on display and being bought by shoppers. The food shelves were full, albeit of brands that were obviously locally produced and based on recognisable brands around the world. The clothes shopping was as enthusiastic as anywhere else. It was a Sunday on my first visit, which I was told was a traditional day for shopping in North Korea, and it seemed like whole families had taken the opportunity to do just that. There was an almost celebratory air to the proceedings, with the aforementioned Art Propaganda Troupe serenading everyone outside, and orderly queues at the cash desk – by the way, the only two currencies that were accepted at this store were either Chinese Juan and the Euro, so the North Korean Won had to be changed at a desk before entering. Of course, cynics might suggest that I was taken to this supermarket because it was the only one in Pyongyang, but what I saw is what I'm reporting. As the guides say: 'Look with your eyes and tell the world.'

Another department store I was taken to sold household goods and clothing, although there didn't appear to be any distinction between the two in terms of presentation. On its three dimly lit floors, washing machines were placed alongside men's trousers, with women's shoes in the same section as garden rakes and shovels. There was no understanding of branding and commercialism, because it just wasn't needed. If you wanted a garden shovel and a pair of trousers, you knew where to get them, instead of being lured in by advertising. It was odd, but strangely comforting too. Despite this, I did fall for the familiar tourist trap in paying far too much for an item. I saw a child's North Korean national dress, which I wanted to buy for my granddaughter. There was no price attached and as I was wandering the department store alone (proving that there is a certain amount of freedom if you visit) the sales lady just made up a figure of 30 Euros. I gladly paid as it seemed reasonable. Only when I returned to my guide did she inform me that the same item could be purchased in my hotel for 12 Euros! So it seems there is a small amount of capitalist drive and eye to profit in the North Koreans too.

This of course gives a rather naïve view of shopping in North Korea, an almost quaint and simplistic way of buying your weekly goods, and it does fail to tell the full story. Shopping in North Korea (and I refer here to Pyongyang because this is where the majority of the goods end up) is very much an as-and-when affair. If a food shop has a certain item that hasn't been available for some time (i.e. fruit, which wasn't available at all during my second visit) then word of mouth is the best way of finding out if it has returned and so the woman of the household queues for hours to make sure her family don't miss out. This can be seen regularly throughout the city, especially if a new batch of food has been delivered. Noodles and rice are the staple diet in the country, but eggs are regarded as a delicacy and are regularly in short supply, unless you're a visiting tourist, in which case they are available in abundance.

To combat the food shortages, especially during the slow recovery after the famine, small markets started to appear on the roadsides selling virtually any commodity that was needed, but mostly home-grown food. These are called *Jangmadang* in Korean and they started to appear at such a rapid rate that the government tried to close them down, citing harm to the national economy, but as food shortages continued, small stalls would re-appear a day after the army had destroyed the previous one. In one of the most swingeing acts, after numerous attempts to curtail them had failed, the government made the decision in 2009 to devalue the North Korean Won by cancelling the final two zeros on every banknote. This meant that a 10,000 Won was now only worth 100 Won, and of course that was disastrous for those who had made a profit from the markets and managed to make some savings. Citizens were given just one week to exchange their banknotes, losing thousands in the process, and were also given a limit of just 100,000 Won that was allowed to be exchanged. This law ruined many and boosted the North Korean economy at the same time. What became of the remaining banknotes is a mystery. They are probably hoarded in people's apartments, now totally valueless. Destroying them would also mean destroying the image of Kim Il-sung, something which would be unthinkable.

Despite this, the markets continued until eventually a veneer of legality covered them as the government privately admitted that they couldn't stop them, and they also couldn't feed their own people by normal methods, so now the market stalls are everywhere in the city. Owners (usually a middle-aged wife as her husband has to be at his place of work) pay a nominal fee to a local cadre and a blind-eye policy is implemented. It's a private economy that not only embarrasses Juche, but also undermines the national economy too. It's estimated that around 70 per cent of the households in the country now indulge in some form of private market economy, from which they derive around 75 per cent of their income.

Away from the major cities and towns, shopping is an almost unheard of activity. In the rural areas, survival is paramount, and so food is grown, clothes are made, and living accommodation is just that, accommodation for living. There are no village shops, or deliveries to rely on, and trips to the local town are an adventure in themselves and probably only happen about once a month, so it's just a case of managing and surviving. A more austere lifestyle is difficult to imagine.

Sports

Being someone who has been involved in sport in some capacity or other for most of my life, I'm always intrigued when visiting a new place or country as to how highly regarded sport is there. When it comes to North Korea, it's something of a mystery, just like everything else. We all know that the DPRK actually participated in the Seoul Winter Olympics in 2018, actually joining forces with the South to create a Korean team in ice hockey, etc., but trying to find any evidence of organised sport in the country is extremely difficult.

In the centre of Pyongyang is the May Day stadium, a huge circular Olympic-sized arena that was completed in 1989 and opened on 1 May of that year. It has been hugely renovated in recent years with the new version re-opening in 2013, and it is an impressive sight both inside and out. According to my guides, it's the largest stadium in the world with 150,000 seats, but the facts are different as the official capacity is 114,000.

It was in this stadium that I sat and watched a 'Pyongyang derby' football match one gloriously sunny Sunday with my two bored-senseless guides. I was excited when I was told the day before that I would be allowed to attend, and so I was expecting a great atmosphere with a packed ground, two sets of fans cheering their teams. You can imagine my disappointment and surprise when I entered the stadium to find there were no more than around 150 spectators huddled together in a small area near the team's dugouts.

It was a sobering experience, even if the football was of decent standard (for the record the league leaders, April 25, scored twice in the first 10 minutes and that was effectively the end of the contest) and it made me realise that sport doesn't appear to be a passion at all in the country.

Alongside the stadium is a football school for children of eight upwards. It's an impressive facility with purpose-made pitches and accommodation of a decent standard for the students, but on my visit there appeared to be only around thirty to forty pupils engaged in the activities. When I asked who their favourite teams were, they replied almost as one with the name of Real Madrid, and that was because of a sponsorship deal that had been linked to the Spanish club. None of them mentioned any of their local teams, yet they had all watched the recent World Cup with fascination.

As I was stood watching, I noticed one particularly talented young player and remarked on it to the local guide. She told me that he was aged twelve and had been at the academy for two years but was probably going to be sent back home within two months. As he was clearly the best player on the pitch, I asked why, and was told it was because he was shorter than all the rest and didn't conform to the regulation height and no amount of training or body building could add to his stature.

For me it was such a shame, as the future for this young boy would almost certainly be a return to rural life where he would presumably work out his life on the land, simply because he was shorter than the rest.

Later, when asking my two female guides which sports they liked, their answers were vague to say the least. They liked to ice-skate and they liked to go bowling, but any suggestion of following a team or player in any given sport was met with blank looks.

It seems though that sport has played a part in the nation's history at times when it's been needed as a way of galvanising the people. Football fans will remember the heroics of the North Korean team at the 1966 World Cup in England, very nearly knocking out the mighty Portugal at Everton's Goodison Park ground. Now the national football team very rarely bother the headline writers, even if they did reach the World Cup again in 2010.

Basketball has certainly won new popularity in recent years due to Kim Jong-un's friendship with Dennis Rodman, who is a regular and controversial visitor, and it does seem to have a history in the country. Kim Jong-il demanded the instigation of a Men's and Women's Basketball League in the late 1990s, even having a song composed called 'Basketball is Exciting', which was constantly played on state radio. It was all part of the 'height-increase campaign' that existed following the years of famine. If one example is enough you could argue it worked as the country boasted one of the world's tallest players in Ri Myung-hun at 2 metres 35.

The Dear Leader was such a huge fan of the sport that he had a video of every single game that Michael Jordan had ever played and was presented with a signed ball when Madeleine Albright visited the country in an official capacity in 1998. The film that I referred to earlier, *The Story of my House*, was about a family of basketball fans and the attempts of one of the younger children to make the national team. Inevitably after an incredible struggle, she succeeded and proceeded to take North Korean basketball to new heights around the world!

Traditionally the more physical sports such as wrestling and weightlifting are the ones that supply the heroes to the North Korean public, especially if they have success at the Olympic Games. Kim Jong-un recently introduced a policy that gives successful athletes perks such as the top-of-the-range apartments in Pyongyang for their efforts. If you asked any North Korean who their sporting hero was, they'd most likely pick any of the three who won medals at the 2012 London Olympics, Om Yun-choi, An Kum-ae or Kim Un-guk. Also, marathon running has a following in the country, and the Pyongyang marathon has run since 1981, admittedly with a few interruptions for political and economic reasons. Today it attracts a huge number of participators from Asia and other parts of the world.

With some spectacular mountains and a love of skiing in the country, it's surprising that there hasn't been more success at the Winter Olympics, but the infrastructure to get a talented individual to international level doesn't appear to be there and this was proved when I was taken to a couple of indoor ice rinks, both of which were melting and not exactly 'user-friendly'. Then again, I attended an ice-dance festival, which was full to capacity and featured some amazing local acts, backed up by foreign stars who perform there every year. Ice hockey has also existed at a professional level in the country since the 1950s with the teams mostly based around Pyongyang, Kaesong and Nampo, but at an international level, there has been little success.

Sport is often used as a unifying force in many countries, the former USSR being an obvious example, so it's surprising how little organised sport there is in North Korea. I can only assume that the priorities are different in a country that has an economy barely able to sustain itself, and another problem must be the lack of television coverage of sport in a country that obsesses over the Supreme Leader and the constant struggle for victory. Even the Winter Olympics of 2018 was given scant media coverage apart from the political ramifications of having an all-Korean team. Having said that, the First of May stadium was built for a reason.

It is an Olympic-approved stadium, although the chances of the Games taking place there are remote. It was built after South Korea was awarded the 1988 Olympic Games and the

North wanted to prove that it, too, was capable of hosting a huge sporting event. The country then successfully bid to host the World Festival of Youth and Students a year later, and so the stadium was part of a huge reconstruction of the city.

The largest sporting event it has hosted was quite odd. In 1995 around 160,000 fans over two days saw a pro-wrestling event organised by the American series, World Championship Wrestling, but its main purpose now is to host the annual Arirang Festival, celebrating the nation and its achievements. This comprises about 100,000 participants involved in mass dances and gymnastics and it continues for hours, well into the evening. It's normally a two-month event, but the sheer task of arranging such a celebration has meant that there was a gap of five years after the last festival in 2013, although it seems to have been incredibly successful as it was still being mentioned in November 2018 when I was visiting. The event is listed in the Guinness Book of Records as the largest gymnastic display with an astonishing 100,090 athletes involved in 2007.

As ever with anything to do with the country, there is a dark side. In the late 1990s, the stadium was apparently used for the public executions of army generals who were involved in an attempt to assassinate Kim Jong-il. As is always the case though, this event is surrounded in myth and mystery. The worst descriptions are of the generals being burned alive in the centre of the pitch, while other stories have them being shot by firing squad. Again these stories are difficult to verify, but I must admit to feeling quite uneasy sitting in a stadium that was reputed to have witnessed such atrocities.

Near the Juche Tower there is another stadium of slightly smaller capacity, the Kim Il-sung Stadium. This is on the exact spot where the Great Leader delivered his speech on

14 October 1945 after his return to the newly liberated Korea. It has some 80,000 seats, and football is the main activity, but sadly on my three visits to the country, I have never seen it open, although I was reliably informed that it plays host to regular matches.

Although there are a great deal of leisure activities in North Korea, especially involving families, sport doesn't seem to play a big part. I saw few football pitches, a handful of basketball courts and hardly any gymnasiums during my visits, but there were numerous table tennis courts at the schools. Only there does there seem to be a desire to train the next champion. In a way that is totally understandable. Table tennis is one of the cheapest sports to get involved with and can be played anywhere there is a space large enough to hold a normal sized table. We may not see North Korea in the next World Cup Final, but we will continue to see North Koreans excel at wresting, weightlifting and possibly table tennis.

Travel

Travelling around North Korea is not easy. The country has an infrastructure that is basic at best and virtually non-existent at worst. As a tourist it's an adventure, but as a local it can be at times difficult and in some cases almost impossible. If you're visiting and you're travelling from one area to the next, then it's just a case of sitting in the official tour mini-bus, which has no air-conditioning in the summer and little heating in the winter, allowing the guides to deal with the numerous military check points and then watching the scenery pass by as the driver negotiates some of the worst highways in the world. This is typified by the road that takes you from Pyongyang to the DMZ, and in fact any trail that is supposed to resemble a country lane in the rural areas. The drivers of the official tour vehicles are nothing short of excellent, as they have to deal with stone-covered tracks that at times even traverse streams, and deal with overtaking other vehicles in almost kamikaze manoeuvres due to the lack of road awareness of the few other drivers travelling the route.

In any developed country, a trip from the main city to the border would be a comfortable journey of a few hours, but North Korea is not a developed country. It has little infrastructure so inevitably going from Pyongyang to anywhere takes considerably longer. Firstly, the highway is completely deserted, which should be a pleasure for those who have to endure the traffic-jammed motorways and auto routes of Europe, but there's a reason for this. Hardly any cars venture outside of the capital due to the almost impossible demands inflicted on any citizen in terms of the papers and passes required to leave Pyongyang. In some cases, citizens are just not allowed to travel outside the main city, depending on their 'standing' in the country. If you're a military cadre, then there are few problems, but if you are just another worker in a factory, then there has to be a very good reason why you want to travel.

The second restriction is that the highway is almost impossible to negotiate at any speed above 20 miles an hour due to the huge potholes that have never been repaired and are getting larger each year. Driving any vehicle on this road takes the utmost concentration as you have to zigzag and weave constantly to avoid serious damage to the suspension or a blown tyre. It's exhausting to watch, never mind to drive.

On the highway that I've described, as indeed with many of the others, there is what resembles a service station, but in fact is a structure that is hardly ever used. The bridge crossing the three-lane route does have a restaurant, but it doesn't appear to have ever been used, with the rest of the building in some sort of decay. It's hardly surprising as on the journey there and back, I saw no more than five other vehicles (excepting military lorries, which are always nearby) and during an equally difficult journey from Pyongyang to the International Friendship Exhibition, I saw a total of two other cars in the six-hour round trip. If you break down, you're on your own.

Car ownership is on the increase in North Korea though, and in the capital the streets are certainly busier with vehicles than ever before, but rush hour is an unknown term and the traffic is made to move freely under the glare of the traffic women at every crossroads – although traffic lights are becoming more and more common too. Unfortunately for the average North Korean family, a private car is almost completely out of their reach, and most of the top-of-the-range makes that can be seen in Pyongyang (imported from China) belong to either the higher ranks of the military, or other well-regarded citizens such as scientists or successful sports stars. In fact, there is a recently built street in Pyongyang called Scientists Street, which of course houses the scientists, designers and architects (part of the 'Constructing a powerful Knowledge Economy' drive) who are so treasured in the country. Despite the fact that most of them own cars, this particular street is nearly always completely deserted, something I never quite understood.

For North Koreans to travel within the towns and cities, the tram system is preferable if the distance is too far to cycle. This is an ancient system relying on an electricity grid that is creaking and in dire need of modernisation, yet somehow it seems to work. It's a common sight to see old Eastern-bloc trams rattling along the street, with sparks flying from the electricity power lines above, and packed with people. There are also buses that provide a service (seriously reduced on Sundays due to 'walking days') but these didn't appear to be as popular when I was there. It's possible that they are more expensive than the trams. Also, as I mentioned previously, there is an extensive metro system in Pyongyang, with a few other towns and cities having smaller versions. It's never packed but it is slow, even if the stations are a wonder to behold.

To travel around the country for a North Korean citizen means there are the usual security forms to fill in and checkpoints to pass. Train travel is by far and away the most popular way of travelling with nearly 5,500 kilometres of track criss-crossing the country. For the most part the carriages are reasonably comfortable, if rather dated by Western standards, but journeys can take some time if there are repairs or electricity shortages in the rural areas.

This is dealt with stoically, as nearly everyone who embarks on a long-distance train journey is prepared for lengthy delays. The train is also one of the most communal ways of travelling and spending any time in a carriage with a North Korean family can be entertaining and enjoyable, although the conversation will always be rather stilted as questions and answers have to be translated by the ever-present guides.

Surprisingly North Korea has eighty-two airports, with the main international one situated in Pyongyang. The other eighty-one are usually landing strips with a Portakabin for a terminal. The main airport in Pyongyang though was totally refurbished and renovated recently and matches any modern airport anywhere in the world. It has three terminals with the usual shops, cafes and bars, but the International Terminal is unique in that it's nearly always empty. For a tourist checking in to fly to Beijing, no more than 45 minutes is required as the aircraft is effectively waiting for you. There is one national airline, Air Koryo, which has the worst rating of any airline in the world, but that's simply because it's not a member of the Federation that rates airlines, the IATA. I have flown with this airline many times and it's like any other short haul carrier, not luxurious but certainly not uncomfortable. The planes are modern, the crew extremely pleasant, but the in-flight entertainment is a macrocosm of the country with constant running of films of singers and dancers entertaining military officers in a concert of propaganda songs. It can be an acquired taste but certainly provides a glimpse of the country if you're on your first visit.

For ordinary North Koreans though, there is no chance of them being able to fly from the International Terminal, and even the air crew has to stay in the aircraft in Beijing before the flight home. North Koreans are simply not allowed to leave the country, unless under the strictest of security – i.e., athletes competing in Olympic Games, or members of the government attending a trade conference. This also includes any train travel across the border to South Korea. The security at border patrols is so severe that few defectors would attempt this route, either by plane or train.

One of the strange vagaries of the country is the almost complete lack of road signs directing anyone anywhere. If you want to catch a train in Pyongyang, then you need to know where the station is, because there are no signs to tell you. Equally the airport's whereabouts is a mystery until you are virtually there. I remember travelling back to the airport on my second visit along one of the main roads leading out of Pyongyang (the airport is approximately 20 kilometres away) and becoming quite concerned that we weren't actually travelling to it as I didn't see any signs. Only with about one kilometre to go did I see a man-made sign on the side of the road with a drawing of a plane and an arrow pointing upwards. It calmed a few of my nerves to say the least and made one of my guides laugh when I told her about it, maybe proving that the people are aware of the country's reputation and find it a little amusing. Only on the main highways did I see the occasional sign with kilometre distances quoted to the nearest town, although that just furthered my frustration as a 30-kilometre sign would invariably mean another two hours of uncomfortable travel. Signposts within the cities and towns are virtually non-existent, so any museum or attraction that you are visiting is found through local knowledge as opposed to helpful signage and directions, and of course there are no apps to help in North Korea, nor access to Google maps.

Finally, owing to the sparse number of vehicles in the country, there are very few petrol stations and those that do exist are almost exclusively based in the major cities or towns. Travelling for any length of time outside of these places requires some serious mathematics to calculate the amount of petrol needed. As a nice aside though, every vehicle is required by law to be washed inside and out before entering Pyongyang after lengthy journeys. This is done by a small group of enthusiastic men and women who are employed by the government, although their attention to detail can be quite exasperating as my shoulder bag was also washed thoroughly when I accidentally left it on the rear seat.

Health

The lingering effects of the famine in the mid-1990s has certainly affected the health of the nation. It's reported that the people of North Korea have a life expectancy of just under

70 years, which is comparable to other low-income countries, but causes of death are different. Cardiovascular diseases and cancer account for a large proportion of deaths, which is not entirely surprising bearing in mind the amount of alcohol men in particular consume, and the fact that most adults smoke, however, malnutrition is still responsible for death in the country, and this isn't necessarily a throwback to the famine, but is caused by current food shortages in the rural areas in particular.

Hospitals in Pyongyang appear to be modern and well-equipped, although the World Health Organisation has expressed its concerns at the quality of treatment carried out, with stories of drugs shortages. Outside the capital city the situation is probably far worse. Some of the towns and villages that I travelled through appear to lack even a basic road system, so the chances of there being clean and modern hospitals is remote to say the least.

It seems that preventative medicine is a government ideal, with mandatory exercise and the regular spraying of public places against disease. As I've already alluded to, the population of the country, especially in the capital, seems to be fit and healthy, but the total lack of any sign of disability or indeed anyone in any type of physical distress is a worrying feature.

There are of course no official figures available for the number of people who may be regarded, in the West, as disabled, just as there are no signs whatsoever of homelessness in the country, but it would be stretching credibility to the extreme to think they don't exist.

Healthy eating is not a term that is even understood in North Korea, as eating *at all* is in itself an activity that the older generation view with utmost respect. With memories of the famine still raw, a guaranteed two meals a day at least is always at the forefront of their minds, and despite the government constantly informing the masses that prosperity is near, the fact is that it is a daily struggle to eat well.

Food is available, and in more quantities than for some time, despite the sanctions, but the quality is poor. The North Korean diet is effectively rice and noodles, with steamed and boiled vegetables as a side dish. Meat is available, but its source is not always known and at times it can be unpalatable, yet when food is served to tourists, it is certainly appealing and nourishing, and also available in abundance. My concern as always is that I might be depriving a normal family of a decent meal.

One strange quirk about the North Korean diet is their distaste for cheese, especially as a pizza topping. Pizza is one of the few Western dishes popular in the country but try and put cheese on it and you'll be regarded as being a little odd to say the least!

Education

I have visited five different schools on my visits to the country. One was an amazing building with marble floors and chandeliers in the absolutely huge reception area with a winding staircase to the first floor, the second a little more run-down in a town outside of Pyongyang and another a bland and unremarkable building that didn't look like a school at all. On each occasion I was shown different classrooms and entertained by the children either dancing, singing, or playing instruments, such as the boy I mentioned earlier with his drum kit. I was shown them using computers.

What struck me was how incredibly seriously education appears to be in North Korea and how much the children seem to like it. This cannot be forced on youngsters as they all have a sense of mischief no matter where they live, but the young students in all of the schools seemed extremely proud of their school and of course their country.

I was taken by the headmistress of one school into the national learning room. This was basically an activity-based area, slightly shabby in parts, with clay models depicting the story of the birth of the nation, and great emphasis placed on the Great Leader, the hatred of America and the victory over the Second Arduous March. It is 'brainwashing' to an extent, yet it isn't questioned by anyone. The pupils wear their lapel badges, sing their homage to the Great and Dear Leaders and also learn Russian and English far quicker than any schoolchild I've seen in the West. They also all, boy or girl, have a smile on their face. Again, I can't believe this is forced upon them.

Education in North Korea is taken very, very seriously. There is an eleven-year free period of primary and secondary education, with 27,000 nursery schools, approximately 15,000 kindergartens and 5,000 each of primary and secondary schools throughout the country. There are also universities and colleges, yet many of the students opt not to go to university but complete their compulsory national service instead.

This is all seems quite normal to Western eyes, but the main difference is in the curriculum. There is a very heavy leaning toward natural science at school level, whereas social sciences are effectively ignored. The ideology of the Juche Theory is taught from an extremely early age, and one of the main differences you notice when you visit any school in North Korea is that the walls aren't covered with the workings of the pupils, in the form of pictures, essays etc., but ideological phrases on Juche and sayings from the Great Leader that the pupils are expected to very quickly learn by heart. In that respect, it's an unforgiving and inflexible system.

Family

The family is a very important part of North Korean culture, but it is also another aspect that is strictly controlled by the government. As we've heard, marriages are nearly always arranged and then the wife moves in with her husband's family and takes over the role usually occupied by the mother, effectively saying goodbye to her maternal family. Due to the severe housing crisis that has been ever-present in the country – although that is being addressed in Pyongyang now – the newly-wed couple will, almost without exception, live in the apartment of the husband's parents.

For a woman over the age of around thirty not to be married is virtually unheard of, and being a spinster is just about the worst thing a woman can be in North Korea. Also, divorce is something that is hardly heard of, especially as in nearly every case the woman inevitably loses out. Women's rights are not exactly at the forefront of social ethics.

There is huge peer pressure for a woman in particular to be married by the time she turns thirty years of age. Nearly every one of her friends or colleagues will be married at this stage and as a spinster, she will be effectively isolated. For those who don't get married, then their lives are less than fulfilling in other's eyes and they will always be regarded with suspicion and sadly, a certain amount of contempt. As I referred to earlier in the book, arranged marriages are still extremely common in North Korea.

Some people look at North Korea and believe it to be a communist and classless society where everyone is equal and each and every citizen shares in the overarching struggle for the benefit of the nation. Actually, this isn't true. Although communist in nature with Juche, the reality is that there are effectively three classes in North Korean society and depending on which one a family belongs to, this dictates the quality of life.

In 1957, The Workers' Party Politburo announced the concept of dividing society into three classes or levels depending on the history of individual families. It is called the songbun system and consists of loyal, neutral and hostile groups. For a family or families to be part of the loyalty group, their ancestors had to have fought alongside The Great Leader in the Korean War or pledged total allegiance to him from the moment the country was born. This also included intellectuals and revolutionaries who had contributed greatly to the creation of the Juche state.

To become, through no fault of their own of course, part of the hostile group, a family has to be descendants of people who were once landowners and capitalists, or have family members who were part of a religious movement, or collaborators with the old Japanese colonists. The sins of the fathers shall be visited up one the sons, 'unto the the third and to the fourth generation', and in this case, beyond. To be in the neutral group means that the family is both of the above, and has settled in between the other two.

These three classes effectively dictate the lives of every citizen, even if they're not aware of what class they are officially in. People can live their whole lives without knowing at what level their standing is, although it would become obvious if one was looking to climb the social ladder. The system is run completely by the government and every facet of a family's life is kept on file, including any indiscretion committed (large and small) by past members. This is tallied up in a points system and the more favourable the number of points the more likely it is that a decent job and living conditions will be available. It also appears to be far easier to have a songbun downgraded by bad behaviour than upgraded by good behaviour. Crimes and anti-state actions stay on file forever and never get expunged, so a child of the twenty-first century can be punished for the actions of its great-grandparents from the times of the Korean War, no matter what level of loyalty that child might possess. It is an unfair system, yet in some ways it's similar on a far more sinister and organised level to the upper, middle and lower-class system that the United Kingdom had, or still has.

The lowest class, the hostile, will find it almost impossible to get on in life. They can't serve in the military or be selected for national sports teams. They won't be found in the top scientific positions and schooling will be basic at best. Similarly, marriage will be almost entirely to another in the hostile class as it would be highly unlikely any arranged marriage would involve a loyalty member with a hostile member. There would be absolutely no gain for a member of the loyalty class to marry a member of either of the other two, and so it hardly ever takes place.

Anyone of the loyalty class attempting to marry someone from the other two classes will have so many obstacles put in their way (not least by the parents) that falling in love hardly seems to be worth it. This can explain in part why in effect North Korea can be regarded as a loveless society.

One of the ways around the unfairness to the lower songbun class would be to pay a substantial bribe, but as many of the hostile groups live in the country and are farmers and peasants, then this doesn't seem feasible. As described earlier, most farmers still use practices that were common in the nineteenth century, with oxen pulling heavy carts and seasonal planting with little in the way of chemical fertilisers or modern-day technology. It's a harsh life and environment, where a trip to the capital city would be as likely as a trip to the moon.

The reason for this class system is quite simple. It gives the government complete control of its people, allowing the ones who are unshakingly loyal to the leaders and the Juche Theory to rise to the top of the ladder and continue to propagate the Isolationist policies. It guarantees total servitude as committing any crime, no matter how small, will almost certainly drop the individual and their family members down to the neutral class, with virtually no chance of returning. It also guarantees that the loyalty class will marry each other and so the constant devotion will be handed down the generations.

Over the past few years the songbun society has been challenged and undermined because bribes have become commonplace. This nearly always involves those with a high songbun (from the loyalty group) who want to get on in life or desire a special privilege for a family member, resorting to bribing high officials. This is such a regular occurrence nowadays that it is part of society and expected if ambitions are to be realised. Although North Korea is not a capitalist society, there are benefits to those who are willing to use capitalist methods to gain a better job or a higher position in their company.

One of the strange quirks of this is that defectors (which we will return to later) once fled the country as genuine economic migrants suffering grinding poverty, especially after the famine, and not necessarily because of the constraints of the brutal government. Now they are more likely to flee because they have reached as far as they can in life, no matter how many bribes they have offered or paid. 'I couldn't develop myself' or '*baljeon mothaettda*' is a phrase that has been commonly heard from those who have defected from the DPRK.

This songbun society is a very good reason why any imminent collapse of the country is unlikely. Devotion to the Kim dynasty is carefully managed and unless the class system is scrapped overnight, then it's going to continue to support the Juche Theory.

Products

When you think of North Korea, inevitably food and material shortages are at the forefront, with pictures of poorly dressed citizens struggling to survive. Well, that is certainly true in the country areas away from the main cities, but in Pyongyang it seems that it couldn't be further from the truth. As I've mentioned, the capital city is modern and pleasant, albeit a lot quieter than others. There are cars on the roads, and most are top-of-the-range, clearly imported from China for use by the more select members of society; I was taken to a local car dealership – which although closed much to the embarrassment of the guide – had all the family vehicles on display in its showroom. The trickle-down effect of whatever wealth there may be can be seen in the everyday attire of the Pyongyang people. Men are smartly dressed in black suits and white shirts when travelling to work, with a slightly more informal look on their days off. Women are immaculate in short skirts and jackets, all of them wearing make-up like any Western woman attending her workplace. Clothes appear to be freely available, yet the fashions are probably some way behind the rest of the world, and jeans and training shoes are frowned upon due to their connection to America. While I was there I didn't see anyone who looked shabby or impoverished, although the clothing was bland.

Of course, the food shortages have been reported widely and are commonplace, but I visited two supermarkets in the city, and both at that time were well-stocked with goods, mostly

own-brand versions of popular makes. The cola that I tried
was a local version of Coca Cola that tasted pretty similar.
There are numerous chocolate bars and sweets, all seemed
appetising and were obviously based on well-known brands.
The shelves of the two supermarkets I visited were full and
being constantly replenished, as the locals were out in force on
their traditional Sunday shopping day. The queues to change
the North Korean Won into Chinese currency were long and
good-natured and housewives were leaving the shops with
bundles of goods.

Now I'm aware this could be an elaborate ploy by the
authorities to show the tourists how successful the economy
is in North Korea, but it really would have been an enormous
amount of work if that was the case, particularly as my visit
(with a few French tourists) was unplanned. I was allowed
to wander the aisles of the market alone and I saw the fresh
bread on sale, the packets of cigarettes, the washing powders
and the household goods on display, in some cases all on
the same shelf! Marketing is still an unknown idea in North
Korea. Away from the main supermarkets, which in some ways
resemble what the first ones must have looked like when they
arrived in the UK in the 1970s, there is a booming street trade
with stalls on virtually every street corner selling snacks and
drinks. These are extremely popular at lunchtime, as they are
in virtually every city in the world. Drinks are normally soda
or bottled water and snacks invariably include cold noodles
or rice cakes – no hot dogs or cheese-and-onion sandwiches
with a packet of crisps. Away from prying eyes though,
there is a black market trade usually run by the woman of
the household, selling vegetables, fruit and rice to those who
cannot afford the supermarket prices.

There are restaurants and bars, the second being plentiful in Pyongyang. Restaurants tend to be owned by families with living accommodation attached, and they completely specialise in North Korean cuisine, so the chances of finding a Chinese takeaway or a pizza parlour are virtually nil. The restaurants are pleasant, if not rather intimate in their layout as personal space when eating doesn't appear to be a priority for North Koreans. Food is more than plentiful and the guilt I felt at not being able to eat everything set out for me on individual plates was tempered somewhat when I was told that the leftovers would be distributed to the charming waitresses, who smile constantly. As a vegetarian I worried about what I would be served, but North Korean cuisine is mostly a rice- and noodle-based diet, although the same meal three times a day and seven days a week did eventually wear me down. Visiting a country that has had one of the worst famines in world history only two decades ago meant I tried not to be ungrateful.

Drinking is a regular occurrence in the city, and it would have been interesting to see official figures for alcoholism in North Korea (but there aren't any, unsurprisingly) as most nights I saw clearly inebriated young men being carried away from a bar to a vehicle waiting outside, presumably for them to to be driven back to their homes. The local beers are excellent and well-priced, and in fact every kind of spirit can be found in the bars, many from different parts of the world. One thing that was clear though, visiting a bar in the evening is not a social event considered suitable for a tourist agenda, as they are invariably located well out of the way. You can make your own mind up as to why. Coffee is quite pleasant, but the one café that I saw and visited was hardly welcoming, despite there being a pinball machine in the corner. The coffee is locally made and can be bought easily enough, but locals tend to drink sweet China tea instead.

In terms of personal entertainment, most of it appears only to be available on the black market. I visited a bookshop in Pyongyang which exclusively sold North Korean propaganda books, usually written by the Great Leader or the Dear Leader; there were no books on any other subject available and certainly nothing from any other country. Entertainment to be viewed at home, such as CDs and DVDs, appears to all be smuggled into the country as the domestic television and radio broadcast nothing but propaganda-style documentaries and musicals. These are normally in the form of scenes of soldiers progressing through fields of 10-foot high wheat as they march towards the liberation of the nation from the Imperialistic Americans, all with accompanying battle hymns.

It's hardly light entertainment, so the locals are now adept at illegally watching Western-style films (many South Korean) on DVDs or memory sticks. *Titanic* was the first great hit of this underground movement and was then actually shown to schoolchildren as part of their education about the West. The constant images of South Korea must surely register with the people of the North, yet the government hasn't attempted to stop this plain to see industry from blossoming.

If all of this gives the image of a city that has no problems or shortages, then so be it, I can only report what I saw. Yes, there are food shortages, as was proved in the moment when I was told that the fruit shop was closed that week as there was no fruit. Yes, I'm aware that when I eat a meal as a tourist I'm inevitably offered far more than is necessary to give the impression of abundance, and yes, I also know that the fashions for the citizens are so bland and conformist that it's difficult to tell whether someone is wearing an outfit that was bought last week or ten years ago. All I can say is that when I've been in

Pyongyang and other cities in North Korea, there hasn't been a sense of deprivation.

Outside the cities it's a different story, of course. It's here that the people struggle with food shortages, lack of oil for heating, and in some cases no electricity, or power cuts at best. There can be absolutely no doubt that living off the land in North Korea is a miserable existence. This is the part of the country that is rarely seen by visitors, yet I was fortunate enough to see large swathes of the arable land as I travelled from one city to the next. With the state taking a large proportion of the crops that are grown and distributing them to the military first, followed by the people, hunger is still a feature of life in outlying areas of the country and the chances of this changing in the near future seem remote.

There are no beggars in the cities, or anywhere else for that matter, as it is strictly forbidden and the punishment for such an action is harsh, but there is a certain dignity that characterises the daily struggle. The pride in the nation seems to surpass any personal discomfort, something that has kept the Kim dynasty in power for so long, and locals seem to take a genuine delight in welcoming tourists and making sure they have enough to eat in restaurants and hotels, plus explaining right down to the smallest detail the item of clothing or other product you may be perusing.

On my one-night stay in a hotel that had no running water, the manager and his wife made a point of actually collecting water from a local tap and heating it at 6am to be delivered to me an hour later. This was something they were willing to do as I was their guest, but of course it was a sobering experience for me and left a huge amount of guilt hanging over me for complaining to myself about the standard of accommodation.

One item that is fast becoming a must-have within the country is a mobile phone. These are widely available now, especially in Pyongyang, and like all Western youngsters, there are street scenes of people with their heads down staring at their screens as they walk. Of course, you can't get the World Wide Web on a North Korean phone, but you can get the country's intranet. You can text (which nearly everyone seems to do) and obviously you can make calls, but the wide variety of apps that we take for granted are not available. For instance, Google maps is not something you are likely to find on a North Korean mobile phone. The supplier is very strict as to where the signal can be accessed, yet still some intrepid people manage to connect to the South Korean networks to give them a glimpse of the outside world. It goes without saying that Western mobile phones do not work at all in North Korea.

Finally, in a country where individualism is just not known, it is remarkable that there seems to be a total lack of curiosity from locals when they encounter tourists in the street or in the shops and cafes wearing Western clothes that are more colourful or fashionable. For the most part you are completely ignored anyway, but on the few occasions when you are standing in a crowd and clearly stand out as a Westerner, there are no envious glances, no admiring looks and certainly no questions.

This could be down to a total lack of interest, and maybe years of living in the Juche-dominated state has taken away any natural curiosity, or it's more likely due to the fact that there is still that fear that someone, somewhere might just report one's interest. Walking through the streets of any city or town in the country as a tourist seems to be one of the safest things you can do, as you are totally unmolested and not bothered in any way.

Your clothes do not appear to be a source of envy for anyone, but then that might have more to do with my own particular style as opposed to anything else! I certainly don't see Western fashions like hoodies, the latest training shoes or baseball caps arriving in North Korea any time soon, and if it were to happen, I think I'd find it rather sad.

9

HUMAN RIGHTS AND PRISONS

No matter what positive spin the country puts out, and no matter how many times I personally enjoy my visits there, the fact is that the name of North Korea conjures up appalling images of human rights abuses and severe punishment for any wrongdoers. The experience of American student Otto Warmbier, who was seemingly tortured to just short of the point of death, made headlines around the world, and again proved that the DPRK is a place where some of the worst abuses have taken place, and by all accounts, still do. Warmbier was imprisoned in North Korea in 2016. In June 2017, he was released in a vegetative state and died soon after being returned to the USA; his parents consulted medical experts, then asked for his feeding tube to be removed.

According to the United Nations Human Rights Council, North Korea has one of the worst records in the world for human rights abuses and one of the most long-standing, without any suggestion that it might improve soon. The worst conditions in the country it seems are those of the prison camps for political prisoners, and not 'normal' prisoners who have been incarcerated for the kind of crimes that can be seen anywhere in the world. It's estimated that there are about 100,000 of these political prisoners, but the fact that the number has been rounded-up to make it what it is, suggests again that little actual information is known. The camps, mostly in the north-east area of the country, are totally out of bounds to visitors and can really only be seen by searching Google maps or other satellite images. They are also not referred to or acknowledged by anyone within the country, but it's fair to say that most people are aware of their existence.

At the heart of the government in Pyongyang is what is called the Ministry of People's Security, MPS, a department that employs in the region of 200,000 people and is used as a task force not only to maintain law and order in the country but as part of a huge spy network that works at every level of society. That network employs around 50,000 officers in the State Security Department, SSD, who are responsible for running the political prison camps and for the brutality that is connected to them. The police officers of the MPS are feared by the populace if a clampdown on a particular area is ordered, but they are also involved in the distribution of food and products, policing the roads and security checkpoints and the day-to-day activities of keeping the people secure. For those latter duties, they are normally admired. The same cannot be said of the SSD, who are regarded in the same way as the Gestapo or Stasi. These are people who spy on citizens and foreign nationals who visit, plus interrogate suspects in a particularly brutal fashion.

The problem of being a political prisoner is not just an individual one, as North Korea uses the guilt-by-association method in which a prisoner's wife, children and brothers and sisters can all be punished for his crimes. The only way a wife could avoid any punishment would be to immediately arrange a divorce, but a married sister would be unaffected as she, by virtue of being married, would now belong to her husband's family.

To become a political prisoner in North Korea seems to be rather easy. There are numerous SSD agents, usually someone who has been in trouble themselves and has been threatened with arrest and torture unless he or she co-operates with the spy network. They are part of any community, be it a workers' group, or a local housing association or part of a famers' collective. They are also usually of the lower songbun, so that they find themselves being exploited by officials because they need extra money to supplement their meagre income.

Once someone has been overheard making any kind of criticism aimed at the Supreme Leader or the two previous leaders, then their details are passed to a sitting committee who decide whether the accusations are serious enough for that person to be investigated. If they are, then special SSD agents access their living quarters and will then do everything possible to make a case against the accused.

It's very rare that the person being investigated is not then arrested and interrogated for hours on their loyalty to the Kim dynasty. The interrogation procedure is harsh at best and unimaginable cruelty at worst. Many defectors have reported that one of the main ways of getting a confession is to make the accused stand in one position for hours without being allowed to move. Any small movement results in severe beatings until the person can no longer stand.

How true all of this is, is of course difficult to determine, but enough former inmates who have been lucky enough to escape the process have defected and reported these events that their accounts must be taken seriously. There are also reports of brutal beatings as part of the interrogation process, with the aim to force the confession as quickly as possible. It's at this point that the life of the accused is effectively over. A confession will be made publicly and to all intents and purposes that person then disappears forever. They are nearly always transferred to one of the appalling camps and will spend the rest of their days doing hard labour until they either die of old age or more likely starvation and deprivation. They can only hope that no members of their family join them.

The camps that hold the political prisoners can be traced back to Kim Il-sung who, emulating Stalin, started to punish political opponents as early as the mid-1950s. As far as the UN is aware, there are only four of these camps still in use, from an original ten some sixty years ago, but despite the drop in numbers, the cruelty and appalling conditions are apparently just as bad.

In some cases, there is what is called a Revolutionising Zone, where some inmates who are deemed to be capable of reform are kept. In these areas the prisoners are subjected to constant propaganda and lessons on the State. These people are mostly relatives of those who have been accused or found guilty.

People held in a Revolutionising Zone can be released after a period of time when they are no longer seen as a risk to society. They will be expected to disown the family member who was found guilty and is presumably rotting away in the other zone, the Total Control Zone. They will never see that member of the family ever again.

The Total Control Zone is for the inmates who have been forgotten, the ones who were found guilty. They have absolutely no rights and are treated sub-humanly, with eventual death their only escape. They will sleep in rooms that are no more than 50 square metres with approximately thirty inmates to a room. Food is scarce; they are fed rice twice a day, although those meagre rations are sometimes withdrawn as further punishment if work quotas aren't met, and in some cases inmates who are too weak to continue are left to die, then buried without any grave markings or any family member present. Torture is commonplace, mostly from sadistic guards. The prisoners are non-people. A more miserable existence cannot be imagined, but it has to be pointed out that the DPRK is not the only country to participate in such cruelty. Many others do, but what makes North Korea unique is the number of its citizens who are arrested and incarcerated in this way.

So how do citizens find themselves in such a position? Well, on top of the informers who are planted by the SSD, there are plenty of actions forbidden by the state can be punished. This means such innocent acts (to our eyes anyway) of folding a newspaper containing the images of the leaders, taking their portrait down from a wall, defacing a statue (although in my experience this would be very difficult indeed with the number of policemen present) or printing any kind of anti-Kim literature and distributing it. Knowing of the penalties, few people would even dream of committing such acts, never mind actually doing them.

High-ranking officials who have found themselves falling foul of the regime aren't necessarily treated in the same way. Most are immediately executed (which might be almost be a blessed relief as opposed to the horrors awaiting them in a political camp) or in some cases are just kept under house arrest, meaning they will never move in the circles they once did. They will stay in their allotted accommodation and hardly ever be allowed out. The fact is that crime, especially political crime, is something that is hardly considered by the populace due to the horrendous punishments.

This is certainly one way of retaining the loyalty of the people, or at least their acquiescence.

Of course, one way of avoiding any kind of punishment is to defect from the country. Not all defectors are criminals, obviously, and nearly all are running away to find a better life, but the reasons are all bound up in the dreadful human rights situation in the country. Later in the chapter we will look at some of the more well-known defections and the reasons and danger behind them.

Below I have included extracts from a Human Rights Watch report published in 2018, the latest one available. It clearly highlights some of the problems but I believe in some cases, it shows a lack of understanding of the country.

North Korea remains one of the most repressive authoritarian states in the world, ruled for seven decades by the Kim family and the Worker's Party of Korea. During his fifth year in power, Kim Jong-Un continued to generate fearful obedience by using public executions, arbitrary detention, and forced labour; tightening travel restrictions to prevent North Koreans from escaping and seeking refuge overseas; and systematically persecuting those with religious contacts inside and outside the country.

A 2014 United Nations Commission of Inquiry (COI) report on human rights in North Korea stated that systematic, widespread, and gross human rights violations committed by the government included murder, enslavement, torture, imprisonment, rape, forced abortion, and other sexual violence, and constituted crimes against humanity.

On 10 December 2015, the UN Security Council discussed North Korea's bleak human rights record as a formal agenda item for the second year in a row, following the COI's recommendations.

On 23 March 2018, the UN Human Rights Council adopted a resolution condemning human rights abuses in North Korea. It authorised the creation of a group of independent experts tasked with finding practical ways to hold rights violators in North Korea accountable and recommending practical accountability mechanisms, including the International Criminal Court, to secure truth and justice for victims. Lawyers Sonja Biserko and Sara Hossain joined the panel, supporting Tomás Ojea Quintana, the new Special Rapporteur on human rights in North Korea.

North Korea has ratified four key international human rights treaties and its constitution includes rights protections. In reality, the government curtails all basic human rights, including freedom of expression, assembly, and association, and freedom to practise religion. It prohibits any organised political opposition, independent media, free trade unions, and independent civil society organisations. Arbitrary arrest, torture in custody, forced labour, and public executions maintain an environment of fear and control.

North Korea discriminates against individuals and their families on political grounds in key areas such as employment, residence and schooling, through songbun, the country's socio-political classification system that from its creation has grouped people into 'loyal,' 'wavering,' or 'hostile' classes. This classification has been restructured several times but continues to enable the government to privilege or disadvantage people largely based on family background, personal performance, and perceived political loyalty. However, pervasive corruption enables some room to manoeuvre around the strictures of the songbun system, even while it burdens people, as government officials regularly demand and receive bribes from those seeking permissions, pursuing market activities, or wishing to travel inside or outside the country.

Freedom of Expression and Access to Information

All domestic media and publications are strictly state controlled, and foreign media allowed inside the country are tightly controlled as well. Internet and international phone calls are heavily monitored. Unauthorised access to non-state radio, newspapers, or TV broadcasts is severely punished. North Koreans face punishment if they are found with mobile media, such as Chinese mobile phones, SD cards or USBs containing unauthorised videos of foreign news, films, or TV dramas.

Inhumane Treatment in Detention

The government practises collective punishment for alleged anti-state offences, effectively enslaving hundreds of thousands of citizens, including children, in prison camps and other detention facilities. Detainees face deplorable conditions, sexual coercion and abuse, beatings and torture by guards, and forced labour in dangerous and sometimes deadly conditions.

Those accused of serious political offences are usually sent to political prison camps, known as kwanliso, operated by North Korea's National Security Agency. These camps are characterised by systematic abuses, including meagre rations that imperil health and can lead to starvation, virtually no medical care, lack of proper housing and clothes, regular mistreatment including sexual assault and torture by guards, and public executions. Political prisoners face backbreaking forced labour, including in logging, mining, and agricultural work. UN officials estimate that between 80,000 and 120,000 people are imprisoned in political prison camps.

Those whom authorities suspect of illicitly trading goods from and into China, transporting people to China, and minor political infractions, such as watching or selling South Korean films, may receive lengthy terms in detention facilities known as kyo-hwa-so, correctional, re-education centres. Detainees there face forced labour, food and medicine shortages, and regular mistreatment by guards. People suspected of involvement in unauthorised trading schemes involving non-controversial goods, shirking work at state-owned enterprises for more than six months, or those unable to pay bribes to officials for various reasons are sent to work in short-term forced labour detention facilities (rodong danryeondae), literally labour training centres. Beatings are common in these facilities, and dangerous working conditions purportedly result in significant numbers of injuries.

Forced Labour

The government systematically uses forced labour from ordinary citizens to control its people and sustain its economy. A significant majority of North Koreans must perform unpaid labour at some point in their lives.

Former North Korean students who left the country told Human Rights Watch that their schools forced them to work for free on farms twice a year, for one month at a time, during ploughing and seeding time, and again at harvest time. A former school teacher who escaped North Korea in 2014 said his school forced its students (aged between ten and sixteen) to work every day to generate funds to pay government officials, maintain the school, and make a profit.

Ordinary North Korean workers, both men and unmarried women, are required to work at government-assigned enterprises. Although they are theoretically entitled to a salary, they usually are not compensated. All North Korean families also have to send one family member for at least two hours per day, six days a week, to support local government construction or public beautification projects, like building structures, fixing roads, collecting raw materials like crushed stone, or cleaning public areas.

The government launched a 70-day 'battle' to prepare for North Korea's most important political event in 36 years, the 7th Korean Workers Party Congress, which took place between May 6 and 10. The government forced people across the country to produce more goods and crops in order to cover the costs of the congress. Posters, billboards, and media broadcasts demanded that North Koreans complete their 'battle plans,' and counted down the days until the congress opened.

Labour Rights

North Korea is one of the few nations in the world that has not joined the International Labour Organisation. Workers are systematically denied freedom of association and the right to organise and collectively bargain.

Since Kim Jong-un's rise to power, the government has sent more workers overseas to earn foreign currency salaries, most of which the government seizes. Although the country does not release official data, some observers estimate that more than 100,000 North Koreans worked overseas in 2015. The treatment of North Korean workers overseas falls short of international labour standards, with no right to freedom of association or expression, control by minders who limit freedom of movement and access to information from the outside world, long working hours and no right to refuse overtime.

During 2017, North Korea fired 23 missiles during 16 tests and conducted its sixth nuclear test, sending tensions between the US and its allies and North Korea to their highest level in decades. Personal insults and threats traded between US President Donald Trump and Kim Jong-un in September and October further worsened the situation.

On human rights, the international community continued to press for action on the findings of the United Nations Commission of Inquiry (COI) report on human rights in the Democratic People's Republic of Korea (DPRK or North Korea) that found the government committed crimes against humanity, including extermination, murder, enslavement, torture, imprisonment, rape and other forms of sexual violence, and forced abortion.

On 9 December 2016, for the third consecutive year, the UN Security Council put North Korea's egregious human rights violations record on its formal agenda as a threat to international peace and security. On 24 March, the Human Rights Council adopted without a vote a resolution that authorises the hiring of 'experts in legal accountability' to assess cases and develop plans for the eventual prosecution of North Korean leaders and officials responsible for crimes against humanity.

The North Korean government restricts all basic civil and political liberties for its citizens, including freedom of expression, religion and conscience, assembly and association. It prohibits any organised political opposition, independent media and civil society, and free trade unions. Lack of an independent judiciary, arbitrary arrest and punishment of crimes, torture in custody, forced labour, and executions maintain fear and control.

North Korea discriminates against individuals and their families on political grounds in key areas such as employment, residence, and schooling by applying songbun, a socio-political classification system that groups people into 'loyal,' 'wavering,' or 'hostile' classes. Pervasive corruption enables some room to manoeuvre around the strictures of the songbun system, and some people who bribe government officials can receive permission, pursue market activities, or travel domestically or abroad.

Vulnerable Groups

North Korea refused to co-operate with either the Seoul-based Office of the UN High Commissioner for Human Rights (OHCHR) or the UN Special Rapporteur on the situation of human rights in North Korea, Tomás Ojea Quintana. However, in 2017, the DPRK engaged with two UN human rights treaty bodies and invited a UN Special Rapporteur to visit for the first time ever.

On 6 December 2016, the North Korean government ratified the Convention on the Rights of Persons with Disabilities, CRPD. From 3 to 8 May, Catalina Devandas Aguilar, UN Special Rapporteur on the Rights of Persons with Disabilities, met with government officials, visited schools and rehabilitation centres, and spoke with some people with disabilities. Although her schedule was tightly controlled, and authorities did not grant her request to visit a mental health facility, Devandas-Aguilar acknowledged the DPRK's commitment to advance the realisation of the rights of persons with disabilities.

Following a long delay in submitting overdue reports required under the Convention on the Rights of the Child (CRC) and the Convention on the Elimination of All Forms of Discrimination against Women (CEDAW), North Korea submitted reports on both in 2016. North Korean officials had their record on children's rights examined by the CRC committee on 20 September 2017 and appeared before the CEDAW committee on 8 November 2017. The CEDAW committee expressed concerns about a broad range of violations affecting women including discrimination; stereotyping; non-criminalisation of marital rape; sexual harassment and violence, including in the workplace; trafficking; lack of political participation; and lack of an independent human rights institution, civil society organisations, or other means to enable independent monitoring and promotion of the rights of women.

Despite such engagement, North Korea often refuses to acknowledge its own rights violations or accept committee recommendations. When the CRC committee raised concerns about the North Korean government requiring unpaid labour from children, subjecting children to physical punishment and violence, and discrimination against children on political grounds, DPRK officials denied these allegations. The government did acknowledge the possibility that schools or individual teachers may have forced children to work, but offered no further details.

Women's Rights

Women in North Korea face a range of sexual or gender-based abuses, as well as violations of other rights in common with the rest of the population. These include punishment for the acts of their husband or other relatives, torture, rape and other sexual abuses in detention facilities, sexual exploitation, forced marriages of North Korean women in China, and other forms of sexual and gender-based violence and discrimination.

Gender-based discrimination starts from childhood, with girls constantly exposed to and compelled to comply with stereotyped gender roles. It is harder for women than it is for men to be admitted to university, or to join the military and the ruling Korean Workers' Party, which serves as the gateway to any position of power. State authorities are sometimes perpetrators of abuses against women and fail to offer protection or justice to women and girls facing gender-based or sexual abuse.

Border Tightening

Kim Jong-un's government bolstered efforts to prevent people from leaving North Korea without permission by increasing the number of border guards, the number of CCTV cameras, and barbed wire fences on its border with China. Tactics included jamming Chinese cell phone services at the border and targeting those communicating with people outside the country. China also increased checkpoints on roads leading from the border. During the summer of 2017, Chinese authorities also apparently intensified crackdowns on both North Koreans fleeing through China and the networks guiding them, resulting in fewer North Koreans being able to complete the arduous overland journey to Laos or Thailand, and from there, most often, to South Korea.

The Ministry of People's Security classifies defection as a crime of 'treachery against the nation'. Harsh punishments apply to North Koreans forcibly returned by China, including potentially a death sentence. Former North Korean security officials told Human Rights Watch that those forcibly returned face interrogation, torture, sexual violence, humiliating treatment, and forced labour. The severity of punishment depends on North Korean authorities' assessments of what returnees did while in China. North Koreans caught working or living in China are sent to different types of forced labour camps, long-term kyo-hwa-so, or short-term prisons, rodong danryeondae. Those discovered trying to reach South Korea are treated as enemies of the country and may disappear into North Korea's horrific political prison camp system, kwanliso, where prisoners face torture, sexual violence, forced labour, and other inhuman treatment.

North Koreans fleeing into China should be considered 'refugees sur place' regardless of their reason for flight because of the certainty of punishment on return. China treats them as illegal 'economic migrants' and fails to meet its obligation to protect refugees as a state party to the 1951 UN Refugee Convention and its 1967 protocol. Beijing regularly denies the staff of the UNHCR the UN Refugee Agency, permission to travel to border areas where North Koreans are present.

Key International Actors

Japan continues to demand the return of twelve Japanese citizens whom North Korea abducted in the 1970s and 1980s. Some Japanese civil society groups insist the number of abductees is much higher.

South Korea has also stepped up its demands for the return of its citizens, hundreds of whom were reportedly abducted during the decades after the Korean War. The North Korean government has also kidnapped individuals from China, Thailand, Europe and the Middle East. On 10 February 2016, the South Korean government closed down the Kaesŏng Industrial Complex (KIC), a special joint venture industrial zone at the southern border of North Korea. On 3 March 2016, South Korea passed the North Korean Human Rights Act, to improve human rights and provide humanitarian aid for current and former North Korean citizens.

In July 2016, US President Barack Obama imposed targeted sanctions for human rights abuses on five institutions and ten North Koreans, including Kim Jong-un. The list included individuals responsible for hunting down North Korean escapees and running labour and political prison camps.

Although this report is predictably quite damning, I personally disagree with the assumption that schoolchildren and families are 'forced' to work on farms and for government-controlled enterprises. In all my conversations with people in the country, I have been given the very strong impression that this is an accepted part of their lives and it is something they would willingly undertake, especially harvesting the crops during the winter. The whole ethos of North Korean society is to work for the benefit of the community and not the individual, so such work is regarded as doing your duty.

Personal testimonies

It's also enlightening to read the first-hand accounts of prisoners who have had to endure the torture and barbarism of some of the harshest prison conditions in the world. However, it must be said that there are various versions of their stories, some of which are contradictory. I have bought books on my travels as well as consulting sources easily available in the West. Below are a few details of their experiences.

Jeong Kwang-il worked as a trader and he made business deals with South Korea in China, thereby associating with the enemy, as far as North Korea is concerned. Jeong was accused of being a spy and was taken to a prison camp where he was interrogated and tortured. During the beatings, he lost all his teeth and his head was badly injured. The torture he endured is known as 'the pigeon' – his hands were cuffed behind his back and he was hung from them, meaning his feet were off the ground. In his own words, he said it was so painful 'that it was better to die'. He eventually confessed to crimes he hadn't committed after ten months of the mistreatment. Eventually he was sent to Yodok – a notorious prison in the country that has the slogan, 'Let's sacrifice our lives to protect the revolutionary leadership of Dear Leader Kim Jong-il.' He stayed in that prison, which housed over 50,000 inmates, for three years before a guard released him on compassionate grounds. When he returned home, he found that his family had all disappeared. He then fled to South Korea.

Jihyun Park and her brother crossed the Tumen River into China. The broker who had arranged her escape sold her to a farmer for 5,000 yuan; she spent six years as his sex slave and never saw her brother again. She had a son, Yong, who was due to be sold but she begged to keep him. When he was only five years of age, she was arrested and deported back to North Korea. She was sent to a labour camp where she was kept in 'unspeakable conditions' and prisoners were 'worked like animals' having to clear trees on hillsides so crops could be planted. Prisoners were not allowed to wear shoes and eventually wounds on her leg and foot became gangrenous. She was released after guards became concerned she could infect others. Once she had regained her strength, she again crossed into China to find her son. Re-united with Yong, she met another North Korean defector, Kwang, who later became her husband. A Korean-American pastor introduced them to a UN officer in Beijing and the three of them were granted asylum in the United Kingdom.

Kang Chol-hwan's grandfather had been declared a traitor by the government, so his whole family was arrested and imprisoned. Kang was nine years old at the time. He found himself sharing a room with other children of his age, all of whom were thin and lacking in vitality. They were 'worse than beggars' according to him in a later interview. He was sentenced to hard labour, carrying large and cumbersome logs on his shoulders from the forest to the camp some 10 miles away. If he was unable to complete his task, then he was severely beaten by the guards, and by the other inmates too. On some occasions he was forced to sit in a tiny cell that was full of cold, muddy water, yet others were forced to endure those conditions for nearly six months. Few survived the ordeal. While in prison, he witnessed two soldiers escape, but both were quickly captured and hanged while the other prisoners were forced to march by their bodies as a warning (similar to the actions by the Nazis in the Second World War) and also ordered to throw rocks at the dying men and shout slogans such as 'Down with the traitors of the people.' Failure to do so would result in yet more severe beatings from the guards. After ten years in the camp, Kang was released and five years later he fled to China and eventually South Korea.

The story of Kim Young-soon is a particularly tragic one. As a young girl she'd danced for the Great Leader, Kim Il-sung, but one day she was summoned by the secret police and interrogated about her knowledge of senior party officials. This interrogation continued for two months before she was taken to Yodok camp, with her four young children and parents. As this was the time of the Great Famine, food was scarce and only small amounts of corn were rationed to the inmates. It was not uncommon for prisoners to supplement their diet with rats and snakes caught in the prison grounds. The food wasn't sufficient, and people started to die of hunger on a daily basis, including members of her own family. Kim stayed in the prison for nine years before being released by a visiting military official who recognised her. She then bought false documents and fled to China before the journey to South Korea, without her family. She later found out why she had been imprisoned. It was because of her close friendship with Sung Hye-ri, who was already married and had a child when she became mistress of the Great Leader Kim Jong-il. The scandal would be too much to be made public so all associates of Sung were arrested and imprisoned.

Ahn Myong-chol was a prison guard and kept that position for over a decade. He was brainwashed into believing that prisoners were not human beings at all and he was ordered to kill anyone who attempted to escape. If a guard shot a prisoner then they would be rewarded, so many innocent men and women were killed so that the guard was given the prize of attending college, something which would normally be out of their grasp. On one occasion, a colleague of Ahn ordered a prisoner to climb the barbed wire fence and then immediately shot him dead. This was the beginning of Ahn's change of attitude towards his job. Later he saw two girls take a piece of noodle from a polluted pond in a rubbish dump, but another guard saw them, caught them and pushed them into the pond, holding them down until they drowned. The final act that really horrified Ahn though was when three dogs escaped from their handlers and attacked five children. Three were killed, while the other two, barely breathing, were buried alive by the guards. At this stage he'd had enough and with his father being detained for making negative remarks about the Leader, he decided to flee the country. He swam to China and now lives in South Korea.

These are all harrowing stories and are completely at odds with the country that I've visited where the population smiles, and the tourist sites are welcoming. I cannot possibly imagine how any of the people I have met could find themselves in these positions, but the fact is, it happens all too regularly. The government of North Korea finds itself in a difficult position – any anti-Kim subversive action has to be punished, but the cost of the upkeep of these numerous prisons is too much, especially for a country that struggles to feed itself, so apparently a new solution has recently been found. It's been reported that any enemies of the state are now taken up a mountain and simply left there to fend for themselves. With a harsh climate and no resources, the offending person is expected to die and would only risk a journey to the nearest town or village as a last resort for fear of further arrest as they wouldn't have the necessary papers. How true this is I cannot say. Certainly, no guide would answer a question on such a subject, and if they were to involve themselves in such a discussion, then they would find themselves in serious trouble. It could be another example of mischievous reporting as I haven't come across any actual cases of this happening, but then North Korea is a mysterious state and so it can't be discounted.

As a final part of this chapter, I quote the 'Fundamental Rights of Citizens' as agreed by the DPRK government and published on its official website. It makes for interesting reading in light of everything you have just read.

The DPRK practically guarantees the people genuine political freedom and rights according to the fundamental requirement of the Juche idea for enhancing man's independence and creativity in every way.

In the DPRK the rights and duties of citizens are based on the collectivist principle, 'One for all and all for one.' The Socialist Constitution of the DPRK specifies that the state effectively guarantees all the conditions for the democratic rights and liberties as well as the material and cultural well-being of the citizens.

All the citizens who have reached 17 years of age have the right to elect and to be elected, irrespective of sex, race, occupation, length of residence, property status, education, party affiliation, political views and religion. They also have freedom of speech, the press, assembly, demonstration and association, freedom of religious beliefs and they are entitled to submit complaints and petitions.

The workers, peasants and other working people, as masters of power, participate in state administration and freely engage in socio-political activities in political parties and public organizations.

The working people have the right to work and rest, the right to education and free medical care and freedom of scientific, literary and artistic pursuits. Women are accorded equal social status and rights with men. The state affords special privilege to mothers and children. Marriage and the family are protected by the state.

The working people are guaranteed inviolability of the person and the home and privacy of correspondence. The rights and freedom of citizens steadily increase with the consolidation and development of the socialist system.

10

TERROR ATTACKS AND UNLAWFUL IMPRISONMENT ATTRIBUTED TO NORTH KOREA

Ever since George W. Bush described the country as being part of the 'axis of evil' following the 9/11 attack, the rogue state of the DPRK has been at the centre of terrorist accusations, some believable and proven, and some frankly laughable. The latter can certainly be said of the so-called hacking of Hollywood's computers after the announcement of the release of the film that ridiculed Kim Jong-un – *The Interview* – which was almost certainly nothing to do with North Korea. Unfortunately though, there are many incidents that are actually attributed to the government of North Korea.

A typical example happened in 1987, a year before the start of the Seoul Olympics. On 29 November, two North Korean spies boarded a South Korean plane in Baghdad, using fake names and passports to pass themselves off as Japanese tourists. They also carried onto the plane a hand-held radio, complete with batteries, something the security agents at the airport were suspicious about. They were right to be a suspicious as it turned out to be a bomb. The two spies left it in an overhead locker and departed from the plane in Abu Dhabi. Soon after, the bomb exploded and the plane – Korean Air Flight 858 – disintegrated killing all 115 passengers, most of them from South Korea. Eventually the spies were tracked down, and both attempted to commit suicide using cyanide-laced cigarettes, but one of them was unsuccessful and she, Kim Hyon-hui, was extradited from Bahrain to South Korea. Even though the attack had taken place nearly a year before the start of the Olympic Games, experts were convinced that there was absolutely no doubt that North Korea was behind the bombing as the government wanted to create an atmosphere of fear around the Games in the hope of preventing people from attending. This had come after a proposal by the North to co-host the Games had been rejected, and in reaction the North Korean government had then arranged to host the 13th World Festival of Youth and Students in 1989 at the newly built First of May Stadium in the centre of Pyongyang.

Talking of the possibility of the North and South co-hosting the Games, the IOC President Juan Antonio Samaranch, had said: 'It is difficult for me to think that North Korea can open its borders to more than ten thousand journalists and the Olympic family.' The proposal was rejected completely, and within twelve months the North Korean government had reacted by the blowing-up of a South Korean airliner.

On 3 May 1988 the CIA released a statement saying: 'Pyongyang's public threats against the 1988 Seoul Olympic Games and its sabotage of a South Korean airliner last November clearly point to North Korea as the greatest challenge to the security of the Games. Seoul is now taking extensive precautions to prevent violence and agent infiltrations, but international air links to South Korea remain vulnerable to sabotage or to serving as transportation to terrorists.'

North Korea then attempted to dissuade their closest allies, the Soviet Union and China, from attending and competing in the Games, but without success. As it was South Korea, which had just come out of dictatorship into democracy, hosted a well-run and extremely successful Olympic Games with absolutely no North Korean participation. To rub salt in the North's wounds, the Soviet bloc countries started to recognise the South diplomatically, something which they had refused to do previously. In a way, that was a defining moment in the history of the DPRK. Historian Sheila Miyoshi Jager argued in the *Politico* magazine that '...the North Korean regime we face today – isolated, belligerent, desperately pumping up its dangerous nuclear programme as its only leverage on the World stage – was born, in part, in 1988, at the Olympics.'

On 30 April 2013 US citizen Kenneth Bae was tried and found guilty of 'hostile acts' against the State, and was sentenced to fifteen years in prison, including hard labour. Two weeks later, a 15 May press release from North Korea's Central News Agency stated that he would serve his sentence in a 'special prison'. Bae, who was a devout Christian, was also the owner of a North Korea tour company and had been in the country with official permission when he was detained on 3 November 2012. He was arrested under the charge of attempting to overthrow the government and was accused of setting up bases in China with the intention of building a team of volunteers for this goal. In reality, Bae was a humanitarian and had founded the NGO named NGI (Nehemiah Global Initiative) with the purpose of rescuing North Korean refugees and abandoned orphans and helping them to rebuild their lives, something which was an immense embarrassment to the North Korean government. Although his case received international attention, there seemed to be little that anyone could do to effect his release.

He was eventually released though, on 8 November 2014, after yet more international publicity had brought his case to the fore, in the form of an unusual personality. The former basketball player Dennis Rodman, who had made less than accurate remarks when visiting his friend Kim Jong-un in January of the same year, was almost unwittingly the reason for the turnaround in Bae's fortunes. Although Rodman had tried to defend the North Korean government's imprisonment of Bae with what he later described as 'drunken comments', the publicity helped Bae to be unexpectedly released.

The whole case was a reminder of another example in 2000. Reverend Kim Dong-shik, a Christian humanitarian and missionary, was hunted down in China by North Korean operatives. He was tortured, starved and died in a North Korean prison. For years his case remained unsolved with the country denying any knowledge of his whereabouts, but eventually a United States court ordered North Korea to pay $300 million in punitive damages. His abduction, along with around seventeen others at various intervals, received huge publicity in South Korea, but gradually his case was forgotten until the arrest of Kenneth Bae. Both of these injustices suggest that the North Korean government is still very sensitive to any outside involvement in its activities, and it is willing to break international law to punish those who do so.

In another case of zero tolerance, we go back to 15 April 1969, the birthday of Kim Il-sung, when two North Korean fighter jets shot down a US reconnaissance plane outside the country's airspace, killing 31 American crewmen. This came just fifteen months after the capture of USS *Pueblo* in international waters, as previously mentioned, and it also came after the aircraft had flown that exact route for the preceding three months. This time though, they made the mistake of flying on an important date for the country. The North Korean government issued a statement congratulating its pilots for their 'huge successes in downing the US plane'.

In more recent years, there have been many incidents that can be linked to North Korea, including the March 2010 torpedo attack on the South Korean Navy's ship *Cheonan* that resulted in the death of forty-six sailors. On 23 November the same year there was the shelling of Yeonpyeong Island – a territory that belongs to the South – during which two marines and two civilians were killed.

These are just a handful of incidents down the years and of course it can be argued very strongly that other countries have been involved in similar atrocities, but it also proves that North Korea is still a dangerous country on the international stage, despite its willingness to open itself up now more than ever.

The Great Leader and the Dear Leader.

Bronze statues of the Great Leader and the Dear Leader. There are thousands of these all over the country.

People preparing to pay homage to the leaders.

Japan treated Korea as its own territory until there was an uprising. This Japanese colour print made from a woodcut by the artist Kobayashi Kiyochika, (1847–1915), shows a Japanese soldier bending slightly under the weight of a fortress, from which Russian soldiers fall, that he has pierced with his bayonet; two men in the background, representing Korea and China, are in awe of the strength of the Japanese soldier. To this day the North Koreans express hostility towards Japan. (Library of Congress)

After the Second World War, all former Japanese colonies were taken from the defeated empire. However, dividing Korea into North and South led to the Korean War. This July 1950 photograph shows South Korean soldiers of the 1st Division, I Corps, preparing and laying an antitank mine somewhere in Korea during the conflict. (Library of Congress)

An unforgettable image of American soldiers during the Korean War.

Entrance to Pyongyang – it's called the Monument to the Three Charters for National Reunification. South Korea is on the left of the monument with North on the right.

The Kim Il-sung Stadium is built on the spot where he made his famous speech following the liberation of the country.

Metro station, Pyongyang: marble floors and chandeliers.

With track 110 metres underground, the Pyongyang Metro is one of the deepest in the world.

Kim Il-sung Square.

The Monument to Party Founding, Mumsu Street, Pyongyang.

The Monument to Party Founding, seen at night. The buildings behind are apparently designed to look like the DPRK flag.

Every year a flower festival is held at the Kimilsungia-Kimjongilia Exhibition Hall, with the focus inevitably being on the leaders.

Pyongyang in the winter.

Above: *Kumsusan Palace of the Sun – both the deceased leaders lie in state in this building.*

Left: *A Monument to the People, Pyongyang.*

Mass dancing. This can be seen on any of the country's anniversaries, such as the birthday of the Great Leader. Dances can last for days.

The entrance of the school where children extend their education after normal school hours. It is mandatory to attend. See page 11 for a picture of the youngsters on stage.

Above: *The masses bowing before the bronze statues of the leaders.*

Right: *On the birthday of the Great Leader, there are huge firework displays over Pyongyang.*

Above left: *This is the main highway from Pyongyang to the Demilitarised Zone (DMZ). The picture was taken from the only service station, about 10 kilometres from the capital.*

Above right: *The axe used in the incident in the DMZ and now on display there.*

Below: *The Demilitarised Zone. The blue huts belong to the US and South Korea, with the silver ones belonging to North Korea.*

Life is quiet outside of Pyongyang.

Right: *This selection of dishes gives an idea of traditional North Korean cuisine.*

Below: *This huge five-star hotel is in the mountains of rural North Korea, and was almost completely empty when I visited.*

One of the many Buddhist temples in North Korea.

Another Buddhist temple, proving that religion is not forbidden in North Korea no matter what is sometimes claimed by people outside the country.

Woljong Temple in the UNESCO biosphere reserve of Mount Kuwol.

This picture shows the state of the roads in the countryside.

Above left: *In the capital city, being a traffic controller is seen as a very important position for a young woman. This picture was taken in winter.*

Above middle: *A traffic controller in her summer uniform; she has complete authority in directing the traffic.*

Above right: *A traditional North Korean wedding.*

Couples dancing in one of the city's squares, with the women wearing their traditional costumes. These colourful dresses are worn on public holidays, and particularly family days out on Sundays.

A school play, North Korean-style. The author was taken to see this production, staged in the Pyongyang school shown on page 7, to illustrate the advancement of education in the country.

Two views of the May Day Stadium. Opened on 1 May 1989, it is the largest stadium by capacity in the world.

Above: *Kim Il-sung Stadium.*

Left: *Juche Tower.*

The entrance to the Victorious Fatherland Liberation Museum.

The captured 'spy' ship, USS Pueblo.

Above: The Ryugyong Hotel dominates the Pyongyang skyline – it has 105 floors but is completely empty.

Right: Old and new. The old residential building is inhabited, but the new hotel is not.

Above: *Based on the national flower, this is one of the many unusual buildings on Scientists Street, Pyongyang.*

Left: *Another interesting building in Mirae (Future) Scientists Street, Pyongyang; the Unha Tower.*

Scientists Street, Pyongyang. Only the elite can live on this street.

The entrance to the Victorious Fatherland Liberation Museum.

Panoramic view of Puyong town.

The Western Sea Barrage or Nampo Dam.

Above: *The Arch of Triumph. Based on the original* Arc de Triomphe *in Paris – but bigger.*

Left: *Ox and cart in the countryside. Virtually no machinery or technology exists for the farmers.*

Above: *A famous image of North Korea in darkness next to brightly lit South Korea. After the fall of the Soviet Union, the lack of imported oil supplies led to electricity shortages. Pyongyang is unusually dim for a capital city, the pale glow emerging from apartments often outshone by the moon. An editorial in* Rodong Sinmum, *the state-run newspaper, put a positive spin on this, saying the country doesn't go in for 'flashy lights' and other countries could soon find themselves following suit.*

Left: *Interior of the Sci-tech Complex, with a rocket as the centrepiece.*

11

TOURISM AND WHAT TO EXPECT
AS A TOURIST

One of the many myths concerning North Korea is that you can't actually visit the place. This is completely untrue, as the government actively encourages tourists. Embassies of many coutries often issue warnings about travelling to North Korea, citing security concerns.

I have on two occasions visited North Korea at a time when the UK government was sending out a strong message with guidelines advising all citizens not to travel there. This has a huge effect on tourist numbers in North Korea, especially those visiting from the United States. One of my guides confided in me that visitor numbers had dropped alarmingly over the past few years from most Western countries, and that of course would have a knock-on effect for her too, as few tourists would mean fewer tours and the alternative forms of employment are not something that could be described as attractive. She never actually explained what she would be required to do, but I read between the lines that it would involve back-breaking work in the countryside.

There are inevitably no official figures for tourism in the country but the fact that there is a large group of highly trained multilingual guides who are ready to meet visitors, and who are normally busy nearly all the year round, suggests that tourism is taken very, very seriously indeed. After all, how can you show your country to the outside world, if no one is allowed to come? I have been fortunate to have visited North Korea on numerous occasions, even when I was still working for the BBC – and although I didn't refer to that on my visa application, my guide knew all about me when I arrived. Background checks on potential visitors are extensive, yet there are few examples of people being refused entry.

To visit North Korea, you have to travel with a government-supported travel agency (of which there are many in Europe and especially the UK) and allow them to apply for your visa. Once this has been granted, and it can take some time, you can pick it up at the embassy or have it delivered with your passport. I personally prefer the former but standing outside the North Korean Embassy in London waiting for the process to be completed doesn't give you the best impression of what you are about to experience.

I have been made to wait for an hour at the sturdy electric gates while the rain has been pouring down, as no UK national is allowed inside the building. Eventually, one of the staff emerges and produces the passport with the visa attached. All of this is done in a very solemn and rather stern fashion, completely the opposite of what awaits you in the country. Anyway, the important thing is that the visa is provided. So, once you have it, what's next?

Air Koryo flies from Beijing to Pyongyang on specific days and flights take around 90 minutes. The airline is very professional with modern aircraft, beautiful and smiling air stewardesses and comfortable seating. What sets it apart is the constant playing of music on the television sets of concerts performed for the military with the usual propaganda hymns, and the fact that the interior of the aircraft is rather disturbingly decorated all in red. Apart from that, it really is the same as flying on any short-haul route – and sandwiches and drinks are provided too. The flights are nearly always full of Chinese 'businessmen' and wide-eyed tourists nervously awaiting their arrival in the country. Once you arrive at the new Pyongyang International Airport, the first thing you notice is that it's almost completely deserted. There are three terminals, of which only one appears to be in constant use, and that caters for the twice-a-week flight from Beijing. Aircraft on the ground are sparse and there doesn't appear to be another airline that uses the airport, which of course is symptomatic of the country's isolationist policies. Air China used to have a Beijing to Pyongyang service, but it has recently been terminated as uneconomic. That is rather surprising, as the majority of tourists to North Korea are from China.

Despite the airport being so modern, the immigration procedure is tedious and very, very lengthy. Expect your mobile phones and any reading material to be taken away for inspection, plus your bags to be thoroughly searched. However, it is done with a smile and a welcome. The North Korean people, including the security officials, seem genuinely pleased to see you, but haste is probably not a word that translates into the Korean language, and as I have failed miserably to learn a single word of Korean, I would have no idea how to say it anyway. Patience is a virtue. It's also advisable, indeed essential, to check the contents of your phone before your arrival for any material that might be deemed offensive to the country. Books are a sensitive issue too. Taking any religious material into the country will almost certainly lead to a lengthy inquisition before you are allowed to proceed.

Once through immigration, though, you are eventually met by your two guides and a driver. For the duration of your stay, these people are like your family. They do not leave your side, they answer every question with knowledge and politeness and they stay with you at every hotel, tourist attraction and shopping venture. They sometimes have their meals with you but, out of respect for your privacy, will also sometimes let you eat at a separate table – but within eyesight and earshot. It's possible to become extremely fond of these people, especially as most of them are specially chosen attractive women for the male visitors, and I have heard stories of some tourists returning every year to see a special guide. It's clearly something the guides have become accustomed to as there are many jokes and amusing stories told about it. They are trained to be as friendly and attentive as they can, within reason of course. During my stays, I have got to know certain guides who have opened up to me about their relationships, ambitions, fears and hopes, all of them living with the same dreams and the same disappointments as we do, but in an isolated nation. No matter where you go, people are the same.

At every tourist attraction, you are normally met by a different guide who is allocated to that particular place, and they take over the duties, showing the same level of friendliness and professionalism. English is spoken with an American accent (which is surprising, bearing in mind the distaste they have for the US) and other languages are spoken fluently too. I felt seriously embarrassed that my French was nowhere near as good as one of the guides, who accompanied me around the Arch of Triumph – I live in France! Built to commemorate resistance to Japan from

1925 to 1945, the Arch of Triumph in Pyongyang is modelled on the Arc de Triomphe in Paris.

Of course the questions I am constantly asked are why are tourists never allowed to wander the streets alone, and can they visit anywhere they want to? The simple answer to the first question is that there is no explanation. It's made very clear to you before you arrive in the country (by the tour company and the North Korean government) that you are strictly forbidden from leaving the guides and exploring on your own. The punishment for such an action would be almost certainly to be immediately deported from the country, but the punishment for the guides may be even harsher. Walking the streets alone would probably not last long, as there enough security officials who would notice and immediately arrest you, albeit in a friendly and charming way.

The assumption of course is that there are certain things that the government would prefer you not to see, but this is never admitted to by the guides when they are asked. On my third visit I was staying in a city centre hotel and could have walked out at any time, but my female guide had asked me quite pleasantly not to 'disappear' so out of respect for her, I didn't. The answer to the second question is again vague. There have been places that I have asked to visit and the guides have immediately agreed and made arrangements, but there are other places where a smile and a shrug of the shoulders suggested that it was not a good idea. I can only surmise that as guides, their job is to show the best parts of the country, but not behind the scenes, very much like a guide in London who would take you to Buckingham Palace, Trafalgar Square or for a boat ride on the Thames but who would be unlikely take you to the parts of the capital that are known for homelessness and drug addiction.

In North Korea certain areas can only be seen from a distance, such as country villages where poverty is still prevalent, while others are presented like shining beacons, such as Scientists Street in Pyongyang where the top professionals live in their gleaming new apartment blocks, all of which have individual styles and look impressive even if slightly weird.

Hotels can go from one extreme to the other. I've stayed in what would be regarded in the Western world as five-star hotels. One particular place was set in the heart of mountain forests and was absolutely amazing, with around 1,000 rooms, marble floors, top-class restaurants and bars, a swimming pool, gymnasium, and the most incredible views from the bedroom balconies over the mist-covered mountains, yet there were no more than twenty people staying there – including me, my guides and driver and one other French group. Sitting in one of the top-class restaurants alone and being waited on by at least six waitresses is a rather uncomfortable experience, especially as you can't even use the 'fail-safe' distraction of staring at your mobile phone!

The locals have no need to stay there, and couldn't afford it either, and the visitors tend not to travel that far, which begs the question – why build it? The same question could be asked of the ghost building that dominates the skyline in Pyongyang. It's called the Ryugyong Hotel. Construction started in 1987. It's an astonishing looking structure tapering to a point, designed as a shining pyramid. The problem is building work stopped in 1992 as the money ran out (and the famine took hold) and so far, it hasn't been completed.

There are suggestions that foreign investment may arrive in the next few years and it will eventually be opened, but that suggestion has been hanging around for some time now. There was also a story reported in the Western media that the construction workers had 'forgotten' to build lifts to the higher floors, but I was assured by my guide that this wasn't the case and it was another example of the myths that surround the country.

What about the opposite end of the accommodation spectrum? Well, it's what you would expect when you visit a state that is effectively still in the dark ages outside of the capital city and developed towns. I stayed in one place in Hoech'ang, called a guesthouse, which was a challenge to say the least. No running water, power cuts from early evening and a bedroom that had the smell of a sewer, the fact that I couldn't leave and walk the streets, or even open the window as it was nailed shut, made it a long evening. I did however fare better than my female guide, who was forced to sleep on the concrete floor in the office as the only other bedroom was occupied by the male guide and the driver. Gender equality does not exist in North Korea, and although I did offer to give up my room, I was told firmly that I was the guest of the country and so I should have the best accommodation. It was certainly an experience.

Food is always abundant for a tourist. This is uncomfortable at times as it's clear that somewhere, someone is not getting anywhere near enough because the food stocks have been diverted to the latest batch of Europeans, Americans (and yes, they do visit) or Chinese.

There's little you can do but accept it and hope that whatever leftovers there are, do somehow make their way to the people who truly need them. By the way, North Korean cuisine is a challenge if you're a vegetarian, as I am, but the hotels always make an effort to accommodate you. Ten days of rice and steamed vegetables can be tiresome, but I felt I needed to accept them with grace and humility, knowing how much others would want them.

One thing that is expected of you is that you totally accept the traditions of the country, and that means constantly bowing to the Great Leaders' statues, photographs or their bodies in the Kumsusan Palace. This is not something I found particularly difficult to do, as complying was always met with a huge smile and a thank-you by the accompanying guide. Not doing so would be frowned on by the local security and might result in your stay being dramatically cut short. As previously mentioned, there is also the rule about not folding a piece of paper with the leaders' images on it, and never touching a photograph or picture frame hanging on the wall.

I remember writing a thank-you note to my guide on the back of a sheet of paper, folding it and putting it into my pocket to give to her when I left – only to find to my horror that I'd written it on the back of a black-and-white photograph of both the Great Leader and the Dear Leader. Not only did I have to quickly rewrite the note on a different piece of paper, but I then had the rather scary prospect of being caught with the original. The temptation was to throw it away, but the knowledge that it could be found after I'd left the country and that some poor unsuspecting local might be blamed for it made me think again, so I hid it deep inside my dirty laundry in my travel bag in the hope that no immigration official would be remotely interested in searching it. Thankfully it worked, and I was able to dispose of the offending piece of paper in a waste bin in Beijing airport.

Being a tourist in North Korea is a fascinating experience. You'll find yourself constantly pushed to the front of queues, or given the best seats in the theatre, something which the locals don't appear to be upset about at all. When you visit schools or any type of educational facility, you are treated like a VIP and specially choreographed displays of dancing, singing or musical instrument-playing are put on for your benefit. At mealtimes, the waitresses hover around you constantly, quickly taking away an empty plate to be immediately replaced by a full one, and when travelling through the numerous checkpoints, soldiers take the time to smile as they wave you past. One thing is for certain, tourists are very welcome in North Korea and it truly isn't the dangerous place that it is constantly reported as being by the Western media. I found travelling to North Korea far safer than travelling to places in Europe.

However, it can go wrong, as was proved by the terrible experiences of Otto Warmbier. The official report was that his imprisonment was due to the fact he allegedly attempted to remove a propaganda poster in a Pyongyang hotel. If this is true, then it was a stunningly naïve thing to do as the warnings about such behaviour are made extremely clear ahead of your visit and removing any poster or image that pertains to the leadership or history of the country is something that is just not going to be acceptable.

Having said that, his punishment for such an act was extreme to say the least, if Western media reports are to be believed. The North Koreans say that he contracted botulism in prison, but doctors in the US found no traces of it, and while his family claimed he was beaten and tortured, again the same doctors saw no evidence, so it seems it will remain a tragic mystery. With the lack of diplomatic channels between North Korea and Western states, finding yourself arrested in that country is the least desirable prospect imaginable.

The economy is based on the Euro if you're a visitor, but the notes have to be in pristine condition as old ones just won't be accepted. That can be a problem so a last-minute trip to a foreign exchange counter is always advisable. Any gifts or souvenirs will be inevitably focused on the country's propaganda. I once bought a poster for a friend that said 'Death to America' in Korean with a drawing of numerous ballistic missiles flying through the air over an image of cheering soldiers. These things are normal in the country, completely at odds with the generosity and friendliness of the population. The quality of the goods on sale does leave a little to be desired, but for a Western tourist, they are remarkably cheap. Anyone who has a scale model of the Juche Tower in their living room and only paid 10 Euros for it is in a rather unique position. I bought my grandchildren two military uniforms, which they proudly wore around the house, even if my daughter made a point of not allowing them out of doors.

When staying in hotels, it's noticeable that you are given the best rooms, certainly better than the ones that the guides have, and nearly always well away from them too. I have stayed on the forty-second floor, while my two female guides were on the twenty-fifth. This separation is a deliberate policy, as is the availability of all news outlets on the television sets, including my former employers the BBC, as those are definitely not available to the guides. A word of advice though – walking into a hotel bar alone as a Western tourist can suddenly cause all drinks to be hit by record inflation in a remarkably short period of time.

I must admit that after my last lengthy visit, I had become rather jaded with the constant images of the leaders and the Korean War as part of my everyday experience in the country and at one stage I asked one of my guides when they would start to forget the latter in particular. She was quite forceful in her response and said that the country and its people will always glorify and respect those who fought in the war, and therein lies the appeal of this country. If you visit, you will be browbeaten (in a nice and charming way) with the images and stories of the heroes of North Korea. The Great Leaders are ever-present, there is always victory and everything in the country is better than anywhere else – even the Arch of Triumph is bigger than its French counterpart – nothing bad is ever reported, the famine was part of a natural progression and so should be celebrated, and the country is self-sufficient, defensively safe and wealthily prosperous.

No matter how many questions you ask, no matter how many times you may disagree and no matter how many times you refuse to believe, nothing shakes the North Korean people from this ideal. That is the country you are visiting.

Dennis Rodman

One of the more famous tourists in recent years has been the former basketball star Dennis Rodman, although his frequent visits to North Korea and his 'friend for life' Kim Jong-un have attracted ridicule and controversy. The former NBA star first visited Pyongyang in March 2013 with three members of the Harlem Globetrotters and a media company making a documentary. The Supreme Leader is well-known as a basketball fan and was a huge supporter of the Chicago Bulls franchise, and so he had invited Rodman to visit in the hope of promoting the sport in North Korea.

The two got along famously and sat together courtside to watch an exhibition game involving the Harlem Globetrotters and nine North Koreans. Only afterwards did Rodman stir up the controversy that followed him each time he returned to Pyongyang. He took a microphone and addressed the crowd:

'I'm sorry that my country and your country are not on good terms, but for me and the country, you're a friend for life.' Clearly, he had been charmed by Kim Jong-un, something which was to be echoed in 2018 when President Trump announced that they had 'fallen in love' when discussing his first summit with the North Korean leader.

Six months later, in September 2013, Rodman returned to North Korea and was allowed into Kim Jong-un's private inner circle. Dennis was photographed holding Kim Jong-un's baby daughter. Then weeks later, in December 2013, he made his third visit and spent some time training North Korean basketball players ahead of an exhibition game to be played in January 2014. Sadly, things deteriorated from there. Following the game, he took to the microphone and sang 'Happy Birthday' to Kim Jong-un, getting all the players and the crowd to join in. If this wasn't embarrassing enough, he then conducted a rambling television interview with CNN in which he tried to defend the North Korean government's arrest and imprisonment of Kenneth Bae, the Christian missionary who was locked away in appalling conditions:

Kenneth Bae did one thing ... if you understand what Kenneth Bae did. Do you understand what he did in this country? No, no, no, you tell me, you tell me. Why is he held captive here in this country? Why?

The next day he apologised for the interview and said he had been suffering from a combination of alcohol and sleeping pills, but he did write a letter to Kim Jong-un asking for Bae to be released, and within a week the American was actually set free.

Rodman didn't return to the country until 2017, when he was sponsored by PotCoin, a cryptocurrency, at the same time as Otto Warmbier was being released by Pyongyang. Rodman presented a copy of the Donald Trump book *The Art of the Deal* to the Supreme Leader. The former NBA star said that he didn't think Kim knew who Trump was up until that point and he hoped the book would help him get to know the new American President.

Finally, leading up to the first historic summit between Kim Jong-un and President Trump in Singapore, Dennis Rodman had allegedly offered his services as some kind of mediator, but they were rejected.

Instead he went to Singapore and conducted many interviews, mostly with CNN, in which he said that his personal appearances in Pyongyang had helped to lay the foundation for the summit ahead:

> I said to everybody, the door will be open. When I went back home,
> I got so many death threats ... but I kept my head up high, brother.
> I knew things were going to change. I knew it. I was the only one.

The last sentence was said as he wiped tears away from beneath his sunglasses during the interview. Rodman was just about the most unlikely ambassador either country could have wished for, and his constant visits caused so much bad feeling in the US, and ridicule around the world, yet he seemed to be a trailblazer for those who really wanted to see the country. He is, after all, one of the few men in the world who can say he is personal friends with both President Trump and Kim Jong-un, and despite his bungling and incoherent interview over Kenneth Bae, he contributed to the early release of the American.

Down the years there have been many well-known visitors to the country, for all kinds of different reasons. The Evangelist Billy Graham went, while political figures such as Madeleine Albright and former US President Jimmy Carter have also made visits. It seems that North Korea is happy to open its doors to anyone who wants to get to know the country better, and that is a good start in the path to openness for this isolationist country.

12

DEFECTORS

One of the reasons we've heard about life in North Korea is because of the number of people who have defected from the country. In the recent past there has hardly been a month go by without the news that a defector was ready to tell his or her story to the outside world including the unimaginable cruelty that they, and the people, have suffered under the Kim regime. This has come about through television programmes, magazine articles and best-selling books. There are some truly harrowing tales. In some cases life doesn't appear to have improved for the defectors, women in particular, who have found themselves sold to the sex trade in China once they'd escaped, but for the most part North Koreans have found a happier life once they've left. What stands out about all of them though is their love of the country that they've escaped from; it's not the country they hate, but the regime that runs it.

Since the end of the 1950–53 Korean War, it's been estimated that up to 300,000 people have defected from North Korea, although other sources suggest a figure of only a third of that number. The peak was understandably during the years of the Great Famine in the mid-nineties, and it's interesting that the highest percentage of people leaving North Korea are female. This could be for a variety of reasons, but it does seem that economic concerns are the main driving force behind women leaving the country. In many cases they are the 'breadwinner' as their husbands may be in the military, or they are having to provide for the whole family of their partner, and the stress and pressure become too much.

Sadly, in many cases, fleeing to China has not always been the improvement that defectors have imagined. As China is a strong ally of North Korea, it does not recognise refugee status between the two countries, and anyone arriving in China who is arrested is almost immediately returned, when they may face a rather unpleasant welcome. Many women after having avoided arrest have been forced into prostitution by gangs who have identified their distress. After initially embracing them with kindness, providing a safe sanctuary, shelter and food, they have then been sold, and their lives become even more miserable than the ones they had left behind. Human trafficking was endemic in the early years of this century, and women could be sold for as much as 10,000 Chinese yuán. Thankfully, this seems now to be in decline as the Chinese government has made great endeavours to stamp out sex slavery in the country.

Despite the continual media reports of defections from North Korea, it appears that they are now slowing down; just over 1,000 were registered for 2018, compared to nearly 3,000 in 2011. The belief is that under the leadership of Kim Jung-un the populace is far more content with their standard of living and genuinely excited about the possibility of the country opening its doors a little more. However, there is also the opposite view that security is stricter now, especially at the borders of China and South Korea, than ever before.

The common destinations for defectors are China, South Korea and Russia, with the first being the most popular. As mentioned, China doesn't give refugee status to North Koreans, and during the famine years in particular would regularly deport hundreds of defectors. Once they returned, they were likely to face severe punishment and perhaps torture. There is a loophole for North Koreans who are fleeing the country into China. In the book *China–North Korea Relations,* no author credited (2008), which I bought in Beijing airport, I discovered that if they get caught and are sent back to their home country they can marry ethnic Koreans in China – normally something which is arranged many months in advance for a fee – then they are repatriated into China as legal refugees. It's estimated that around 40,000 North Korean defectors live in China because of this.

South Korea has a far more welcoming attitude to anyone who flees from the North because it's obviously a great propaganda victory for the country if someone decides to cross the border, and they have an official government agency to deal with defectors. The South's Ministry of Unification is a department that is in charge of preparations for the unification of the two countries into one Korea. This agency handles all immigrants from the North; they ensure there is a smooth transition process into South Korean society, and an understanding of resettlement policies. Up until 1993, there were generous aid packages for North Korean defectors who were establishing their new homes in the South. Money was provided (under a strict selection process based on need) and in some cases free apartments were made available, plus the guarantee of employment. Soon though, this became unsustainable and most of the aid was slashed by the government. In 2004, new measures were introduced to slow down the number of asylum seekers that were now coming from China, all of North Korean origin, as the numbers were becoming too high.

Unfortunately for defectors fleeing from the North to the South, life is still a struggle. The stigma of being a North Korean is still high in the southern part of the country, where a lack of money or work skills prohibits them from climbing the social ladder. North Koreans are regarded as being undereducated by their southern counterparts, and so discrimination is rife. According to a poll by the National Human Rights Commission of Korea, around 50 per cent of defectors said they had experienced discrimination because of their background; the two major issues were their inability to afford medical care and poor working conditions. Many complained of disrespectful treatment by journalists. The North Korean belief in that there is 'One Korea' is not necessarily shared by the South.

Russia is another destination for defectors from North Korea, but this remains the harshest of environments in which to start a new life. Most people who flee the country are from work camps, as the Russian border is the closest, but there is little if no aid available to anyone who wishes to settle. It's estimated that around 10,000 of these people living in the east of Russia, but there also doesn't appear to be an official resettlement policy in the country so they can live peacefully and undisturbed.

There are also people known as 'double defectors', particularly from families forcibly repatriated after the birth of North Korea. These are the third- or fourth-generation members of the families who left to live in China or Japan, and who now want to relocate to the home of their ancestors. There are few statistics available, but the numbers are said to be on the increase. The Supreme

Leader has recently started to offer inducements for people to return to North Korea after defecting, in the shape of housing and employment and also financial promises, with figures of around 40,000 Euros being suggested. Once they return, they denounce their previous lives in television appearances and in newspaper interviews, exactly mirroring the behaviour of those who flee to the South.

One of the less frequently reported results of defecting are the reactions of North Koreans who genuinely seem to miss their old country. Once they have been subject to the commercialism and competitiveness of other countries, starting with their neighbours in the South, then there is, in some cases, a real desire to return. If you leave a society where 'cradle-to-the-grave' care is part of life, then leaving that behind and being forced to survive in an alien environment is not always as appealing as you might at first have thought. The old saying 'the grass is always greener' seems to apply.

Norbert Vollertsen, a German doctor, was given a Medal of Freedom by the North Korean government after he donated grafts of his own skin to help a workman with serious burns. Vollertsen was expelled in December 2000 after accompanying Madeleine Albright with a media tour company. Since then, he has become an outspoken critic of Pyongyang, and recently he has called for the discontented people of North Korea to just walk out of the country en masse. Despite his obvious good intentions, it seems a rather naïve thing to call for, especially as he compared it to the mass migrations following the fall of the Berlin Wall and the change of government in Cuba. In Berlin after the wall fell, all the Eastern Germans had to do was to walk into another part of Germany, while there was little in the way of resistance for most Cubans at a time when there was more freedom being offered to them. The thought of a mass exodus doesn't exactly appeal to China either, but the idea that North Koreans would simply get up and leave the country they love so dearly is ridiculous. On a day-to-day basis, their lives are so strictly controlled by the ideology of Juche and the power of the personality cult of Kim Jung-un, that there barely seems a moment when such an act would be considered. Even if it were, the chances of even a hundred or so protestors attempting to cross the border, especially through the DMZ, are minuscule at best with the strict security and the shoot-to-kill policy of the military. There will, however, always be individuals who will risk everything to flee the country.

How defectors escape from North Korea varies. It could be the death-defying soldier who runs across the DMZ avoiding gunfire, or the case of professional workers simply asking for asylum once they reach the South. In many cases, defectors take a huge risk, especially when they cross the border into China in the Liaoning and Jilin provinces, as these are heavily patrolled and major rivers and forests have to be traversed. One thing is for certain, once a defector leaves North Korea, he or she is effectively leaving behind everything they have ever known and are unlikely to see again. Family, friends and lovers are left behind and the chances of reuniting with them are slim.

13

NUCLEAR WEAPONS

The one subject that keeps North Korea in the news more than any other is nuclear weapons. Virtually every television and newspaper report takes the stance that the DPRK has armed itself with a nuclear capability so great and powerful that all it will take is a single push of a button to spark an attack on the US and the beginning of World War Three. The truth is rather different.

North Korea didn't really take nuclear ability seriously until the 1990s, and at that time it was being supplied by the Pakistani government – or rather the nuclear warhead is what was supplied, as the ballistic missile had already been designed by North Korean scientists. Pakistan's partnership with the country – something which was kept hidden until the early years of the twenty-first century – meant that slowly the DPRK began to build up a network of nuclear weapons unseen by the rest of the world. There is of course a shady and secretive narrative here, but it's been made clear time and again by the leaders that the nuclear arsenal is for defence purposes only; in a way that in my opinion can be believed, as there can be no suggestion that any nuclear strike by North Korea against the US could be remotely successful as the ramifications would be too devastating for the country and its people. Having said that, the tensions have been there in the past, and remain to this day.

As far as back as 1994, President Bill Clinton was seriously considering a strike on the nuclear base of Yongbyon, but was stopped after the US military put forward some pretty strong statistics suggesting that the conflict that would follow could see up to a million casualties, and the cost would be astronomical. Even President Obama looked into the possibility of surgical strikes, but he, too, was unsure as to the risks involved as there was no real military intelligence about the location of nuclear warheads. Now President Trump, after exchanging childish insults with Kim Jong-un, seems to be taking a more radical approach with his face-to-face meetings with the Supreme Leader. These came after it was announced that North Korea had tested a hydrogen bomb that was supposed to be ten times more destructive than the one that was dropped on Hiroshima.

The question is of course, why are the North Koreans so eager to have nuclear capability? The answer really stretches back to the end of the 1950–53 Korean War and the obsession with self-sufficiency. After the armistice was signed, the US placed hundreds of nuclear weapons in South Korea, all aimed at the North, threatening that they would use them should the newly named Democratic People's Republic of Korea even think of invading the South. Since then, the country has always felt under threat and it has been one of the reasons for the build-up of the military, and of course the nuclear arsenal. I have been taken to science complexes where grainy black-and-white films of early warhead testing have been shown, with the familiar images of military officers wildly waving their arms in the air as the missiles have shot up into the sky. They were then followed by state-of-the-art digital special effects as the latest rockets with nuclear warheads attached are also fired into the air, landing at a place far enough away to suggest that both South Korea and Japan are within reach. There are even reports by the Western media that they now have the capability of reaching the US, but that is again subject to conjecture. Delivery of a nuclear warhead on target is now more difficult than creating the warhead itself. One thing that is certain is that every single North Korean person I spoke to talked of defending their country and never of attacking another.

Another reason for the DPRK's paranoia over nuclear capability is the experience of Iraq and Saddam Hussein, summed up in this interview with Vladimir Putin in *The Putin Interviews*, a four-part, four-hour television series by Oliver Stone, first broadcast in 2017. It was based on several interviews with Putin between 2015 and 2017, and later turned into a book:

> Everybody remembers what happened to Iraq and Saddam Hussein. Saddam abandoned the production of weapons of mass destruction. Nevertheless, under the pretext of searching for these weapons, Saddam Hussein himself and his family were killed. The country was destroyed, and Saddam Hussein was hanged. Everybody is aware of it and everybody remembers it. The North Koreans are also aware of it and remember it.

The same can be said of the experience of Libya and Mohammed Gadhafi. He came to an agreement with President Bush to stop making nuclear weapons and was promised better diplomatic relations and economic aid from the US, yet eight years later was killed during his overthrow, which was heavily supported by the US. North Korea has since said that the diplomatic efforts to make Gadhafi give up his weapons were an indirect invasion tactic and illegal.

Kim Jong-un has tested more missiles than either of his predecessors and will continue to do so. It seems that no amount of sanctions or threats or promises will deter the country from becoming a fully fledged nuclear state, and indeed the last four American Presidents have tried numerous methods in dealing with the country.

Bill Clinton agreed a deal where North Korea would cease making weapons in return for oil. It didn't last. George W. Bush joined the six-party talks – involving the US, China, North and South Korea, Russia and Japan – with the aim of ending the proliferation of missiles in the DPRK. It didn't work. Barack Obama seemed to take the route of no contact and showing patience while imposing sanctions, but that too seemed to have no effect. Now Donald Trump is continuing with sanctions while engaging with the leadership. Only time will tell if he will be more successful.

The race to become a nuclear state is something that is taught in all schools and is as much a part of the curriculum as maths or foreign languages. This suggests that the 'problem' is being handed down through the generations and is not likely to go away any time soon. In one of the very few conversations I had with my guides concerning the nuclear issue, they said the same thing that I heard being declaimed in schoolrooms. If the US, Russia, Europe and many other nations can have a nuclear capability for their defence, then why can't they? It was stated to me again, quite forcibly, that North Korea had never, ever invaded another country in its entire history, but had been the victims of numerous periods of oppression and invasion. This was the reason why a nuclear capability was necessary in today's world, just as the latest warships were required in the nineteenth century, or the latest cannons in the centuries before. It's a means of defence. As someone who has been a regular visitor to the country, I can testify to the peace-loving nature of the population, despite the images of massed armed soldiers parading through the central square and the propaganda images of the missiles being fired into the sky. Unfortunately, these images do the North Korean leadership no good whatsoever, and therein lies the problem as I see it. The posturing and the threatening makes the country look far more dangerous than it actually is.

14

WHAT WILL CHANGE?

This is usually the chapter where the author is ready to make some major announcement as to how he or she believes the brutal and cruel dictatorship will finally topple and the people will rise and claim their freedom. Well that's not the way I see it. As I've explained, North Korea is not a military dictatorship. Yes, there are some appalling human rights abuses and the people live in a society that provides only a small part of what is expected in other parts of the world, but the North Korean people seem to be very, very happy. The adoration they have for the Great Leader, the Dear Leader and now the Supreme Leader is not forced or false. They truly believe that these three people are the guiding forces behind their lives and every single day is a tribute and homage to them as they lead North Korea towards a greater and more prosperous future. Even in the days of The Second Arduous March – the famine of the 1990s – the Kim dynasty was not challenged by the people. Kim Il-sung, Kim Jong-il and Kim Jong-un are the driving forces behind every single action taken on every single day by virtually every member of the population of North Korea. They are worshipped. They are adored. They are revered.

I am sure there must be small pockets of citizens who might actively rise up against the Kim dynasty if such a time arrived, but with little knowledge of the outside world, it's difficult to know how this might come about. With a naïve belief that 'Imperialistic' America is evil and North Korea is good and there is nothing in between, then the chances of relying on foreign intervention is as unlikely as democratic elections being announced in the country. I have walked through streets with propaganda hymns extolling the leaders blaring out from loudspeakers on every corner, looked at the hundreds of posters that adorn virtually every building with a slogan that promotes Juche and watched as everyone bows to the statues, cars slow down as they pass an image of the leaders and people have tears in their eyes as they attach the lapel badge of the leaders to their jackets. It could be a form of brainwashing, but it's brainwashing that started in 1945 and has continued every day since. I've seen children in nursery school perfectly recite the poem that describes the Great Leader and his single-handed victory over the US in the 1950–53 Korean War, and I've spoken to articulate and intelligent adults who have nothing but total and undying love for the Great Leader, the Dear Leader and the Supreme Leader. To my Western mind, it is still something I find hard to understand, even after so many visits, but it will not change.

It is my belief that if there was ever any kind of regime change and the Kim dynasty was toppled, then North Korea would no longer function. The collective sense of grief that the people would feel would ensure that virtually the entire infrastructure would break down and stop within days. People would no longer have the reason for starting each day and their lives would become meaningless. The fight and spirit that they have shown so many times down the years when their country has been invaded just wouldn't exist anymore. This may sound like a huge exaggeration but being with these people and seeing how they behave and feel means for me it's not too far from the truth.

It's entirely possible that a world superpower may have their own reasons to effect change in the country, but the fact that North Korea has existed this way since 1945 and has outlived the fall of the Soviet Union, the collapse of the Berlin Wall, the change of political society in neighbouring China, and the toppling of dictators in Romania, Libya, Iraq, Chile etc., and still survived, are telling reasons why I feel it won't happen.

If change were to happen, it would be gradual and it would be based on the economy. Kim Jong-un has already started to open up with respect to dialogue with other leaders. He appears to be aware that the country cannot survive on its own and needs help, albeit with strings attached. He has allowed trade to take place that had been forbidden by his grandfather and he seems to have a more 'Westernised' outlook than the two previous leaders. Of course, the human rights abuses continue and retribution for wrongdoing is as ruthless as ever, but the moment he allows a multinational corporation to come through what is now only a crack in the door – I'm thinking of a McDonald's or a Starbucks in the first instance, not Google, Toyota or even Huawei – will be the moment that the country will change. For better or for worse? I'm just a tourist so my opinion doesn't count and it will be the people who will decide after they've tasted their first hamburger or drunk their first latte. In a way I hope they don't, but is that preserving their unique way of life, or tightening the shackles even more?

North Korea is one of the most confusing and fascinating countries in the world. It's just about the last place on earth that can be discovered by the intrepid traveller – providing you discount undiscovered parts of the rainforest – and it can be done far easier than expected. Each time I returned, I noticed a slight change with just a hint of Westernisation creeping in – a hotel that has piped Western music, or the pinball machine in a café sponsored by Chelsea Football Club. Little but important things that suggest the country is now opening itself to the outside world, albeit at a snail's pace.

I'm reminded of the Dutch tourist who had first started visiting North Korea at the turn of the twenty-first century, when there was nothing in the way of transport infrastructure, electricity was hit-and-miss (as it still is outside of Pyongyang) and running water brought its own hazards. He told me that he didn't like the 'new' North Korea and probably wouldn't visit again as it had become so modernised, so who knows what it will be like in ten years' time?

My fear is that eventually the country will bow down to the inevitable onslaught of commercialism. Although the people aren't envious of the outside world (Nothing to Envy!) they are curious, and that curiosity could eventually make a difference in subtle ways. I see the contentment in the faces of the people as they go about their daily business, but I can't see into their minds (or into their apartments for that matter) so I genuinely don't know if there is a sadness deep inside. All I can do is relate what I've seen and what I've seen is a country completely at peace with itself. Everything is black-and-white, in that there is good and evil in the world, and the United States fulfils the obvious role of evil. With this mindset, there seems little likelihood of immediate change, but just as the wind can move a forest inch by inch, so the attitude of the people can also move with just a little prodding. For the time being though I take my guides' advice. 'Look with your eyes and tell the world.' That's what I've tried to do.

North Korea Timeline

1945 – With the surrender of the Japanese at the end of the Second World War, occupation of Korea ends. The 38th parallel is chosen by two inexperienced American soldiers and the northern part of the division is now controlled by the Soviet Union.

1946 – With the backing of the Soviet Union, the Korean Workers' Party is founded, and military leader Kim Il-sung is made its head.

1948 – The Democratic People's Republic of Korea is the new official title of the northern state, and the Soviet Union and China lend their backing to the new country, while the United States and her allies continue to support the new state in the south, the Republic of Korea.

1950–53 – One of the bloodiest and costliest wars ever fought, the Korean War, takes place between the two countries over a three-year period, 25 June 1950 to 27 July 1953. Millions of soldiers and civilians were killed and injured with more bombs dropped in the Pacific than during the five-year Second World War. The devastation caused to Pyongyang is almost complete, and the city has to be completely rebuilt. In 1953 an armistice is signed and a demilitarised zone roughly along the 38th parallel is created. The armistice is still in place as the war hasn't 'officially' ended. North Korea continues to this day to claim victory.

1955 – Kim Il-sung makes the first mention of his new philosophy, the Juche Theory, in a speech to the Workers' Party.

1956 – The August Faction Incident takes place, in which virtually every opponent of the Great Leader is purged in ruthless fashion. This proves that he is now in almost complete control of the country, despite the concerns of both China and the Soviet Union.

1963 – The Juche Theory now becomes official political and social policy of North Korea.

1972 – Hopes for peace between the North and South Koreas are raised after a joint statement is issued hoping for peaceful reunification.

1974 – Eldest son Kim Jong-il is designated the official successor to the Great Leader, as and when Kim Il-sung dies. Tensions flare between the North and the South after a failed assassination attempt on the South Korean President Park Chung-hee, which is blamed on North Korean agents.

1977 – Sweeping agricultural reforms throughout the country mean that landowners are stripped of their land as property is now nationalised. This forces many landowners to attempt to flee the country, many without success.

1985 – North Korea becomes a member of the International Nuclear Non-proliferation Treaty, meaning the country is forbidden from building nuclear weapons.

1986 – A nuclear research reactor in Yongbyon becomes operational.

1987 – The North Korean government denies strongly any involvement in the destruction of a South Korean civilian airliner in which 115 people are killed. Tensions rise between the two countries once more.

1991 – North and South Korea are invited and both join the United Nations.

1993 – Pyongyang test fires a ballistic missile into the Sea of Japan, breaching the terms of the Nuclear Non-proliferation Treaty.

1994 – Military first is officially implemented as part of the Juche Theory. Shortly afterwards, the Great Leader suffers a heart attack and dies. His elder son takes over but doesn't assume his duties as president immediately. He is given the title of Dear

Leader. One of the first things he does is to agree with the United States a framework whereby North Korea freezes its nuclear programme in return for oil.

Mid-1990s – The country is hit with the Great Famine, or The Second Arduous March as it is now referred to. Hundreds of thousands, if not millions, of people died from starvation as crops failed and foreign aid – mostly from the now defunct Soviet Union – dried up. Floods and drought exacerbated the results of ill-advised farming methods. Only after about two years did the government reach out for international aid as it became clear that the country could not feed itself.

1996 – The 43-year-old armistice signed between the North and South is nearly broken as Pyongyang sends thousands of troops into the DMZ. Skirmishes follow, and a North Korean submarine is captured off the South Korean coast. 25 sailors are killed, while 17 South Korean soldiers are also killed in clashes along the border.

1998 – The Dear Leader becomes president as Kim Jong-il takes power officially. His father Kim Il-sung is declared eternal president, meaning he will forever be with his people, even after death. There are also more skirmishes between the two divided countries as another North Korean submarine is captured with all inside killed. At the same time, Pyongyang fires another long-range rocket that lands in the Pacific Ocean, further than expected.

2000 – Following years of tension, Kim Jong-il and South Korean President Kim Dae-jung meet at a summit. In an act of goodwill, prisoners from both sides are given amnesty and are freed to return to their home countries.

2002 – Following 9/11, President George W. Bush describes North Korea as part of the 'axis of evil' for their intention to build 'weapons of mass destruction'. Pyongyang does not react to the statement. At the same time, tensions flare again between the North and South resulting in The Second **Battle** of Yeonpyeong in the Yellow Sea, with casualties on both sides.

The Japanese Prime Minister Junichiro Koizumi visits the country for the first time, and Pyongyang admit that Japanese citizens had been abducted during the 1970s and '80s. This causes a temporary freeze on aid from Japan to North Korea until the four remaining survivors are released.

All oil shipments from the USA and Japan are stopped after it is discovered that North Korea is developing a uranium-based nuclear weapon, despite promises of a halt to its nuclear programme. United Nations inspectors are refused admission to the facilities in Yongbyon and are subsequently expelled.

2003 – Unsurprisingly, North Korea withdraws from the Nuclear Non-proliferation Treaty. It also withdraws from the 11-year-old agreement with the South to keep the peninsula free of nuclear weapons, so alienating itself internationally even more. China threatens to reduce aid to the country following disparaging comments made about the country in the Pyongyang newspapers. China also announces that it believes North Korea now has the capability and materials to build six nuclear bombs.

2006 – Pyongyang continues to test nuclear weapons, including one at an underground facility, although experts suggest that it was less than successful. It also fires seven missiles into the sea during the year with varying success, forcing the United Nations to impose yet more sanctions against the country.

2007 – A second summit between North and South Korea takes place as South Korea's President Roh Moo-hyun walks across the DMZ to meet Kim Jong-il. Later in the year passenger trains cross the border for the first time since 1951, which was during the Korean War.

2008 – The health of the Dear Leader is under scrutiny as it's reported he has suffered a stroke. Officials now speculate about his successor. The USA removes the country from its terrorism blacklist, and in return North Korea grants access to the Yongbyon nuclear facility.

2009 – After launching what it describes as a communications satellite, which the UN says is a long-range rocket, North Korea walks out of the six-party talks with the USA, Russia, South Korea, Japan and China. It then confirms it will restart its nuclear programme, testing underground once more.

Later in the year it reaches out to South Korea by releasing four prisoners and resuming family reunions, which had been suspended. It also sends a delegation to the funeral of the South Korean President.

Domestically, the local currency is devalued, causing thousands of wealthier citizens to lose money. This causes the first real unrest in the country to be seen since the days of the famine.

2010 – Kim Jong-un is appointed to numerous political posts. As the youngest son of the Dear Leader, it was not expected that he would be so favoured, but this is a clear indication that he will take over from Kim Jong-il.

There are yet more skirmishes between North and South Korea. A South Korean warship is sunk and shots are fired over the DMZ border, resulting in the deaths of soldiers in the South.

2011 – The Dear Leader, Kim Jong-il dies and the country is thrown into mourning with citizens wailing and crying in the streets. Kim Jong-un takes over and is given the title of the Supreme Leader.

2012 – On the 100th anniversary of the birth of the Great Leader, there are mass celebrations all over the country. Pyongyang fires another long-range Taepodong missile into the air, but it fails spectacularly, the film of this event being shown all over the world. The embarrassment is great, but North Korea insists it was trying to launch a satellite.

2013 – Kim Jong-un shows his ruthlessness by executing his uncle, Chang Song-thaek, after he was found guilty of attempting to overthrow the State. This act is greeted by horror all around the world as Chang had been one of his closest advisors. Meanwhile, the UN imposes yet more sanctions against the country after another nuclear test is discovered. The third test is said to be the most powerful and successful to date.

2014 – More ballistic missiles are tested, and more UN sanctions are imposed. On a less serious level, cyberattacks hit Hollywood as a spoof film on Kim Jong-un is about to be released. North Korea is accused, yet absolutely no evidence is released to back up the accusation. Experts doubt whether the country has the ability to engage in cyberattacks, bearing in mind there is no internet link to any other country. The film is a flop and some critics suggest the hacking story was a way of creating publicity for it.

2015 – North Korea reopens the Yongbyon nuclear facility after eight years with the intention of building more weapons. The US imposes more sanctions.

2016 – North Korea claims it has tested its first hydrogen bomb, although this is not believed by the outside world. The Workers' Party has its first congress since 1976, where Kim Jong-un is elected as its new leader. The UN imposes yet more sanctions.

2017 – The country is in the news again as Kim Jong-un's half-brother, Kim Jong-nam, is killed at Kuala Lumpur airport. He is covered with a highly toxic nerve agent in what was described initially as a 'prank'.

Later in the year a US aircraft carrier is positioned off the coast of North Korea after another long-range missile is tested.

China imposes sanctions and the UN says it will come down strongly on the country if nuclear testing continues.

The American student Otto Warmbier is returned to the United States after being imprisoned. He dies shortly afterwards following accusations of torture.

2018 – The country agrees to participate in the Seoul Winter Olympics as part of an all-Korea team in selected events. The singing and dancing troupe of girls that follow the team becomes instantly famous around the world.

Kim Jong-un and President Trump meet face-to-face in an historic meeting. Promises of nuclear disarmament and withdrawal of sanctions are made, but no official commitments are made on either side. President Trump says of the meeting: 'We fell in love.'

2019 – The Supreme Leader Kim Jong-un makes his traditional New Year's Day address to the people, clearly stating that this year (Juche 108) is an extremely important one for North Korea and its international relations.

Dear people and service personnel of the People's Army across the country,

Dear compatriots,

Dear comrades and friends,

Having seen out the year 2018, in which we adorned the history of the motherland, the revolution and the nation with meaningful events leaving another indelible imprint in the history, we are seeing in the new year 2019 full of hope.

As we see in the new year, I extend heartfelt greetings to all the people and service personnel who devoted their all for the cause of socialist construction sharing the same mind and pace with our Party in the eventful days of last year, and wish that homes across the country will brim with affection, hope and happiness.

My warm new year greetings go also to the compatriots in the south and abroad, who shared our will in writing a new history of reconciliation, unity, peace and prosperity of the nation.

I wish success in the work of heads of state and other foreign friends who are making efforts for social progress and development and global peace and justice.

Comrades,

The year 2018 was a historic year, in which remarkable changes took place in the internal and external situations and our socialist construction entered a new stage thanks to our Party's line of independence and strategic decision.

The Third Plenary Meeting of the Seventh Party Central Committee held in April last year constituted an occasion of pivotal significance in developing our revolution onto a new stage and continuing to speed up the advance of socialism on the basis of the great victory of the line of promoting the two fronts simultaneously. Following the road of arduous struggle with faith in certain victory of socialism, our people provided by their own efforts a sure guarantee for defending their sovereignty and achieving peace and prosperity, and became able to set out on a grand revolutionary advance to attain still higher goals for the construction of a prosperous country.

Thanks to our proactive and positive efforts, a peace-oriented current was created on the Korean peninsula and the international prestige of our Republic continued to be raised, and in the midst of this we celebrated the 70th anniversary of the founding of the glorious DPRK in splendour with great dignity and self-confidence.

Through the celebratory events held in September, the might of the DPRK, which achieved the ideological oneness of the whole society and the single-hearted unity of the Party and the people and which possesses a reliable self-supporting economy and self-reliant defence capabilities, and the ardent will of the heroic Korean people to fight to the end for the victory of the socialist cause were fully demonstrated in front of the eyes of the world.

Last year all the people further consolidated the foundations of the self-supporting economy by turning out in the struggle for carrying out the Party's new strategic line of concentrating all efforts on economic construction.

Meaningful and valuable advances were made in the struggle for implementing the line of making the national economy Juche-oriented. The generation capacity of the Pukchang Thermal Power Complex was increased remarkably, the Kim Chaek and Hwanghae iron and steel complexes and other metallurgical works built on their successes in establishing the Juche orientation in production, and dynamic efforts were made to strengthen the independent foundations of the chemical industry. The quality of various vehicles and light-industry products that give us pleasure at sight as they were made by our efforts, technology and resources was raised to a higher level and their mass production was realized, bringing delight to our people.

The working class in the coal-mining industry, in defence of the lifeline of the self-supporting economy, conducted a do-or-die campaign for production when everything was in difficulty, and the agricultural sector waged an unremitting struggle for increased cereal production, thus producing a large number of high-yielding units and farmers even in adverse weather conditions.

The munitions industry, in hearty response to our Party's militant call for concentrating all efforts on economic construction, produced a variety of farm machinery, construction equipment, cooperative products and consumer goods, thereby giving an impetus to economic development and the improvement of the people's living standards.

Last year the gigantic construction projects, geared to adding glory to the era of the Workers' Party according to the Party's long-term plan and operations, proceeded in a three-dimensional way and on a grand scale. This demonstrated in reality the stout mettle of socialist Korea that never flinches in the face of any adversity but achieves victory after victory by surging forward more forcefully, as well as the inexhaustible potentials of our independent economy.

True to the decision of the April Plenary Meeting of the Party Central Committee on bringing about a revolutionary turn in science and education, the sector of science and technology presented valuable research findings conducive to accelerating the growth of hi-tech industries and revitalizing the national economy; the efforts to make education modern and scientific gained momentum, the teaching conditions and environment being updated at many universities, colleges, middle and primary schools across the country.

The sector of art and culture produced and staged a grand mass gymnastics and artistic performance, evoking positive response from at home and abroad and vividly showing the advanced level of Juche-oriented art and its peculiar features and advantages.

Comrades,

Through the struggle of last year, which added a new page of proud victory to the annals of our revolution, we have been convinced once again of the validity of our own cause and the invincible strength of our state. Thanks to our people's indomitable fight against the challenge of injustice, our state's might of self-development has increased on a steady basis and the cause of building a powerful socialist country is progressing at a faster pace.

Availing myself of this opportunity, I should like to extend my heartfelt thanks, once again, to all the people including the service personnel of the People's Army for advancing non-stop along the road of victory indicated by the Party and thus performing feats that will shine brilliantly in the history of our country.

Comrades,

Having grown seasoned and powerful amid the struggle to glorify the new era of the Juche revolution, our Party and people are launching the new year march full of greater confidence and ambition.

This year we are faced with the task of expanding the country's capability of independent development to open up bright prospects for taking a step forward towards socialist construction.

We have the strength and foundations to bring forward a brighter future of socialism by our own efforts, and we have also developed our own strategy and creative methods to this end. When we strive hard with an indefatigable spirit on the principle of self-reliance by adhering to the Party's new strategic line, our country's strength will redouble and our people's dreams and ideals will come true.

'Let us open a new road of advance for socialist construction under the uplifted banner of self-reliance!' – this is the slogan we should uphold. We should bring about a revolutionary upsurge on all fronts of socialist construction by regarding self-reliance as a treasured sword for prosperity, a spirit which has always been a banner of struggle and driving force for a leap forward in the whole course of the Korean revolution.

The might of the independent socialist economy should be further strengthened.

We should rely on our own technical forces and resources and the high creative spirit and revolutionary enthusiasm of all the people so as to succeed in attaining the strategic goals of national economic development and enter a new stage of growth.

We should properly plan and thoroughly implement the national operations aimed at maintaining, reinforcing and reenergizing the national economy as a whole.

Strategic measures should be taken to give full play to the potentials of the self-supporting economy and utilize the new elements and driving force for economic development, and the manpower and material resources of the country should be enlisted in economic construction in a cost-effective way. We should focus on the main link in the national economic work, reenergize the other links of its whole chain and promote the long-term development of the economy, so as to push forward its revitalization.

The management method should be innovated to satisfactorily realize the unified guidance of the state over the overall economy and give fullest play to the voluntary enthusiasm and creative abilities of the working people. The Cabinet and other state and economic guidance organs should improve planning, pricing, and monetary and financial management in line with socialist economic law and make sure that economic levers have a positive effect on the revitalization of production and expanded reproduction in enterprises. They should adjust the structures and system of work to raise the efficiency of economic work and to make enterprises smoothly conduct their business activities.

Talented personnel, science and technology are our major strategic resources and weapons with which to bring about a great leap forward in socialist construction.

The state should promote talent training and sci-tech development purposefully and increase its investment in them.

It is necessary to improve the quality of training talented personnel, who will shoulder the socio-economic development, by improving the teaching contents and methods in conformity with the world trend of developing education and pedagogical requirements. We should set a high goal of developing new technologies and concentrate our efforts on the research into core technologies of great practical and economic significance, so as to secure the leading force of economic growth. We should also take institutional measures so that scientific research institutes and enterprises, in close cooperation, can boost production and technological development and enhance intellectual creativity.

Every sector in the national economy should give impetus to hitting the targets of the five-year strategy for national economic development.

We should direct primary efforts to relieving the shortage of electricity to make a breakthrough in revitalizing the national economy.

One of the most important and pressing tasks in socialist economic construction for this year is to radically increase the production of electricity.

By focusing state investment on the electric-power industry to maintain and reinforce its existing foundation and making maximum and effective use of it to renovate and modernize one by one badly needed sectors and projects, we can, for the present, raise power generation to the peak year level.

We should take the problem of easing the strain on electricity as an undertaking of the whole state, step up the construction of hydroelectric power stations including Orangchon and Tanchon power stations and create a capacity for generating tidal, wind and atomic power under a far-reaching plan. Provinces, cities and counties should develop and utilize in an effective way various energy sources available in their local areas.

The coal-mining industry is a primary front in developing the self-supporting economy.

Only when coal is mass-produced can we resolve the problem of electricity and satisfy the demand for fuel and power for different sectors of the national economy including the metallurgical industry.

The coal-mining industry should channel efforts, first and foremost, into supplying coal to thermal power stations so that they can normalize electricity generation without let up.

The whole country should render active ideological and spiritual, material and technical assistance to coal mines, and the state should take stringent steps to provide in a responsible manner facilities and materials needed for coal production and good living conditions for coal miners.

A greater development should be achieved in establishing the Juche orientation in the metallurgical and chemical industries, the two pillars in economic construction.

The metallurgical industry should lower production cost to the minimum by perfecting the scientific and technological aspects of the Juche-oriented iron- and steel-making processes and ensuring their normal operation, and work out and implement an operations plan for providing them with full amounts of iron ore, refractories and ferro-alloys to meet their increased production capacity.

The chemical industry should step up the building of the phosphatic fertilizer factory and the establishment of the C_1 chemical industry, develop the glauberite and synthetic fibre industries and convert the existing equipment and technical processes into energy-saving and labour-saving ones. This year a nationwide effort should be made to run the chemical fertilizer factories at full capacity and boost production at the February 8 Vinalon Complex.

Rail and other transport sectors should launch an intensive campaign to strengthen discipline and increase their carriage and traffic capacities to ease the strain on transport. The machine-building industry should upgrade designing and processing techniques to develop and produce a variety of modern machinery and equipment in our own way to suit our actual conditions.

Improving the people's standard of living radically is a matter of greatest importance for our Party and state.

The agricultural front, the major point of attack in socialist economic construction, should conduct a campaign for increased production.

The Cabinet and other relevant sectors should give effective scientific and technical guidance for each farming process and supply sufficient amounts of materials needed for this year's farming, thus increasing cereal production decisively. They should respect the opinions and interests of farmers, masters of farming, and meet the demands of the socialist principle of distribution properly.

It is necessary to adhere to the four key factors set forth by the Party for the development of livestock farming, modernize and reenergize stockbreeding bases like chicken farms, and encourage the joint stockbreeding by cooperative farms and the side-line stockbreeding by individual farmers so as to supply the people with more meat and eggs.

The fishing sector should consolidate its material and technical foundations, put fishing and aquatic culture on a scientific basis and protect and increase aquatic resources, so as to open a new path for developing the fishing industry.

The sector of light industry, by consistently upholding the banner of modernizing production lines, obtaining at home everything needed for production and improving quality, should produce and supply various kinds of consumer goods that are favoured by the people, and ensure that provinces, cities and counties renovate the condiments factories and other locally run plants and maintain their regular operation by relying on the locally available raw materials and other resources.

This year, too, we should push ahead, in a bold manner, with huge construction projects for national prosperity and the people's wellbeing.

The whole Party, the entire army and all the people should turn out to transform Samjiyon County into a model of modern mountainous city, an ideal socialist village, and complete on the highest possible level the construction projects that would represent the present era, including the Wonsan-Kalma coastal tourist area and other new tourist areas. It is important to steadily improve architectural designing and construction methods, and ensure domestic production and better quality of finishing materials, so as to build all the architectural structures magnificently and in our own style and provide our people with a cultured, happy life. With the national-level construction projects underway on an extensive scale, we should build up the capacity of producing cement and other building materials as planned.

We should make proactive efforts to implement the tasks for the second stage of the forest restoration campaign, improve landscaping, urban management and road administration, and take every precaution against environmental pollution.

All sectors and all units should fulfil their quotas of the national economic plan in all its indices by identifying and enlisting every last reserve, possibility and potential and by increasing production and practising economy.

The politico-ideological strength of our socialist state should be increased in every way possible.

It is necessary to unite the broad sections of the masses solidly around the Party by thoroughly applying the Juche-oriented view on the people, a people-oriented philosophy, in Party and state activities.

Party and government organs and working people's organizations should give top and absolute priority to the people's interests whatever they plan and whatever they conduct; they should lend an ear to their sincere opinions, prioritize their wants and anything beneficial to them, and strive to translate them into reality without any conditions attached. Anywhere, anytime and under any circumstances, they should make selfless, devoted efforts for the good of the people, direct primary attention to their livelihood, and ensure that everybody benefits from the politics of affection and trust, the one of embracing and taking care of them all. They should intensify the struggle to eradicate both serious and trivial instances of abuse of power, bureaucratism and corruption, which would wreak havoc on the harmonious whole of the Party and the masses and undermine the socialist system.

However the situation and circumstances may change, Party members and all other working people should cherish the principle of our state first as an element of their faith and step up socialist economic construction in our own way. They should glorify the country's great history by working with sincere devotion and a patriotic desire for developing their homeland by their own efforts before the eyes of the world, the precious land of socialism which they have defended from generation to generation.

We should accelerate the building of socialist civilization.

A revolutionary habit of studying and a way of cultural and emotional life should be established throughout society, so that all the people possess versatile knowledge and cultural attainments as required by the developing times. The sector of art and literature should create splendid works including films and songs that reflect the times and reality and touch the people's heartstrings, thus enriching the spiritual and cultural wealth of the nation and giving a powerful impetus to today's grand revolutionary march.

We should ensure that all the people realize the advantages of the socialist public health system by modernizing pharmaceutical and medical appliance factories, upgrading medical institutions and raising the level of medical service. Mass-based sporting activities should be conducted briskly and specialized sporting techniques developed to ensure that the whole country brims over with vigour and optimism and the sportspeople continue to demonstrate the wisdom and might of Koreans in international competitions.

We should launch a powerful drive to establish a socialist way of life and ennobling moral discipline, thus ensuring that no immoral and uncultured practices that run counter to our people's emotions and aesthetic view are revealed. By doing so, we can turn the whole society into a large, harmonious family filled with moral excellence and tender feelings.

The national defence capability should be solidified.

The People's Army should reliably defend the Party and revolution and the security of the country and the people and continuously perform miraculous feats at all sites of socialist construction as in the past by consistently holding fast to the four-point policy for developing it into a powerful army. By doing so, it should demonstrate to the full the might of the revolutionary army, the invincible might of the army of our Party.

The Korean People's Internal Security Forces, as befitting the red shield of the revolution, should defend unto death our Party, system and people, and the Worker-Peasant Red Guards should effect a turn in strengthening its combat efficiency in this year of its 60th founding anniversary.

Powerful self-defence capacity is a cornerstone of the existence of a state and a guarantee for safeguarding peace.

The munitions industry should, on the one hand, steadily raise the national defence capacity to that of the world's advanced countries by stepping up the effort for making the defence industry Juche-based and modern, therefore guaranteeing the peace on the Korean peninsula by force of arms, and, on the other, should actively support economic construction.

In order to successfully carry out the militant tasks facing us this year, officials, leading members of the revolution, should make redoubled efforts and struggle with determination and courage.

It is none other than the masses of the people that constitute the motive force and are responsible for carrying out Party policy, and they know actual conditions better than anybody else. Officials should always immerse themselves in the pulsating reality, seeing everything with their own eyes and conducting a comprehensive analysis of how matters stand; they should go deep among the masses, sharing board and lodging with them and motivating them to resolve bottlenecks if any. They should set their ideals and ambitions in keeping with the Party's plans, and steadily improve their practical abilities and widen their horizon; in this way they should become competent organizers and hands-on workers who make persistent efforts to achieve everything perfectly at the standard demanded by the Party. They should throw themselves into doing any challenging task, burn the midnight oil pondering on how to bring benefit to the country and people, and find the worth of their work in the people's happy laughter.

Today young people should play a large part in promoting socialist construction.

With the same spirit and mettle which they displayed in recent years to create legendary tales of the new era in response to the Party's militant appeal, they should honour their title of vanguard at the revolutionary posts where the Party wants them to be. In the present stirring era they should become pioneers of new technology, creators of new culture and pathfinders for a great leap forward; they should make sure that youthful vigour and stamina are overflowing wherever they work.

It is needed to decisively increase the role of Party organizations.

Party organizations at all levels should conduct political and ideological work in a progressive manner in line with the requirements of the times and the developing revolution in order to make our people give full play to the strength of their indomitable spirit on all fronts of socialist construction.

They should give a boost to administrative and economic officials so that they can map out plans and provide guidance for implementing Party policy in a responsible way, and fire a zeal for collective innovation and competition in their sectors and units. Provincial, city and county Party committees should wage a powerful struggle to bring about a turn in the development of farming, education and local industries.

Comrades,

Last year was a stirring year which witnessed a dramatic change unprecedented in the history of national division spanning over 70 years.

With a determination to usher in an era of national reconciliation, peace and prosperity by putting an end to the abnormal state on the Korean peninsula which had suffered a constant war crisis, we took proactive and bold measures to effect a great turn in north–south relations from the outset of last year.

It is unprecedented that three rounds of inter-Korean summit meetings and talks were held in a year amid great expectations and interest of peoples at home and abroad, and this clearly showed that north–south relations entered a completely new stage.

The Panmunjom Declaration, the September Pyongyang Joint Declaration and the north–south agreement in the military field, which were adopted by reflecting the firm resolve and will to usher in an era of peace in which war exists no longer on the Korean peninsula, are of great significance as a virtual nonaggression declaration in which north and south have committed themselves to terminating fratricidal war based on force of arms.

While sportspersons of north and south displayed the wisdom and strength of the nation by jointly entering international competitions, artistes came and went to Pyongyang and Seoul to fire the enthusiasm for national reconciliation and reunification.

We took the significant first step towards common prosperity of the nation by promoting cooperation projects in various fields including railways, road, forestry and public health while resolutely overcoming manifold obstacles and difficulties.

The surprising changes which took place in inter-Korean relations last year convinced all the fellow countrymen that when they join minds and efforts, they can turn the Korean peninsula into the true home of the nation, which is the most peaceful and will prosper forever.

Though it was the initial step, north and south pooled intentions and wisdom to surely reverse inter-Korean relations in the utmost extremes of distrust and confrontation to those of trust and reconciliation and make in a short time eye-opening achievements which were unimaginable in the past. I am very satisfied with that.

In the New Year 2019 we should make greater strides in our efforts to boost inter-Korean relations, achieve peace and prosperity and reunify the country on the basis of the priceless achievements we made last year which was wonderfully adorned with unprecedented events.

All the nationals should hold high the slogan 'Let us usher in a heyday of peace, prosperity and reunification of the Korean peninsula by thoroughly implementing the historic north–south declarations!'

It is our steadfast will to eradicate military hostility between north and south and make the Korean peninsula a durable and lasting peace zone.

North and south, as they agreed, should take practical measures proactively to remove military hostility on the whole of the Korean peninsula, including the ground, airspace and sea, as a follow-up to its ending in the areas of confrontation.

Given that north and south committed themselves to advancing along the road of peace and prosperity, we maintain that the joint military exercises with foreign forces, which constitute the source of aggravating the situation on the Korean peninsula, should no longer be permitted and the introduction of war equipment including strategic assets from outside should completely be suspended.

It is also needed to actively promote multi-party negotiations for replacing the current ceasefire on the Korean peninsula with a peace mechanism in close contact with the signatories to the armistice agreement so as to lay a lasting and substantial peace-keeping foundation.

All the fellow countrymen should unite as one, being conscious that the master of peace on the peninsula is our nation, in order to wage a powerful struggle to check and frustrate all the moves that wreck peace and incite military tension on this land.

Inter-Korean co-operation and exchanges should be expanded and developed in an all-round way so that national reconciliation and unity can be consolidated and all the fellow countrymen can practically benefit from improved north–south relations.

For the present, we are willing to resume the Kaesong Industrial Park and Mt Kumgang tourism without any precondition and in return for nothing, in consideration of the hard conditions of businesspersons of the south side who had advanced into the

Kaesong Industrial Park and the desire of southern compatriots who are eager to visit the nation's celebrated mountain.

When north and south join hands firmly and rely on the united strength of the fellow countrymen, no external sanctions and pressure, challenges and trials will be able to hinder us in our efforts to open a broad avenue to national prosperity.

We will never tolerate the interference and intervention of outside forces who stand in the way of national reconciliation, unity and reunification with the design to subordinate inter-Korean relations to their tastes and interests.

North and south should not pass up the favourable atmosphere of today when all the nationals' interest in and aspiration for reunification are growing unprecedentedly, but actively try to find a peaceful reunification plan based on nationwide agreement and direct sincere efforts to this end.

All the fellow countrymen in north, south and abroad should further accelerate in high spirits the nationwide advance for implementing the north–south declarations, and thus glorify this year as a historic one when another radical change is brought about in the development of inter-Korean relations and implementation of the cause of national reunification.

Comrades,

Last year, our Party and the government of our Republic exerted responsible efforts to safeguard the peace and security of the world and expand and strengthen friendship with different countries.

The three rounds of our visit to the People's Republic of China and the Cuban delegation's visit to our country were remarkable events in boosting strategic communication and traditional ties of friendship and cooperation among the socialist countries.

Last year, frequent visits and exchanges were made on Party, state and government levels between the DPRK and many countries of the world, with the result that they deepened mutual understanding and confirmed the stand and will to promote sound development of the international community.

The historic, first-ever DPRK–US summit meeting and talks brought about a dramatic turn in the bilateral relationship which was the most hostile on the earth and made a great contribution to ensuring peace and security of the Korean peninsula and the region.

It is the invariable stand of our Party and the government of our Republic and my firm will to establish a new bilateral relationship that meets the demand of the new era as clarified in the June 12 DPRK–US Joint Statement, build a lasting and durable peace regime and advance towards complete denuclearization.

Accordingly, we declared at home and abroad that we would neither make and test nuclear weapons any longer nor use and proliferate them, and we have taken various practical measures.

If the US responds to our proactive, prior efforts with trustworthy measures and corresponding practical actions, bilateral relations will develop wonderfully at a fast pace through the process of taking more definite and epochal measures.

We have no intention to be obsessed with and keep up the unsavoury past relationship between the two countries, but are ready to fix it as early as possible and work to forge a new relationship in line with the aspirations of the two peoples and the requirements of the developing times.

As evidenced by the reality of north–south relations that made rapid progress last year, nothing is impossible to a willing heart, and dialogue partners will reach the destinations that are beneficial to each other without fail if they put forward fair proposals on the principle of recognizing and respecting each other by abandoning their dogged insistence broadmindedly and conduct negotiations with a proper stand and the will to settle issues.

I want to believe that our relations with the United States will bear good fruit this year, as inter-Korean relations have greeted a great turn, by the efforts of the two sides.

I am of the opinion that, while meeting and holding talks beneficial to both sides with the US president in June last year, we exchanged constructive views and reached a consensus of understanding for a shortcut to removing each other's apprehensions and resolving the entangled problems.

I am ready to meet the US president again anytime, and will make efforts to obtain without fail results which can be welcomed by the international community.

But if the United States does not keep the promise it made in the eyes of the world, and out of miscalculation of our people's patience, it attempts to unilaterally enforce something upon us and persists in imposing sanctions and pressure against our Republic, we may be compelled to find a new way for defending the sovereignty of the country and the supreme interests of the state and for achieving peace and stability of the Korean peninsula.

The stabilized situation on the Korean peninsula and in the region is never something that has been created with ease, and the countries that are truly desirous of peace have the common responsibility for setting great store by the current situation. The neighbouring countries and international community have to support our sincere stand and efforts for promoting the positive development of the situation on the Korean peninsula and fight against all practices and challenges that wreck peace and run counter to justice.

Our Party and the government of our Republic will continue to bolster up unity and cooperation with the socialist countries and develop relations with all countries that are friendly to us under the ideals of independence, peace and friendship.

Comrades,
We are beginning the journey of the new year as we brace ourselves once again with the resolve to work devotedly for our country, our motherland, and the happier laughter of younger generations.
What we are convinced of once again as we proudly review the past year when we made rapid progress while paving our way by our own efforts with belief in our own strength in the face of harsh economic blockade and sanctions, is the truth that our state is fully capable of dynamically advancing along the road of development of socialism of our own style by dint of our people's great strength and efforts, without any external assistance or any other's help.
This year, too, we will face constant obstacles and challenges in our progress, but no one can change our determination and will and stop our vigorous advance and our people will successfully achieve their beautiful ideals and goals without fail.
Let us all work energetically and with one mind and will for the prosperity and development of the genuine people's country, the socialist motherland.

Some of this reads like a communication from another world, or perhaps another time.

15

CONCLUSION

I don't pretend for one moment to be an expert on this strange land, but I do know that I am in the unusual position of having visited numerous times and of having seen how the country operates. I am also in the rather interesting position of being an ex-member of the media (some 26 years) and so I do know how stories are, in some quarters, fabricated or exaggerated to suit the news agenda. This does not by any means suggest that all media stories on North Korea are 'fake news', as most of what is written or reported is entirely accurate, but there are some glaring examples that I have seen that make me shudder at the lack of knowledge.

North Korea is not the secretive society that it is portrayed as being. The people are not starving and dying on the streets, and there are no spies standing on each street corner ready to immediately take action should any local, or tourist, misbehave. It just isn't true. Having said that, it is not an open society and there are some very strict rules governing people's behaviour. There is huge poverty in the countryside, particularly in the areas where the Great Famine started in the mid-nineties, but there is little evidence of starvation, and there are members of the government who watch affairs closely, especially tourists visiting rather more controversial spots.

When walking through the streets of Pyongyang in particular, it's noticeable how everyone just carries on with their daily routine and ignores the Western man staring at the odd-looking buildings. In the countryside, it's a different story. Places like Nambo hardly see visitors from outside their own country, so it's an event that needs to be shared!

The people are extremely friendly though and always greet you with a smile and an outstretched hand to shake. They are genuinely proud of their country and are always ready to explain some latest advancement or show you the building of a new entertainment complex, etc. They are totally immersed in the wonders of North Korea and their real and sincere love for their three leaders is beyond question.

It is not the military dictatorship it is portrayed to be by those who have never visited. There is an adoration for the dynasty that has made their country great and their lives so special. It just looks and feels odd to outsiders, and even after my visits, I still find it difficult to comprehend. As someone who has faith, I find it hard to suggest they worship these men, but that in effect is what it is. Total worship. Total adoration. Total obedience. I honestly believe that if somehow a regime change was to take place due to forces from outside of the country, then North Korea would collapse. It would fail to function as the whole focus of the people would have been taken away, and I don't think I'm exaggerating to say that they would collectively lose the will to live.

Of course, asking anyone in the country about their missile programme and relations with the United States is guaranteed to result in furtive looks and a change of subject. There are some things that just won't be discussed publicly, and especially with a Western tourist, but what I was told time and again by my guides was that the people do not want war. They want peace, but they want to be left alone to live their lives in their own way.

There is no envy of the outside world – in fact 'Nothing to Envy' is a mantra that was repeated regularly when I was there – and there is very little interest in other countries. Few of my guides showed much curiosity about the United Kingdom, or France where I live, they knew of Brexit and they knew about the European Union, but they actually weren't really that bothered. The UK is described as an ally of the 'Imperialistic USA' and so regarded with some suspicion, but at the same time North Koreans are incredibly grateful that tourists from Europe travel so far to see their country.

The dilemma that you face when you travel to North Korea is understanding the economy and how some things can be justified. Every building that has a connection to the 1950–53 Korean War and the leaders is effectively 'paved with gold' and has cost many millions of dollars. They are all in pristine condition, guarded by the world's most sophisticated security, and manned by hundreds of workers from guides to military personnel and gardeners.

At the same time, there are apartment blocks and other living accommodation that look run-down at best, but to be fair, a huge renovation programme is taking place in Pyongyang which is already making it one of the most modern (and architecturally unusual) in the world.

While the top scientists and sportsmen and women ride around in government-owned limousines, the daily worker has to contend with rattling 1970s Czechoslovakian trams, or bicycles. Also, while there seems to be food aplenty in the cities (with the exception of fruit which seems to be the main lack due to the regular sanctions imposed on the country), farmers and peasants in the countryside are involved in the back-breaking work of ploughing the fields without any machinery or technology. Failure to meet the deadlines for bringing in the crops results in near-starvation for the community, so harvesting is a family affair.

This is all played out among a homogeneous population. I don't remember ever seeing a black face in North Korea, but then with the total lack of immigration and integration since its inception, that is not surprising. I don't remember seeing a single disabled person either. There are no facilities for the disabled as far as I could see, with no ramps for wheelchairs, no special parking spaces or any type of acknowledgement of disability. If there are blind or deaf people, I wasn't aware of them. I just didn't see them and it's as if they don't exist. I can only let you draw your own conclusions. This is what was reported to the UN Human Rights Council recently:

As early as 2003 the Commission on Human Rights expressed deep concern at the 'mistreatment and discrimination against disabled children.' Since 2006 the General Assembly has consistently decried 'continuing reports of violations of the human rights and fundamental freedoms of persons with disabilities, especially on the use of collective camps and of coercive measures that target the rights of a person with disabilities to decide freely and responsibly on the number and spacing of their children.' Whereas in 2006 the Special Rapporteur noted, 'to date, the situation facing those with disabilities are sent away from the capital city, and particularly those with the mental disabilities are detained in areas or camps known as 'Ward 49' with harsh and subhuman conditions.

The other thing that stands out about walking the streets of any town or city, and especially in the countryside, is the complete lack of domestic animals or pets. This presumably has a lot to do with the Juche Theory and the belief that man is above everything and so animals are there for working and eating, but I was assured by one of my guides that some North Koreans do indeed keep pets, but they are normally far too busy and so it's not a popular exercise. You certainly won't see old ladies carrying pooches under their arms or tattooed men walking a bulldog through the street!

North Korea is a paradox and some thing don't make sense. It shouldn't exist due to its constantly failing economy, but it does. It shouldn't be able to feed itself because of the centuries-old farming practices, but somehow it does, albeit with international aid still required.

The extreme communism ideal that is a basic part of the Juche Theory shouldn't work as it has failed in virtually every place around the world, but it still does, and the leaders shouldn't still be in power as so many other 'dictators' have been toppled elsewhere, but they are.

The Supreme Leader is stronger and more loved now than ever. His judgement is never questioned, and his orders are obeyed without hesitation.

The country continues to follow the path of isolationism and there is absolutely no suggestion that this is likely to change in the near or distant future. The country chose its path after the Korean War and has stuck resolutely to it ever since.

Visiting North Korea is probably like no other visit you will have made before, unless you were in China in the 1960s or the Soviet Union in the 70s, and today there is no country on earth like it. It's fascinating and disturbing. Exciting and slightly worrying. An adventure and a challenge. It's like nothing else in this world, and I love it.

Appendix

IMPORTANT SITES IN NORTH KOREA

Kumsusan Palace of the Sun

'The Kumsusan Palace of the Sun is the supreme sanctuary of Juche that is associated with the enabling revolutionary careers and exploits of President Kim Il-sung and Chairman Kim Jong-il.' That is the way it is described in the tourist guide handed out at the reception of the resting place of the two leaders. A more imposing and grandiose building is difficult to imagine. This is the supreme palace for all North Koreans to honour, as it holds the bodies of their two leaders.

It was originally the Kumsusan Assembly Hall where Kim Il-sung, the founding father of the socialist Korea and the creator of the Juche Theory, worked during the period from 1976 to 1994 – or Juche 65 to Juche 83 as it is stated in the leaflet. After he died though, the Dear Leader, Kim Jong-il, had the building completely renovated and renamed the Kumsusan Memorial Palace, where the Great Leader lay in state. He also decided that it was no longer to be a working or residential palace, as it had now received the blessing of the President, and so it became a shrine to the life of Kim Il-sung.

After the Dear Leader passed away, Kim Jong-un – now in power – renovated the building again and built a new hall where Kim Jong-il also lies in state, this time with the opportunity for the people of the country and tourists to visit and pay their respects.

The whole complex is absolutely huge. The building itself in the region of 115,000 square feet, with two of the halls nearly a mile long. The palace is set in immaculate gardens, and lakes with a moat completely surround it. It is spotlessly clean and its staff includes hundreds of guides, security guards and members of the military because it is the focus for the mass homage that the citizens pay to the statues of the two leaders. It is also the largest mausoleum dedicated to communist leaders anywhere in the world.

Foreign visitors can only access the building after receiving an official invitation from the North Korean government. Visits can only take place on set days, usually Tuesday and Thursdays. It is an intimidating and a fascinating experience for any first-time visitor, but one that will stay in the mind for years to come.

Firstly, all foreign visitors have to line up outside in rows of three and only proceed when the strict security guard calls them forward. You then have to walk in an almost military fashion before entering the building where you are immediately told to leave all of your personal belongings in the cloakroom. Dress is strictly formal. For instance, no jeans or trainers are allowed, and any fancy form of adornment (even the fake fur on a winter coat) has to be either removed or hidden from view. You are then taken through a security entrance that makes any airport feel like a stroll in the park, before standing on a moving walkway for nearly half-a-mile. Again, you are strictly forbidden to walk on this travellator as the views of the gardens outside are of the utmost importance. At the same time, there are literally hundreds of soldiers watching you sternly, with barely a smile among any of them.

Soon you find yourself entering one of the many huge halls that hold every artefact or memento connected to the two leaders. There are numerous halls where the gifts that have been given down the years are displayed, there is a 3-D display of Kim Il-sung and Kim Jong-il standing in front of Mount Paektu and there are separate rooms displaying the train carriage where the Dear Leader passed away, preserved exactly as it was when he died. There are also numerous cars, planes and carriages that were used by one or both of them.

Eventually you come to the two separate halls that house the bodies of the two leaders. After going through a cleansing machine that is supposed to blow away any dust particles from your body, you are then required to stand at the feet of the body and bow graciously. This is repeated at the left and the right of the body, but not at the head. It's worth practising this ritual as the guards do appear to be watching very closely indeed. I was told on my first visit that one tourist had decided to perform a handstand at this very moment – something which he had done at all famous buildings around the world – and as a result was immediately arrested. As there doesn't appear to be any official record of this act, I can only assume he was dealt with leniently.

It's with a huge sense of relief that you leave the building as the atmosphere inside is solemn to say the least. Even the guides seem to be on edge throughout the hour or so it takes to walk the full tour, but once outside – and after you've been reunited with your personal belongings – you can then happily take photographs, something that is totally forbidden inside the palace. It's an incredible place to visit and I can only compare it to Buckingham Palace in terms of its sheer size and importance to the nation. I can also only assume that once Kim Jong-un passes away (something which is a totally taboo subject in the country) then the palace will be extended even further. It's a wonderful place to visit.

The Arch of Triumph

At the foot of Moran Hill, on the site of the Triumph Square, stands the Arch of Triumph. This is an instantly familiar structure, as it is based on the Arc de Triomphe in Paris, but in typically North Korean style, it's actually taller and bigger, although second in size to a similar arch in Mexico. Despite the guides' intimate knowledge of all the monuments in the country, they actually had no idea that the one in Paris was almost exactly the same, which was surprising.

The Arch of Triumph was built in 1982 (Juche 21) in honour of Kim Il-sung's triumphal return after achieving national liberation against the Japanese and it was inaugurated on his 70th birthday. The 60-metre tall arch has around 10,500 granite pieces with the numbers 1925 and 1945 carved into them. These dates signify the year when the Great Leader started on his road to the nation's freedom, and the date when it was achieved. Also, the hymn 'Song of General Kim Il-sung' is etched into the face of the building. Each individual block signifies each day of the life of the Great Leader between 1925 and 1945.

To enter the arch, you have to use a rather rickety lift, before being taken to a room where a film of the building of the structure is shown. Rather surprisingly, there isn't a lift to the viewing platforms at the top, but once the six flights of stairs are overcome, there are spectacular views of the city, especially the Kim Il-sung Stadium immediately adjoining the Arch. The whole structure is lit up at night – as most monuments are and none of them suffer from electricity power cuts – and it can be seen from most places in the city.

The Juche Tower

Situated on the banks of the Taedong River, the Juche Tower was also built in 1982 (Juche 21) for the 70th birthday of the Great Leader. It is 170 metres (560 feet) tall and the second largest tower of its kind in the world. As it tapers to a point, a flame sits atop the structure, and this torch is always illuminated. Along both the west and east of the tower, the letters 'Juche' (in Korean) are etched into the side and can be seen clearly. In front of it there is a statue that personifies the people who built North Korea; in their hands they hold the tools used to achieve this – the hammer denotes the worker, the sickle illustrates the peasant, and the writing brush, the intellectual. Behind the tower on the river stand two fountains that are lit up at night.

At the entrance to the structure there are 82 friendship plaques from supporters all around the world, including my home town of Nice in France. Once inside, you are shown a film covering the building of the tower.

The lift to the top is slow and cramped and the floors in between the ground and the top are strictly out of bounds with no explanation as to what is on them. Once at the top, though, the narrow viewing platform gives sensational views all over the city. Like the Arch of Triumph, this monument was based on another structure – this one being the Washington Monument – but unlike the Arch, the Juche Tower isn't quite as tall, something not always admitted to by the guides. My last visit there was enhanced considerably by the local guide deciding to recite the hymns extolling the powers of the Great Leader for my entertainment. She did this gladly, even though I hadn't asked, and with a smile on her face. I wish I'd made a video of the event, but it was such a personal and intimate moment that it may have been inappropriate if I had.

Victorious Fatherland Liberation War Museum

This is one of the most astonishing and impressive tourist sites in the country, and a museum that must rank highly on the list of great museums in the world. It is a building that is so vast, so full of artefacts and displays and so awe-inspiring that it would be no exaggeration to say it would take at least a week to see everything.

The new renovated museum was reopened in 2014 alongside the Pothong River, but it is so large that it actually spans the river, where the captured 'spy' ship, USS *Pueblo,* is moored. The building has a 360-degree diorama at the top, where you can watch parts of the 1950–53 Korean War played out using impressive CGI and models.

The museum is all about the Korean War, hence the name, but of course you have to accept that it is completely seen from the North Korean point of view, and the US and her allies (including the UK) are given little sympathy or understanding. For that reason, it is probably best to experience it *as an experience,* and not as a record of history. The sheer splendour of this place should take away any doubts about visiting it as it is truly an astonishing place.

You enter through security-patrolled doors at the front of the complex, nearly a kilometre from the main building, and walk through the immaculately presented gardens. You are then met by a female guide, who works for the military but is not recognised as a soldier, and firstly taken to a display of captured enemy tanks and weapons. This display is in the form of trenches that you walk through, before having every piece of machinery explained to you including where it was captured. The list is impressive with Pershing, Sherman and Chaffee tanks all stored in their faded glory, plus the remains of downed helicopters from both the US and the UK.

Following that, it's on to the captured USS *Pueblo*. As explained earlier, this ship was taken in January 1968 and caused an international crisis with the sailors taken prisoner and only released after they signed statements that confirmed their roles in espionage. The ship has never been released, despite numerous requests from the US government, which ever since has repeatedly denied that it was involved in spying.

Inside the ship – which to all intents and purposes looks like a spy ship with the amount of surveillance equipment that is proudly shown to you by your guide – you are required to watch a 30-minute film of the capture and the subsequent international fall-out. It's worth putting on your best poker face for this as not only the very pleasant guide, but her military companions (all who refuse to smile) watch you intently as you listen to the propaganda. Most of it seems to be true, but there are moments of almost comic exaggeration.

Then you are taken into the museum itself, starting with the main reception hall. This is of stunning architectural beauty. A main feature is the Victory statue, with Kim Jong-un's inscription honouring 'The Great Years' clearly visible. Alongside are numerous sculptures of the leaders plus countless propaganda sayings emblazoned on the wall. There are huge chandeliers hanging from the ceiling and two ornate marble staircases leading to the first floor. Unfortunately, no photographs are allowed inside the building, which is an enormous frustration as words truly cannot convey the sheer magnitude of the museum. Sadly, you'll just have to take my word for it unless you get the chance to visit yourself.

The tour for foreign visitors is strictly adhered to and does not change over the years. I have been three times now, and each guided tour is exactly the same, only covering around 20 per cent of the whole museum, which again is a source of real frustration. Once again, there is a film to watch of the start of the Korean War (obviously from their point of view) where you are observed closely for any reaction. There are then numerous rooms to walk through with displays so full of detail that it could take you a couple of hours to read everything in just one small room. As it is, you take the word of the guide who explains everything in near-perfect English. This continues for at least five more rooms, but bypassing others where locals are being escorted. For reasons that I've never established, these other halls are not available to foreign visitors. At one stage you are walked through a re-creation of an underground tunnel, similar to the hundreds that were built for the soldiers during the war. This is so realistic that a sense of claustrophobia can easily creep in.

The final act is to take the lift to the top of the building and enter the 360-degree diorama. This is an amazing experience as you sit comfortably and allow the images to pass slowly by as they tell the story of one particular conflict in the war. The special effects wouldn't be out of place in a Hollywood film and the small-scale model of the battleground is made in intricate detail. A great way of ending your visit.

The last time I visited this place, I plucked up enough courage to ask my main guide afterwards to how much of it she believed. She replied unequivocally that she believed absolutely everything in the museum, because why would they lie? It's an interesting question, and if you find yourselves fortunate enough to see the place yourself, then it might be a question you may ask too. The other conundrum that baffles me is the obvious one – for a country that at times has struggled to feed its own people, how can the cost of building such a place be justified? The answer is quite simple for most North Koreans. The 1950–53 Korean War totally defines the country, and it will simply *never* be forgotten. So, no matter how long it takes you to make your first visit to the country, the Victorious Fatherland Liberation War Museum will always be there.

Kim Il-sung Square

One of the regular images seen in Western television news reports about Pyongyang is the one that shows thousands of North Korean soldiers goose-stepping in unison, while huge missiles are carried on the back of trucks, accompanied by tanks and other weapons during one of the many military displays. These are watched by thousands of locals and are of course overseen by the Supreme Leader Kim Jong-un. Well, this all takes place in Kim Il-sung Square, an area of about 75,000 square metres and at the centre of the capital city.

Built in 1954 (Juche 43) during the complete reconstruction of Pyongyang, it is based on Tiananmen Square in Beijing, China, and has spectacular views towards the Juche Tower and the nearby River Taedong. Surrounding the square are many government buildings, which are all lit up at night, and at its head is the Great People's Study House from where government officials, the military and Kin Jong-un watch the military processions. The square is also the location for many mass dances and these can be seen being rehearsed for weeks in advance leading up the big day. On all buildings on the three sides that surround the square, there are the usual portraits of Kim Il-sung and Kim Jong-il, with the propaganda messages adorning the balconies.

It is said that all roads in North Korea start at the centre of the square and the road network (for what it is) has its starting point there, but if you stand in that spot at night and look towards the Juche Tower and the Taedong River, then you can see how each individual road stretches away in grid-like fashion. Like Tiananmen Square, the Kim Il-sung Square is open to the public, but unlike Beijing, there are no tourist stalls, or gift merchants patrolling the streets. There is a bookshop attached to the square, which seems to open irregularly, and sells only propaganda material in many different languages, with English being the most popular. On the opposite side of the street, there is a café. This is the only café that I know of in Pyongyang, although I was assured there was another one being built near the Koryo Hotel, and it does sell reasonably enjoyable coffee, albeit in a rather bleak and unwelcoming setting. Kim Il-sung Square is great for photo opportunities and of course on the days of the parades and processions, but on other days don't expect to be distracted for more than half-an-hour by the place, as there really isn't a great deal to do.

International Friendship Exhibition House

In the North Pyongan Province of Myohyangsan, some three hour's drive from Pyongyang, lies the International Friendship Exhibition House, a huge museum complex holding all the gifts the leaders have received from foreign dignitaries down the years. Why this is located so far from the capital is a mystery to me, as the journey there by car is a challenge in itself, but its setting is spectacular. In fact Kim Il-sung composed a poem about it in 1978, just two months after it was built:

> On the balcony I see the most
> glorious scene in the World...
> The Exhibition stands here,
> its green eaves upturned, to exalt
> the dignity of the Nation,
> and Piro Peak looks higher still.

Hardly Keatsian, but as someone who has sat on that very balcony at the end of the tour (with a cup of scalding but almost undrinkable coffee in my hand) I can testify to the sheer splendour and beauty of the scene he describes. The peaks of the mountains that surround the building can be seen above beautiful green foliage and gentle mist rolling down the hills. It really is a moment to savour, as indeed is the magnificent museum.

It opened on 26 August 1978, and if the building itself doesn't look overly impressive from the outside, then indoors is where you get a sense of the dramatic. There are more than 150 rooms, of which I probably saw around thirty in my 2-hour visit. The first thing you are greeted with is a security guard who points to a plaque that states that the Great Leader built the museum in three days. He didn't. It took hundreds of builders over a year to complete it.

You are then informed by the local guide that there are about 200,000 gifts on display, which is a lot more believable as each room is packed with gifts, all displayed in a tasteful and chronological fashion.

These can range from an aeroplane donated by Chairman Mao, a bulletproof limousine given by Soviet leader Josef Stalin, to a tea cup set from the German Chancellor and a rugby league ball from Wigan Warriors!

Heads of State who have donated gifts range from Romania's Nicolae Ceausescu, Libya's President Gaddafi, Fidel Castro of Cuba, Palestine leader Yasser Arafat and US Secretary of State Madeleine Albright, plus literally hundreds of others. The whole enterprise is a way of showing the North Korean people that their leaders are admired universally, without admitting to the fact that all leaders exchange gifts on meeting. In fact, another plaque that stands next to the statues of both the Great Leader and the Dear Leader states that the gifts are 'Proof of the endless love and respect towards the Great Leader Kim Il-sung and the Dear Leader Kim Jung-il.'

No matter how extreme the propaganda attached to this complex, it really is an essential place to visit if you want to see the real adoration the people have for their leaders. There is a smaller and more intimate exhibition in Pyongyang called The National Gifts Exhibition House, which has by and large a similar theme, but concentrates on gifts and presents donated from Asian countries. This is not as impressive, but if you can't visit the main building in Myohyangsan, then the second one in Pyongyang will give you a taste of it.

Chollima Statue

The tourist guides explaining the significance of the Chollima Statue state that it can be seen from every part of the capital city, Pyongyang. That's not true as I had to search for it when I was being walked through the streets on an earlier visit. It is quite impressive though, standing some 46 metres high. It is cast in bronze and shows a male worker holding aloft the 'Red Letter' from the Central Committee of the Workers' Party of Korea, and a female worker holding a rice sheaf in her arms, both of them riding on the legendary steed Chollima soaring high into the sky with its wings spread wide. It's fair to say that everything built in the country has some kind of symbolic importance and is nearly always aimed at the glorification of the people's struggle spearheaded by the Great Leader and then the Dear Leader. It was built in 1961 and given as a gift by the people to Kim Il-sung on his 49th birthday, 15 April, and according to the plaque at its foot, it was inspired by a speech the Great Leader had made on that very spot called 'Let Us Further Develop Popular Art' on Mansu Hill. It's impressive, but again with so many monuments and buildings aimed at the leaders, this is one that could easily be overlooked or forgotten during a hectic visit.

May Day Stadium

There are two big stadiums in Pyongyang. The smaller one is the Kim Il-sung Stadium that holds around 80,000 spectators in its all-seated interior. It is famous for being built on the exact spot where the Great Leader made his debut speech in 1945 (Juche 34) at the birth of the nation. The second, and far more important, is the May Day Stadium – or First of May Stadium – which holds anything from 110,000 to 150,000 depending on who you listen to. When I visited in 2017 to watch a local football 'derby' that had an attendance of approximately 150, I was told that it was the largest stadium in the world and held 150,000 spectators seated. It clearly doesn't and when I looked at a locally produced tourist guide, it stated that it held 135,000. Other figures are as low as 110,000, but no matter how big it is, it's a pretty impressive looking structure.

It was opened on 1 May 1989 and the first event was the 13th World Festival of Youth and Students (a direct response to the

Seoul Olympics held in South Korea one year previously) and since then has been mostly used for the Mass Games that take place at irregular intervals, plus the occasional badly attended football match.

It's actually been designated as an Olympic stadium, even if the chances of the Games taking place in North Korea are extremely remote. The stadium has a unique design – it is made up of sixteen huge arches, set in such a way to resemble a magnolia blossom, the national flower of the country, as seen from above. There are eight storeys of which there are three tiers for spectators watching the events.

Behind them are training halls, swimming pool, conference halls, hotel rooms and numerous restaurants, making it one of the most modern stadiums in the world.

The history of the stadium is both exhilarating and disturbing. It's the place where the incredible Mass Games take place with more than 100,000 participants and a similar number of spectators. These events are now legendary in the country, with spectacular displays and dancing celebrating the country and its leaders, which can go on for days and are the highlight of the year for locals in Pyongyang. The 2007 version was officially recognised by the Guinness Book of Records as the largest gymnastic display in history with exactly 100,090 participants, something which is proclaimed proudly when you are given a tour of the stadium. Rather oddly, the largest attendance registered was for an American World Championship Wrestling event in 1995 where around 160,000 attended over a two-day period. By contrast, the stadium is reputedly the place where many of Kim Jong-il's opponents were publicly executed after failed assassination attempts on the Great Leader. The details of these executions are horrific to say the least, and I must admit to feeling slightly uncomfortable sitting in the stadium one bright and sunny October Sunday afternoon watching a football match, knowing that this was the space where so many people had been murdered.

More recently, the South Korean President Moon Jae-in gave a speech in the stadium; official figures suggested that 150,000 North Koreans had attended in September 2018, although I was there just one month later, and this was never referred to at any stage by my guides, so the figures may have been exaggerated.

It is an astonishing complex and certainly rivals some of the great stadia in the world, and even if you don't like sports, then it's still worth a visit. Thankfully it was completely renovated in 2013, so the place where the executions took place in the mid-nineties doesn't look quite the same now.

Ryugyong Hotel

There is one building that totally dominates the landscape of Pyongyang and cannot be missed from any point in the city, towering above the Juche Tower and the Arch of Triumph, yet it is completely and utterly useless. That building is the unfinished Ryugyong Hotel. This pyramid structure was first started in 1987 and was given the nickname of '105 building' due to the fact that it has 105 floors, but nowadays there are less proud names applied to it. It is a huge white elephant in the city that is both a source of pride and embarrassment to the government.

The building is of course quite amazing, reaching 330 metres in height, with the pyramid tapering to a point where there is a red light constantly burning. Inside there are 105 floors of bedrooms and executive suites, none of which are finished. It was intended to be completed by 1989 for the World Festival of Youth and

Students, as mentioned previously. Unfortunately, the money quickly ran out. If it had been finished, then it would be officially the world's tallest hotel, but sadly it now holds the record as the world's tallest unoccupied building.

When it was designed, it was meant to include around 7,000 rooms with five revolving restaurants, but none of this came to fruition. As recently as 2011, the exterior was finally completed with glass windows after a resumption of construction three years previously. It had been left to decay since 1992 when the government halted all construction projects as the economic problems started to take hold, leading of course to the Great Famine. At the time it had cost in the region of $750 million, 2 per cent of the GDP of the country, and for many years it stood there as a rusting bare shell. There was no money to complete it and no money to demolish it either.

One of the great myths told about the building by the Western media was that the hotel had been built without any lifts, which was partially true as it hadn't been completed anyway, and so lifts were to be the final thing added. As it was, nothing was completed and so it still stands there as a testament to the problems the country has experienced and the over-ambitious nature of the project.

Today it is lit up at night with LED displays showing propaganda slogans and mini-firework displays, so at least it is now being recognised as existing, as up until just a few years ago it was completely ignored. It didn't appear on any street map of the city, was erased from any photograph of the skyline and wasn't referred to by anyone in the government. In a way that's all rather impressive, bearing in mind the sheer scale of the hotel. Even my guides seemed to be rather uninterested in it and knew little about its interior, suggesting that most people 'close their eyes' to it when they walk the streets of Pyongyang – again an almost impossible task when you see it towering above you.

There are more suggestions that in 2019 construction will restart, but I have to say I saw absolutely no evidence of any work being done either to the building or the infrastructure around it. The whole complex is closed off with sturdy metal fences and nothing happens behind the barriers. It's unlikely to be demolished as it will cost a lot in terms of finance and pride, but it's also unlikely to be completed, meaning no one will get the chance to see inside. It does make for a great photo opportunity though, if you can persuade your guides to allow you to take some.

Nampo Dam

The Nampo Dam – or the West Sea Barrage as it is more commonly known – is not an immediate tourist destination, but if you are taken to it, then its construction is certainly something to marvel at. Built from 1981 to 1986, some 15 kilometres west of the city of Nampo, it spans more than 8 kilometres and was constructed to stop the intrusion of seawater into fresh water and also to help irrigate land in the arable region of the country. It now completely closes off the Taedong River from the Yellow Sea, although it has been the subject of criticism outside the country with some experts saying that it played its part in the arrival of the Great Famine due to the loss of farmland.

It's hardly a thing of beauty and for me it was made worse by visiting on one of the greyest days I've seen in the country, not helped by the rather tedious film shown to all tourists. This was of the remarkable construction of this barrage in what can only be described as horrendous circumstances. Watching a film of the Great Leader arriving in 1982 and urging the construction workers to increase their efforts, despite the hardships that were being endured, is a disturbing experience, but the North Koreans are very proud of the structure.

The film was unintentionally informative as it was clear that the faces of the cheering workers were gaunt and the physique of each man appeared to be unhealthy, if not emaciated. Whatever hardships they had endured up to that point were clearly of no interest to the Great Leader as he stood tall with his arms stretched out wide, seemingly using the force of his presence to urge them to harder and more productive labour. The huge earthmoving machines such as excavators and bulldozers dwarfed everyone in an almost apocalyptic vision, and it was these terrifying metal monsters that were carving up the countryside, driven by the constantly enthusiastic workforce. A more uncomfortable promotion video could not be found. The dam was estimated to have cost in the region of $4billion, and although there are no references anywhere to the human cost, it is inconceivable that there wasn't any, bearing in mind the primitive conditions the thousands of workers were working in and the sheer might of the machinery used to reclaim the land.

Finally, the dam is in the heart of both beautiful natural countryside and dour industrial areas. The journey from Pyongyang to Nampo, which takes around 2 hours, provides a perfect example of the wide-ranging scenery.

Woljong Temple

As I mentioned previously, religion is still alive in North Korea, and that is proved by the number of Buddhist temples that still exist. I've visited a few, but the one that left an immense impression on me was the Woljong Temple in the UNESCO

Biosphere Reserve of Mount Kuwol. This is a popular tourists' destination for locals, who visit the mountain mostly in the ninth month of September when it is said to be at its most beautiful, but it's the Temple that is the National Treasure of the country (number 75 according to local guides). It was built in the ninth century during the Joseon period and has been lovingly restored and preserved ever since, as recently as the 1980s when it was visited by Kim Jong-il.

The temple comprises traditionally designed buildings and is set on the side of the mountain, among forests and streams. It is one of the most beautiful and tranquil spots I have ever seen. It is overseen by a monk who has lived there for more than forty years with his family, while his father had been there for many years before. During his time – and even during the Great Famine – the monk has rebuilt virtually every piece of the area. Every day he maintains the temple, while welcoming tourists too. It now has protected status in North Korea and is financed by the government, something which was heartening to hear.

The visit was especially memorable as the monk invited me, the two guides and our driver into his home where we enjoyed lunch and his extremely potent homemade wine. During my time there, he told me many stories of his struggle, especially during the famine years, when the lack of food left him almost too weak to continue his work. He also answered my question about why he wore the badge of the leaders, bearing in mind he was a man of faith.

He replied that it was because of the generosity of Kim Jong-il and Kim Il-sung that the temple was allowed to continue. He also told me that Kim Jung-un had contacted him to say that it would continue to be protected and financed by the North Korean government.

There are few places in this world where you are guaranteed complete peace and silence, but for me this is definitely one. When I left, we exchanged gifts and I would love dearly to return one day. During my time there, I only saw one other group of visitors, and they were North Korean women who were enjoying a Mother's Day outing. They ignored the Temple to climb up to the peak of the very high hill next to it.

Finally, this was one of only two places where I was aware of a North Korean government employee lurking in the background. It was all rather tame, and he smiled at me and said goodbye when we left, but it did remind me that this is still a feature of tourism in the country.

Songam Cavern

Songam Cavern is situated in Kaech'ŏn-si in the South Pyongan Province and is a well-known tourist destination. It consists of seventeen brightly lit caves, which all have some connection to the Great Leader in North Korean culture.

There are some obvious highlights among the stalactites and stalagmites, such as the flower gate, called Kkotmun Dong, a wonderful waterfall that gives a superb photo opportunity, Phokpho Dong, and an area that resembles a snowy mountain, called Solgyong Dong.

It's clear that a lot of time and money has been put into creating this tourist attraction, but I must admit that I felt quite sorry for the pleasant female guide who told me she worked there for eight hours each day, in the cold and damp. It didn't help that as she was telling me, we had a brief power cut, leaving the cavern in darkness before the emergency generators kicked in. Still, it's a pleasant place to visit – and not too far from the International Friendship Exhibition House.

Korean Revolution Museum

The Korean Revolution Museum is situated in the centre of Pyongyang, and it's the focus for the people to pay tribute to the leaders as their huge statues are situated at the entrance – the Mansu Hill Grand Monument. I have watched hundreds of locals stand in line and bow in unison to the statues on the anniversary of the birth of Kim Il-sung and leave flowers and gifts while dressed in their traditional costumes.

The museum itself was founded in 1948 and tells the story in chronological order from 1860 of the resistance the people have shown against all invaders, including the Japanese. Great victories such as the Battle of Height 1211 in the Korean War are featured, in which Supreme Commander Kim Il-sung naturally utterly out-fought and out-thought the enemy, and his troops found time to 'make musical instruments in the tunnels and trenches'. The building is approximately 250,000 square metres, which, according to local guides, makes it one of the largest in the world, and it has over 90 rooms of artefacts relating to the eternal struggle. It had a complete renovation in 2017 and is definitely a place to visit, even if the constant propaganda theme of the place can become slightly overwhelming after a while.

It's believed that the museum has received around 27 million visitors from North Korea and abroad, and it was one of the busier places that I visited. It was also the place where the local guide sang the ode to the Great Leader to me after I asked what the words meant on the wall. Her voice was melodic and pleasant and there was absolutely no sense of embarrassment on her part. It was certainly a highlight of my tour. The sheer number of items is overwhelming, and each slogan is patiently translated. Another amazing place to visit, providing you can understand and accept that propaganda is what motivates these places.

Sci-Tech Complex

When you walk around the streets of Pyongyang, you can't help but feel you've been parachuted into an episode of the cartoon *The Jetsons*. The buildings are of irregular shape and often resemble a flower, a rocket, or the North Korean flag, but none of the apartment blocks can match the sheer weirdness of the Sci-Tech Complex built on the Ssuk Island in the Taedong River in the heart of the capital city. It is one of the strangest looking buildings I've visited, both inside and out.

It was opened on 1 January 2016 and was a personal interest of Kim Jong-un, who wanted to showcase to the world the advances in technology that are happening in the country. The local guide told me the story of how the building works were on schedule, but after a visit from the Supreme Leader, productivity increased threefold and the whole complex was complete nearly a year ahead of expectation.

The huge structure is in the shape of an atom with three overlapping buildings portraying the paths of electrons. The fact that it was virtually empty when I visited makes it even more intriguing. At more than 106,000 square metres and about 300 metres in diameter, it certainly dominates the landmass of the island, and once you step inside, you are immediately greeted with the sight of a mock-up rocket stretching to the tip of the domed roof. The complex includes an 'Earthquake Experience Hall'.

The guidebook describes the place like this:

Sci-Tech Complex is a comprehensive e-library that can serve the materials of the recent national and worldwide technological achievements. It also contains the books of science and technology published in Korea from the past. All of them are electronically processed in a comprehensive and systematic way. It's furnished with massive databases and many e-reading rooms so anybody can have access to the materials they wish. Moreover, the Sci-Tech Complex has an on-line service and everyone, including scientific research sectors, educational institutions, factories, enterprises as well as private users can get access to the Sci-tech materials and publications without leaving home.

There are numerous halls, such as the Children's Dream Hall, the Fundamental Science and Technology Hall, the Virtual Lab, the Indoor Sci-Tech Exhibition Hall and a hotel that has 23 storeys and more than 500 rooms. It's impressive, but it's empty.

I was there being given the grand tour for nearly two hours, where all kinds of technological advancements were being explained to me. I was shown the Virtual Reality Hall where all types of wonderful experiences were at my disposal. I was shown the Fundamental Science and Technology Hall with its hundreds of computers switched on to the country's intranet service, and I was shown the vast library that housed hundreds, if not thousands, of books in virtually every language. I was also taken to the top of the building with its 360-degree panoramic view and walked around the grounds where there were parks and gardens and quiet spaces for reading and studying, and I hardly saw another person. It was as if it had been opened – and no one had remembered to tell the public about it.

There was the occasional student sitting at a desk deeply engrossed in the intranet (no World Wide Web in North Korea remember as the intranet is all that is needed, according to the official line) and a few studious young men perusing the library, but the rest of the place was deserted. Even the rather exciting Children's Dream Hall was all mine to explore without the disturbance of any actual children.

Of course when I mentioned this to the local guide on site, she explained in a rather patronisingly patient way that everyone was either working or at school, and if I returned at a different time then I would see how popular it was, but it was a disturbing insight into the over-extended ambition that the government sometimes seems to inflict on the country. There are no records of the cost of building such a complex, but it must be in millions of dollars, yet it was hardly being used. Most homes in the major cities in North Korea now have their own personal computers, which are strictly regulated of course, so there seems to be little point in visiting a huge educational project such as this, unless on a school trip, so the question is why was it built? It has a lot to do with the image that North Korea now wants to project to the outside world, showing how their technology is advancing at the same rate as everyone else's. Whatever, the reason, they could do with a few more locals showing an interest too.

Pyongyang International Airport

I wouldn't normally recommend an airport as a place to visit, because they're nearly all the same, but Pyongyang's is interesting because it will be the first glimpse of the country you will have after landing, and also because it's virtually completely empty, despite if being an international airport. There's a theme here.

Up until 2011 the airport was rather run-down and only regularly welcomed domestic flights, as most international airlines had stopped travelling to North Korea. Only Air China continued, along with the North Korean airline Air Koryo, and so the airstrip at Sunan was under-used. Once Kim Jong-un came to power, he started a period of modernisation in the country, and that included the international airport. A second terminal was designed and built very quickly, using what was described as the 'speed campaign', which basically meant that civilians and the military were enlisted to construct the building in rapid time.

From the outside it looks like a bustling, busy international airport with arrivals and departures on two separate floors. It's only once you enter that you see how under-used it actually is. Checking in is a relaxed affair as there is usually only one international departure, to Beijing, and that normally only on Tuesdays and Thursdays. It means that you are not expected to arrive until 90 minutes before your flight, and that also means that all the tourist gift shops in the departure lounge are totally empty as no one has the time to browse before boarding their flight. Only in North Korea...

Although no one noticed, the airport was closed on 15 September 2017 as an early morning missile was fired from the runway. It travelled around 2,500 miles before crashing into the sea.

The infrastructure leading to and from the airport consists of potholed roads without any road signs (but then that is the case throughout the country) and a train station that is close by, but the trains do not seem to follow a timetable with any consistency. Of course, with an international airport there comes an international airline and North Korea has its own with Air Koryo. I have flown on numerous occasions with this airline and I find it to be safe and comfortable, if rather unusual with the constant repetition of propaganda hymns as the in-flight entertainment. The aircraft seem to be clean and modern and the staff are courteous and professional, yet if you read reviews on social media (always questionable in my opinion) then Air Koryo is just about the most dangerous way to travel in the world ever. It seemingly only has a one-star rating with Skytrax, a United Kingdom–based consultancy which runs an airline and airport review and ranking site.

The European Union put a ban on it in 2006, which was only rescinded four years later. The aircraft are Russian, the Tupolev Tu-204 being the only aircaft Air Koryo operates that is currently allowed into EU airspace. There are many safety concerns from aviation authorities, but I can honestly say that flying Air Koryo was like flying any other short-haul airline and caused me no concerns or problems, except for the rather gaudy red interior of the planes.

FURTHER READING

Books

China–North Korea relations. China, 2008.

DPRK–USS Showdown. Foreign Language Publishing House, North Korea, 2014.

Korea 20th Century in 100 points. Foreign Language Publishing House, North Korea, 2002.

Panorama of Pyongyang. Foreign Language Publishing House, North Korea, 2017.

French, Paul. *North Korea: State of Paranoia.* Zed Books Ltd., 2015. ISBN 978-1-78360-573-6

Kim Jong-il. *The Juche Idea,* Foreign Language Publishing House, North Korea, 1982.

Kim Il-sung. *Reminiscences: With the Century,* Foreign Language Publishing House, North Korea, no date of publication provided.

Napoleoni, Loretta. *North Korea: The Country We Love To Hate.* UWA Publishing, Crawley, Western Australia, 2018.

Tudor, Daniel and James Pearson. *North Korea Confidential: Private Markets, Fashion Trends, Prison Camps, Dissenters and Defectors,* Tuttle Publishing, 2015.

DVDs
Nation and Destiny. North Korean production, part of a thirteen episode 3-hour series.
The Story of my House, North Korean production.

Newspapers
Pyongyang Times
The New Yorker

Periodicals
Human Rights Watch, United Nations, 2018.
Politico magazine
Time magazine

INDEX

38th parallel 25, 30, 36, 38,
  221, 222

A

Arch of Triumph 196, 197,
  203, 257, 258, 268
Armistice, 1950–53 War 36,
  37, 214, 222, 234, 243
Axis of evil 9, 188, 224
August Faction Incident 53, 222

B

Bae, Kenneth 190, 191, 204,
  205
Beijing 10, 35, 71, 123, 138,
  151, 180, 183, 194, 195,
  200, 209, 262, 263, 278
black market, see economy
Buddhism 102, 107, 108, 110,
  112, 271

C

China –
  1950-53 War 12, 33, 35. 38,
    58
  border 70, 75, 100, 179,
    180, 183, 184, 185, 212
  ally to North Korea 12, 14,
    31, 33, 58, 83, 102, 208,
    222
Chondoism 107, 108, 109
Christianity 18, 92, 93, 106,
  107, 108, 109, 111, 112,
  190, 191, 204
concentration camps 42, 69,
  148
Confucianism 81, 95, 107,
  110
countryside –
  farming 11, 85, 104, 127,
    131, 251

living 11, 85, 101, 104, 113, 116, 126, 127, 131, 251
cuisine 130, 162, 199

D
Defectors 69, 103, 151, 159, 169, 172, 208, 209, 210, 212
Demilitarised Zone (DMZ) 37, 38, 39, 40, 41, 42, 128, 147, 212, 224, 225, 226
Dennis Rodman 203, 205
disability 153
Donghak Peasant Revolution 12, 109

E
economy –
  failing 14, 26, 82, 83, 100, 145, 250
  black-market 141, 159
entertainment 121, 123, 125, 133, 151, 163, 249

F
family –
  traditions 88, 113, 121, 125, 126, 133, 150, 156, 208
  tragedies including imprisonment 16, 69, 97, 154, 157, 159, 170, 171, 182, 183, 226
famine, Second Arduous March mid-90s 11, 64, 82, 87, 97, 98, 99, 100, 101, 102, 103, 104, 130, 131, 140, 152, 153, 154, 159, 184, 198, 203, 207, 209, 218, 224, 248, 269, 270, 272
fashion 28, 118

H
health 51, 152, 153, 238, 242
Hermit Kingdom 9, 14
hotels 10, 105, 127, 164, 198, 199, 202
human rights, accusations by the UN and other organisations and governments 69, 76, 111, 167, 172, 173, 175, 176, 177, 178, 180, 181, 210, 218, 220, 251
Hyon Yong-chol 76

I
Internet 86, 107, 108, 174, 227

J
Jang Song-thaek 75
Japanese annexation of early Korea 13, 14, 15, 20, 21, 22, 50, 106, 196
Juche Theory 11, 53, 66, 70, 79, 80, 83, 86, 89, 90, 91, 92, 94, 95, 98, 155, 159, 160, 222, 223, 252, 252 and see Military first

K
Kim Hye-sun 49
Kim Il-sung –
  personality 25, 30, 33, 34, 35, 37, 38, 39, 44, 46, 47, 48, 49, 50, 51, 52, 53, 54, 55, 57, 58, 59, 60, 61, 62, 64, 66, 67, 69, 78, 85, 92, 98, 99, 107, 108, 111, 131, 141, 170, 184, 191, 218, 222, 223, 224, 225, 254, 256, 265, 266, 272, 283

buildings named after the
  Great Leader   50, 62, 74,
  93, 146, 257, 262, 263, 269
Kim Jong-il   41, 55, 60, 61, 62,
  66, 69, 70, 71, 72, 74, 84,
  88, 89, 91, 109, 131, 144,
  218, 223, 224, 226, 255,
  272
Kim Jong-suk   49, 67
Kim Jong-un   66, 69, 73, 74,
  76, 77, 78, 95, 115, 117,
  144, 172, 176, 191, 203,
  204, 205, 215, 218, 220,
  226, 227, 228, 257, 277
Kim-Sung-ae   49
Korean Air Flight 858   189

L
living conditions   121, 157,
  235
London   44, 114, 115, 134,
  145, 194, 197

M
Mao, Chairman   52, 56, 58,
  59, 69, 264
marriage   121, 123, 158, 187
Military first and Juche
  ideology   37, 52, 81, 84, 86,
  87, 88, 90, 162, 223
mobile phones   165, 195
Moscow   53, 66
Mount Paektu   61, 256

N
New York   43, 44, 69, 114
nuclear weapons   35, 75, 213,
  214, 215, 216, 245

P
power cuts   113, 164, 199
public holidays   131, 136
Pueblo, USS   29, 40, 42, 192,
  259, 260
prison camps   63, 167, 168,
  174, 180, 181, 182

R
religion   13, 106, 107, 108,
  109, 110, 11, 112, 173, 177,
  186, 271
Ri Sol-ju   77
Rodman, Dennis   77, 144,
  191, 203-205
Russia –
  1950–53 War   27, 31, 36, 49
  ally to North Korea   31, 49,
  53, 54, 58, 95, 99, 190, 222
  border   210
  and see Soviet Union

S
Shamanism   106, 107, 109,
  110
schools   12, 22, 61, 113, 119,
  147, 154, 155, 175, 178,
  179, 200, 216, 231
Seoul   17, 25, 31, 33, 35, 36,
  41, 107, 134, 142, 178, 188,
  189, 228, 242, 267
shopping   138, 139, 140, 141,
  161, 196
Sinuiju   70, 71, 101
songbun system   157, 158,
  159, 169, 173, 177
South Korea –
  border   25, 128, 209, 215,
  225
  tension with   31, 73, 75,
  181, 189, 225

Soviet Union   12, 23–7, 31, 34,
     36, 41, 50-54, 58, 62, 83,
     95, 98, 99, 102, 104, 107,
     190, 220, 222, 224, 252,
     264 and see Russia
sport   142, 143, 144, 145, 147,
     203

T
technology   83, 85, 230, 231,
     233, 275, 276, 277
tourists and tourism   28, 29,
     38, 41, 46, 55, 57, 89, 108,
     115, 129, 139, 147, 150,
     165, 185, 193, 196, 199,
     200, 202, 237, 248, 250,
     259, 263, 265, 266, 270,
     273, 278
transport   115, 133, 221, 235

travel for local populace   26,
     135, 147, 148, 149, 150,
     151, 172, 173, 177, 180
Trump, Donald, US President
     77, 176, 204, 205, 216, 228

U
USA –
     1950-53 War   12, 34, 37, 41,
     42, 214, 219
     current relations with   12,
     22, 96, 107, 155, 196, 213,
     215, 216, 219, 225, 226

V
Vollertsen, Norbert   211

W
Warmbier, Otto   77, 167, 201,
     205, 228

Also available from Amberley Publishing

Available from all good bookshops or to order direct
Please call **01453-847-800**
www.amberley-books.com